At Home in Diaspora

Critical American Studies Series

George Lipsitz, University of California–Santa Cruz, series editor

At Home in Diaspora

Black International Writing

Wendy W. Walters

Critical American Studies

University of Minnesota Press
Minneapolis
London

A different version of chapter 3 appeared as "Limited Options: Strategic Maneuverings in Himes's Harlem," *African American Review* 28, no. 4 (Winter 1994): 615–31. Reprinted in *Contemporary Literary Criticism* 108, ed. Debbie Stanly (Detroit: Gale Research, 1998) and in *The Critical Response to Chester Himes*, ed. Charles P. Silet (Westport: Greenwood Press, 1999).

Published by the University of Minnesota Press
111 Third Avenue South, Suite 290
Minneapolis, MN 55401-2520
http://www.upress.umn.edu

Library of Congress Cataloging-in-Publication Data
Walters, Wendy W.
    At home in diaspora : Black international writing / Wendy W. Walters.
        p.   cm. — (Critical American studies series)
    Includes bibliographical references and index.
    ISBN 0-8166-4491-8 (hc : alk. paper) — ISBN 0-8166-4492-6 (pb : alk. paper)
    1. American fiction—African American authors—History and criticism.
2. Wright, Richard, 1908–1960—Criticism and interpretation.   3. Himes, Chester B., 1909—Criticism and interpretation.   4. West Indian literature (English)—Black authors—History and criticism.   5. Phillips, Caryl— Criticism and interpretation.   6. Cliff, Michelle—Criticism and interpreta-tion.   7. Njami, Simon—Criticism and interpretation.   8. Blacks—West Indies—Intellectual life.   9. African Americans in literature.   10. Inter-nationalism in literature.   11. Exiles in literature.   12. African diaspora.
I. Title.   II. Series.
PS374.N4W356   2005
809'.8896—dc22   2005000433

Printed in the United States of America on acid-free paper

The University of Minnesota is an equal-opportunity educator and employer.

12   11   10   09   08   07   06   05   10   9   8   7   6   5   4   3   2   1

Contents

Introduction

Diaspora Consciousness and Literary Expression

In 1940 W. E. B. Du Bois described his books *The Souls of Black Folk* and *Darkwater* as "written in tears and blood." *Dusk of Dawn: An Essay toward an Autobiography of a Race Concept*, he said, "is set down no less determinedly but yet with a wider hope in some more benign fluid."[1] In this reference to ink in the opening "Apology" to *Dusk of Dawn*, Du Bois calls our attention to writing as a hopeful space where concepts of race and identity can be expressed. In the following chapters, I will show how ink and the varieties of narrative forms that have made up African American, Caribbean, and Black European literatures are important sites where contemporary writers continue Du Bois's project of tracing "a race concept" that may be called *diaspora*.[2] The history of African American literature alone has evidenced a shifting between writers claiming an American identity, experiencing a form of racialized exile in their American homeland, and seeking diasporic connections to other black people in the world. Very often this seeking occurs in the pages of their texts, as writers use their prose to construct alternative homelands. Black writers' texts often look beyond the nation-state, demanding reading strategies that see connections in other frameworks. In the introduction to *The African Diaspora: African Origins and New World Identities*, Isidore Okpewho defines *diaspora* as "a global space, a worldwide web, that accounts as much for the mother continent as for wherever in the world her offspring may have been driven by the unkind forces of history" (xiv). At

Home in Diaspora examines writing by contemporary black authors living on several continents, analyzing the ways they define themselves in relation to the multiple communities that claim them.

Though this study is concerned with late twentieth-century African diasporic narratives, the literary story of diaspora is certainly not new. We can see international leanings and longings in slave narratives by Olaudah Equiano and Mary Prince, for example, and in the abolitionist writings of Frederick Douglass.[3] Early nineteenth-century African American novels by Sutton Griggs and Martin Delany continued this project.[4] The Harlem Renaissance was an international cultural movement whose guiding spirit was never confined to the neighborhood for which it was named.[5] Langston Hughes, Alain Locke, Claude McKay, Zora Neale Hurston, and Countee Cullen all looked beyond the borders of the United States—frequently toward Africa and the Caribbean—for a cultural identity for black people, an identity they claimed in their diverse narrative practices. In the early 1950s, Richard Wright, James Baldwin, Chester Himes, and other African American writers physically displaced themselves from the racial discrimination they experienced in the United States, relocating their cultural work in Europe and yet consistently "writing back" about U.S. political life, African American urban life, and African independence movements. Black Aestheticism, or the Second Black Renaissance, also looked to Africa and the Caribbean, seeing in those places guiding examples of resistance and opposition to racist exclusion. Contemporary writers such as Paule Marshall, Michelle Cliff, Audre Lorde, and Caryl Phillips use their writing to construct Caribbean identities that are not bounded by the borders of the Atlantic or the islands that dot its waters.

Focusing on the link between displacement and narrative, I suggest that displacement creates a distance that allows writers to encode critiques of their homelands, to construct new homelands, and to envision new communities. For all the writers in this study, the displacement is physical, as in the case of Chester Himes, who migrated permanently to Europe in 1953 and yet never stopped writing to and about the United States. This physical distance enables, via the double displacement of both racial exclusion and exilic or diasporic travel, an intellectual distance that allows critique. Jamaican-born Michelle Cliff, for example, writes novels about Jamaica from the United States, and is thus able to articulate a Caribbean feminism that acknowledges homophobia in her homeland, social stratifications in Jamaica based on race or skin color, and the U.S.-dominated economic policies that contribute to the dire pollution of the island. Distance, then, couples the longing of nostalgia with the liberty of critique. These entanglements and complications are fruitfully articulated in literary narratives.

The principal claim of *At Home in Diaspora* is that diaspora identity is performed in writing even as it precedes the act of writing itself, indeed in the less benign fluids of tears and blood that Du Bois references. When I speak of "diaspora identity," I am largely influenced by Stuart Hall's essay "Cultural Identity and Diaspora." Hall writes:

> Diaspora does not refer us to those scattered tribes whose identity can only be secured in relation to some sacred homeland to which they must at all costs return. . . . The diaspora experience as I intend it here is defined, not by essence or purity, but by the recognition of a necessary heterogeneity and diversity. (235)

Hall's emphasis on heterogeneity defines part of the focus of this book. That is, I am not looking for commonalities of expression in the literatures of these writers, but am interested rather in examining the multiple ways in which they write about home, community, and exile. In *The Black Atlantic: Modernity and Double Consciousness*, Paul Gilroy analyzes a variety of texts (literary, musical, and otherwise) to gain insight into "those structures of feeling that might be termed the inner dialectics of diaspora identification" (23). Gilroy's reference to affect is important for understanding the ways that these writers imagine home, often in registers of both nostalgia and resentment. Avtar Brah further provides a helpful conceptualization of what she calls *diaspora space*, stating, "'Diaspora space' (as distinct from the concept of diaspora) is 'inhabited' not only by diasporic subjects but equally by those who are constructed and represented as 'indigenous.' As such, the concept of *diaspora space* foregrounds the entanglements of genealogies of dispersion with those of 'staying put.'"[6] Perhaps authorship allows these writers to construct a *diaspora space*, a space more habitable than the spaces of exclusion in particular home countries.

I intend this book to show how the articulation of diaspora identity in writing is more than a literary performance; it is, in fact, a political act. Speaking specifically of the importance of writing by black women, Abena P. A. Busia states, "*In its very existence . . .* our literature can be read as a political body of works, and we have a contingent need for a criticism to read and interpret it."[7] Nation-state categories of identity are at odds with the social practices of migratory/diasporic communities as delineated in their cultural production. Lisa Lowe and David Lloyd's introduction to *The Politics of Culture in the Shadow of Capital* urges us, in this transnational era, to reconceive culture as a key site for political contestation, as the expression of resistance to exploitation. They argue for expanding the concept of political agency and the need "to reconceive the 'social'—as the terrain in which politics, culture, and the economic are related, in terms radically other than those given by post-Enlightenment rationalizations of Western society" (3). The following chapters argue that literature still carries the weight of cultural capital, and as such it represents an important location for the staging of resistant identities. Writing a counterhegemonic story about identity, for diasporic writers, is staking a claim through the medium of ink, as opposed to tears and blood.

One way to approach the concept of diaspora and literature is to state that the condition of exile/diaspora is the material condition that produces particular (perhaps repeated) literary responses. There are many important works that delineate certain themes taken up by diasporic writers. Another way to view the topic is to say that the condition of exile/diaspora is itself constituted in literature via these themes.[8] My argument encompasses and yet goes beyond these two claims. My central claim about diaspora identity is that it is revised in the works of black international writers. I refer to Richard Wright, Michelle Cliff, Chester Himes, Simon Njami, and Caryl Phillips as black international writers specifically because their lives and their texts exceed the boundaries of the countries in which they were born. I am not suggesting, however, that all are acculturating immigrants or cosmopolitan global citizens. Rather, I am interested in the particular ways that they use their writings to define and desire spaces of home. By focusing on writing by black authors living in the West, either in exile or expatriation, I seek to unsettle and complicate the typical construction of home and diaspora as binary opposites. That is, in general usage one cannot be at home and in diaspora at the same time. My argument is that the authors in this study create prose writing that performs a home in diaspora, and that these performances have important political and epistemological implications for all of us.

The circulation of texts in transnational markets—the ability of ink itself to travel—means also that a diasporic community is created through these literary acts. This is a community that is often not recognized by nation-states or by traditional models of literary study, yet it exists as a resistant social practice. For example, when Chester Himes, living in permanent exile in Paris, writes a detective novel set in Harlem, the work is read by many disparate audiences, from black European novelists to continental African critics. Chapters 3 and 4 show how the conversations that Himes's texts create can be seen as a diasporic network. I am not suggesting that the concept of diaspora allows black writers to live outside either the hegemonic powers of nation-states or the nation-bound categorizing of literary audiences, publishers, reading communities, and so on. Rather, their work can be read as resistance to this hegemony and thereby it presents us with ways to think beyond both the nation-state and transnational capital as organizing forces of identity. When writers like Richard Wright and Chester Himes produce imaginative work that takes them to places where they materially conceive of themselves as extra-national, they are creating and describing a "third space," which can be called *diaspora*. Citing Fanon, Homi Bhabha reads this "third space" as "a space of being that is wrought from the interruptive, interrogative, tragic experience of blackness, of discrimination, of despair."[9] Looking beyond despair, the following chapters also show how writing allows authors and readers to transform these experiences into oppositional and resistant identities that move away from the tragic. I hope this book shows how the articulation of diaspora in literature points to "a practice of dwelling (differently), as an ambivalent refusal or indefinite deferral of return, and as a positive transnationalism," held out perhaps as a hope against the despair that Bhabha cites.[10]

My analysis emphasizes the "evidence of experience," as well as the discursivity of race and the performativity of identity.[11] That is, in discussing racial discrimination and exclusion, we must never lose sight of the actual tears and blood behind Du Bois's hopeful prophecy. Bhabha asks, "How do strategies of representation or empowerment come to be formulated in the competing claims of communities where, despite shared histories of deprivation and discrimination, the exchange of values, meanings, and priorities may not always be collaborative and dialogical, but may be profoundly antagonistic, conflictual and even incommensurable?"[12] Like Stuart Hall, Paul Gilroy, and others, Bhabha warns against using shared experiences of discrimination to expect generalizable or consistent articulations of diaspora identities. And yet as Michael J. C. Echeruo argues, "[W]hat the history of the black diaspora teaches us is that black identity must always be predicated on black experience."[13] It is this marking out of a ground between essentializing diaspora as a unified or seamless identity and analyzing shared strategies of resistance through fiction that readers must successfully negotiate. I argue for the importance of seeing literary narratives as crucial ongoing sites where diaspora claims are made, unmade, contested, and reinforced.[14]

The Politics of Diaspora: Writing and Location

Literary studies, as a discipline, has for a long time defined its subjects in national terms characterized by a cartographic ordering of cultural production: Japanese Literature, British Literature, American Literature, and so on. This book is part of a project of comparative cultural studies that seeks to intervene in this geographic ordering, attending to movement instead of stasis and migration instead of dwelling. In "Traveling Cultures," James Clifford describes how the institutionalized disciplines of anthropology and ethnography have "privileged relations of dwelling over relations of travel" as "the ethnographer has localized what is actually a regional/national/global nexus, relegating to the margins a culture's external relations and displacements" (99, 100). Clifford's important move, shifting ethnography's focus from dwelling to a nexus of regional/national/global travel, can also be applied to literary studies and must be applied to the study of diaspora literatures. Responding to feminist critiques of his formulation of diaspora experience, Clifford opens up his definitional terms in his 1994 article "Diasporas," qualifying his earlier assertions: "When diasporic experience is viewed in terms of displacement rather than placement, traveling rather than dwelling, and disarticulation rather than rearticulation, then the experiences of men will tend to predominate" (313). This book intends to hold sight of the multiple tensions in both dwelling and traveling, studying the ways that black international writers both construct homes, via their writing, and critique the exclusions of home(s). Michelle Cliff, for example, uses her fiction to both embrace and critique gendered notions of the homeland and the requirements of gender and class position that are exacted from her main character. Barnor Hesse's work redefining notions of "settling" in relation to diasporic communities is important as he argues that "the contours of Black settlements are . . . always more than residential, they are cultures of movement. . . . The articulation of community itself is a discursive investment in time-spatial constitutions within and beyond the nation-state."[15] At Home in Diaspora examines the ways this discursive investment is articulated in literature, though clearly literary narratives are not the only site where diaspora discourses emerge. Several recent cultural studies works have focused on other sites where this "discursive investment" can be seen.[16] Wolfgang Iser has written about the noise that literature still provides in our contemporary culture: "For a technocratically organized culture [i.e., the United States], the noise of literature carves out a space for the unpredictability and invention that allows an unfettered imagination to impinge on cultural circulation."[17] This book listens to the noise produced by literature, seeking the diverse (and sometimes messy and entangled) ways that prose narratives perform diaspora identifications.

At Home in Diaspora focuses on the work of African diasporic writers who do not live in their "home" country and are thereby doubly displaced: first by the discrimination suffered by people of color in any country organized explicitly or implicitly around principles of white supremacy, and second by an actual movement out of that country, away from a place that they (or their parents) may once have called home. This book specifically intends to unsettle the binary between home and diaspora, opening up both terms for redefinition. One understanding of the term diaspora implies a collective cultural identification in which Africa represents a putative original home or pure origin. In "An African Diaspora: The Ontological Project," for example, Echeruo argues that "the burden of Return" should be seen as the "primary condition for the possibility of a diaspora," and that this return is to "a covenanted forever home . . . the source, root, final location for a determinable lineage" (13). What I am suggesting, however, is that we can read contemporary diasporic literature as shifting from the concept of the origin as the site of Return to the concept of the diaspora itself as a home to which a writer experiencing racial exclusions might return, via their writing, through the literary construction of alternative narratives of identity.

Contemporary critical discourse has taught us to be skeptical of concepts like purity, authenticity, and even home itself.[18] What, then, does it mean to identify either a writer or his/her cultural expression as African diasporic? Given that Africa may not represent a singular, recoverable meaning to many diasporic writers, what kinds of qualities can the writing be said to possess in common with the work of other diasporic writers? It is important to avoid essentializing either the writers or their work by referring back to a monolithic notion of blackness or even African "diasporic-ness."[19] In their seminal work on women's diaspora literatures, both Abena P. A. Busia and Gay Wilentz separately address the dangers of essentialism. Though Busia reminds us that "the willingness to embrace a commonality might blind us to the uniqueness which distinguishes the separate peoples of the desired whole," her work argues that there are "common themes in the literature of black women in the diaspora," and she shows that a "rebellious process of self-definition and redefinition" is repeatedly evidenced in these texts.[20] Gay Wilentz's work stresses the ways in which diaspora studies remains "dialectic," not "essentialist."[21]

What the term *diaspora* captures, then, and why I want to retain the term and the specificities it entails, are the memories of enforced migration, displacement, and racial slavery or colonial dominance that emerge in the cultural expressions of diasporic peoples.[22] This history could also be called the Fact of Slavery. In Du Bois's chapter "The Concept of Race" from *Dusk of Dawn* he writes, "[A]s I face Africa I ask myself: what is it between us that constitutes a tie which I can feel better than I can explain?" (117). By way of an answer Du Bois concludes:

> [O]ne thing is sure and that is the fact that since the fifteenth century these ancestors of mine and their other descendants have had a common history; have suffered a common disaster and have one long memory. . . . The physical bond is least and the badge of color relatively unimportant save as a badge; *the real essence of this kinship is its social heritage of slavery; the discrimination and insult.*[23]

In *Dusk of Dawn*, Du Bois revises Booker T. Washington's 1909 framing of diaspora. In *The Story of the Negro*, Washington had written:

> There is, however, a tie which few white men can understand, which binds the American Negro to the African Negro; which unites the black man of Brazil and the black man of Liberia; which is constantly drawing into closer relations all the scattered African peoples whether they are in the old world or the new. There is not only the tie of race, which is strong in any case, but there is the badge of colour, which is specially important in the case of the black man. It is this common badge of colour, for instance, which is responsible for the fact that whatever contributes in any degree to the progress of the American Negro, contributes to the progress of the African Negro, and to the Negro in South America and the West Indies. (33–34)

Du Bois revises Washington in suggesting that the "badge of colour" itself is less important than the experiential history (the "social heritage") that it may signify.[24] Black international writing traces out this kinship of experience, rather than a kinship based on blood or genealogy, and *At Home in Diaspora* attempts to describe the ways that diasporic authors use their writing to resist, explore, and revise "the social heritage of slavery" as it is lived in contemporary discrimination. Against the "social death" of slavery and the social negations of contemporary racisms, black writers embrace authorship as a means of reinstating not one but sometimes multiple resistant selves. In *Turning South Again: Re-Thinking Modernism/Re-Reading Booker T.*, Houston Baker explains the power of authorship: "What I shall call memorial and performative writing is our rite of black revisionary survival par excellence. In the most profound ways, writing, and especially revisionary writing, is our key to sanity, our prophylaxis against civil and social death" (5). Like Baker, Du Bois, too, holds out this hope in the "crooked marks" of his pen, the writing that was so central to his life, in the final words of *Souls of Black Folk:* "[M]ay infinite reason turn the tangle [of racism] straight, and these crooked marks on a fragile leaf be not indeed The End" (217).

In *Modernity at Large: Cultural Dimensions of Globalization,* Arjun Appadurai sees a "postnational imaginary," coupled with a territorial attachment to a homeland, as diasporic peoples' response to "displacement and exile, migration and terror" (176–77). While I agree with Appadurai's idea of a postnational imaginary as part of the formation of what he calls the *transnation* and what others might call *diaspora,* one of the aims of *At Home in Diaspora* is to show the ways that a territorial attachment to a homeland may be a conflicted concept for African diasporic writers. Focusing on writers who are doubly displaced, that is, writers who are diasporic first and migrant second, I examine how their work problematizes the concept of a homeland at the same time that it stakes out a territory we might call *postnational.* By analyzing literary performances on the stage of the page, indeed studying the critical distance that displacement allows, this book argues that literature is a key site where diasporic authors engage or debate concepts of racial identity, diasporic community, and postnational citizenship.

What does it mean to study the work of writers who have migrated from their homes? Indeed most people in the world have made such migrations, whether far or near. *At Home in Diaspora* argues that the processes by which black writers living in the West define identity are in many ways influenced by their sense of "home." The reasons that many black writers have left their homes have everything to do with the material experiences, as well as the cultural memories, of slavery, colonialism, and contemporary racism— Du Bois's "tears and blood." Thus their identities as diasporic peoples compose an important element of their later status as migrants. None of the writers I study seeks to enact a collective return to a particular home or country of origin. Rather, their very status as migrants in many ways represents a rejection of that national identity. Contemporary critical discourse in the fields of cultural studies, literary studies, anthropology, and geography has pointed to what Angelika Bammer calls "the instability of 'home' as a referent."[25] "[T]his instability," says Bammer, "is manifesting itself on a staggering—some believe, unprecedented—scale both globally and locally. On all levels and in all places, it seems, 'home' in the traditional sense (whether

taken to mean 'family,' or 'community,' or 'homeland'/'nation') is either dis-
integrating or being radically redefined."[26] In examining these authors' various negotiations of their relationships to "home," I suggest revising the
concept of "home," rather than jettisoning it altogether. By acknowledging
the persistence of a desire for home, perhaps especially among diasporic
peoples, we can trace its redefinitions and identify the ways that this persistent desire influences the cultural production of black writers living in the
West. Rosemary George's examination of contemporary postcolonial and
colonial literatures, *The Politics of Home*, claims that "[t]he search for the
location in which the self is 'at home' is one of the primary projects of
twentieth-century fiction in English.... [This literature] is not so concerned
with drawing allegories of nation as with the search for viable homes for
viable selves" (3, 5). My argument here is similar and also explains the ways
that diasporic writers use literature to critique the places they might call
home. Further, I want to ask in what sense we might think of the diaspora
itself as a home, thereby uniting the two terms, which are typically viewed
as mutually exclusive.

Most commonly, one's diasporic location is juxtaposed with the concept
of a perhaps imagined original homeland from which one is now displaced.
By *uniting* the terms, however, we may suggest that in the absence of any
recoverable singular homeland of origin, the diaspora itself—a plurilocal
(also imagined) community of peoples politically self-identified within its
scope—represents a home. This is a home that is not bounded, singular, or
exclusionary. The following chapters question the idea of a singular community with an implied "collective consciousness." Barnor Hesse defines the
diasporic imaginary as "itself vitally emergent in the conditions set by the
'inability of collective consciousness to absorb' the enormity of the traumas
associated with slavery and also the ultimate impossibility of a collective
consciousness."[27] I think the notion of diaspora can represent a multiple,
plurilocal, constructed location of home, thus avoiding ideas of fixity,
boundedness, and nostalgic exclusivity traditionally implied by the word
home.[28]

This book analyzes the ways that black writers construct a home in diaspora via their literary production. Looking further at the constructed nature
of home, Bammer presents the provocative idea that perhaps home is best
understood as an "amalgam, a pastiche, a performance."[29] She refers to home
as "an enacted space within which we try on and play out roles and relationships of both belonging and foreignness."[30] It is this very enactment
that the following chapters analyze. But precisely what is this "enacted space"

in which one's relationship to home or not-home is constructed, negotiated, and repeatedly revised? I suggest that one important realm is discourse and, specifically, literary production. As Khachig Tölölyan states, "[L]ike the nation, the diaspora is not just an organized but also an imagined community whose ligatures are discourse and representation, ideology and the reproduction of a subjectivity of belonging."[31] In seeking to understand the role of discourse in the performance of home, I would turn briefly to Judith Butler's work on the discursivity of gender. In *Gender Trouble*, Butler asserts that "genders can be neither true nor false, but are only produced as the truth effects of a discourse of primary and stable identity." In fact, the gendered body can be seen as performative, since "it has no ontological status apart from the various acts which constitute its reality" (136). This is similar to what I am claiming about the nature of diaspora identification, in that there need not be an ontological "Africanness" to which a diasporic identification refers.[32] And yet, conversely, the desire to claim a home occurs in the language of literary narrative as a direct result of experiencing racial exclusions "at home."

Black writers living in the West repeatedly describe a feeling of statelessness resulting from a lack of state protection. Mari Matsuda explains that racist speech is an example of the exclusions enacted at home and she identifies the affective dimension to this exclusion when she says that racist speech "hits right at the emotional place where we feel the most pain." But when the government appears to sanction such racist speech or acts, the emotional pain may become a sense of statelessness:

> When hundreds of police officers are called out to protect racist marchers, when the courts refuse to redress for racial insult, and when racist attacks are officially dismissed as pranks, the victim becomes a stateless person. Target-group members must either identify with a community that promotes racist speech or admit that the community does not include them.[33]

Chester Himes, James Baldwin, W. E. B. Du Bois, and others have all indicated this state-sanctioning of racism as the reason for their migrations and exiles away from their "home" country. Though there are far too many examples to mention, I provide two passages here that discuss ideas of belonging and the sense of exclusion caused by racist practices. In the second section of his autobiography, Wright writes, "Negroes are told in a language they cannot possibly misunderstand that their native land is not their own."[34] Decades later, black feminist legal scholar Patricia Hill Collins writes of her own childhood:

I now see that I was searching for a location where I "belonged," a safe
intellectual and political space that I could call "home." But how could
I presume to find a home in a system that at best was predicated upon
my alleged inferiority and, at worst, was dedicated to my removal? More
important, why would I even want to?[35]

The perception of a state-sanctioned racism has been the reason that black
writers continually ask in what sense the United States can be a *home* to
people of color.

Writing diaspora, then, is part of the construction of an alternate community, part of the "search for viable homes for viable selves" in opposition
to this experience of statelessness.[36] Peter Ekeh explains the relationship
between state exclusions and the construction of alternative communities
this way:

> [K]inship disappears from societal structures whenever alternative institutions,
> principally states, provide for individuals' basic security needs. If states fail
> to do so, kinship becomes a source of security for the individual, acquiring
> the status of surrogate statehood in some instances. Indeed if the state
> becomes the source of individuals' insecurities, if the state persecutes
> individuals, they will construct a kinship system that will enable them to
> survive the state's transgressions.[37]

Against these hurts, writers construct other forms of community and identification, as Hesse reminds us that "[t]he affirmation of Black community is its
politicization. . . . Categoric distinctions between public and private, personal
and political, local and national, are blurred in the activities of diasporic
identification."[38] The following chapters show how diaspora identifications
exist within, across, and outside nation-states, neither evading nor embrac-
ing the nation-state as the ultimate horizon of social membership. If we
read, however, with solely national concerns, we risk missing the politically
performative power of writing diaspora. These performances are always multiple, and as readers we must attend to the different accents and valances
with which diasporic writers invest their writings of home(s).

Writing Home: More Than "Crooked Marks on a Fragile Leaf"

The identification with a particular place as home is something that can be
claimed in discourse, but that may have little or no ontological status. An
obvious argument here is that certainly there is an empirically verifiable
recourse to geography: home is where you were born. But this phrase may

have a conflicted meaning for many diasporic peoples. Consider Toni Morrison's literary example in *Beloved* of a child born literally on the run to an escaping female slave somewhere in or near Ohio. Or consider the case of black writer Caryl Phillips, who was born in St. Kitts but emigrated to England with his family before he was one year old. Of course, there are many more examples of ways that a geographic answer attempts to unite space and place and to fix this with a notion of time: in many instances, however, one's entry into the world becomes an insufficient answer or an incomplete explanation for either what is home or what is one's geographic (or national) identity.

Because a study of diasporic literature unsettles a nation-based configuration of American literature, *At Home in Diaspora* enters into conversation with comparative American studies. Stuart Hall reminds us that America begins as "the New World . . . [that] has to be understood as the place of many, continuous displacements. . . . [I]t is the signifier of migration itself."[39] Vè Vè Clark says that "all cultures in the 'New World' are diasporic. The singular memory that we 'Americans' share in the hemisphere originates from histories of resettlement, emigration, and displacement."[40] *At Home in Diaspora* examines several narrative genres from diverse late twentieth-century authors whose work and lives crisscross a space now commonly referred to as the Black Atlantic. When diasporic movement becomes a subject of study itself, then American studies must take into account the various and varied transatlantic crossings that inform its literary productions. This book examines both canonical and lesser-known writers, men and women who reside primarily in the United States, Britain, and Europe. Clearly, not all of these performances will reach the same conclusion, be read (seen) by the same audience, or construct the same stagings of diaspora. The differences in the performances are complicated and instructive and often have much to do with gender and sexuality. My readings are informed by a feminist politics that takes note, for example, of the ways that Simon Njami's male protagonist claims a freedom in Paris unavailable to expatriate African women and Michelle Cliff's protagonist rejects prescribed gender roles in the Jamaican society of which her family is a part.

This book examines the space of prose narrative as a site in which black writers enact their relationship to various notions of "home." By necessity, then, such a project must move beyond traditional national boundaries secured by a geopolitical ordering of world events and spaces. Instead, by paying attention to both movement and settlement, we can deconstruct the linguistic binaries in such paired terms as colony and metropole, dominant culture and subordinated culture, homeland and adopted land. It is in the ever-shifting interstices of these terms that diasporic identities are constituted, and these in-between spaces inform the cultural production of diasporic peoples. What I hope the following chapters show is that the texts of diasporic writers give us new ways to conceive of community and resistance to oppression and domination.

The Politics of Nostalgia

While geographic displacement from a putative homeland can be seen as a common condition uniting many diasporic writers, I am more interested in examining the moments of movement (lived or invented) that inform a writer's work. That is, rather than posit a reified homeland from which each writer has been "displaced," I instead probe the ways that transatlantic shuttling between European, African, and "New World" locations informs these writers' literary production. These "movements in time, space, and memory" reconstitute "archaeologies of places of attachment or bewilderment, which are reinhabited in order to comprehend contemporary settings."[41] Here Barnor Hesse's words provide a key description of the way that Chester Himes's detective novels revisit a Harlem constituted perhaps solely in his nostalgic imaginings—a place he was attached to in a sense filled with bewilderment, having never lived there, yet desiring to journey there in memory, creating a community of African American resistance to police invasion. Himes's literary attachment to Harlem can be understood by way of Stuart Hall's notion of a "homeland" as a symbolic imaginary, an "infinitely renewable source of desire, memory, myth, search, discovery" that therefore "fuels the engines of nostalgia and fetishization."[42] Indeed, for a writer like Himes, the very notion of "home" itself is problematized. Himes has said that he experienced "a sort of pure homesickness" in writing his detective novels, a homesickness that was also an intense "pleasure." From a position of expatriation—hurt by U.S. racial injustices and yet longing for the familiar streets of home—he invents a hyperbolic Harlem landscape he can control. But the facts of Himes's life make the ground of familiarity slip away: Himes never lived in Harlem. Through a fictive Harlem marked by named landmarks, streets, and neighborhoods, Himes transports himself to a mental space he desires to call "home." His detective novels bear witness to the power of nostalgia as symbolic imaginary. And yet it is important to delineate the political elements of this nostalgia. In other words, rather than condemn Himes's nostalgia as a facile, potentially regressive state of consciousness, I aim to show in chapter 3 how Himes's re-creations of what was paradoxically both home and not-home enable him to stage a political critique of that very location.

To take another example, Clare Savage, the protagonist of both *Abeng* (1984) and *No Telephone to Heaven* (1987), is, like author Michelle Cliff, a light-skinned Jamaican who has lived in Jamaica, the United States, and London. Clare struggles with her nostalgic longing for her Jamaican birthplace, what Cliff has called "this landscape of her identity."[43] And yet Cliff's texts also refuse to construct Jamaica as idyllic or pure, instead presenting a critique of class politics and homophobia on the island. I am interested in the ways that diasporic writers negotiate their relationships to the various places they call home, and I hope to show the ways they use writing to perform a sense of home in diaspora. How does such a trajectory strain against the overdetermined discourses of nation, race, and family by which the modern self is so often defined? My purpose is not to illuminate an imaginary construct, a fixed finality of selfhood that an author may achieve in and through narrative, because few performances end so simply. Rather, I explore the discursive strategies these authors adopt and the literary performances they enact, studying the ways their texts represent a space of negotiation with a place called "home."

Literary performances that speak in the registers of nostalgia are complicated when they encounter notions of accountability, however socially constructed and discriminatory those notions may be. Judith Butler cautions, "[I]f one always risks meaning something other than what one thinks one utters, then one is, as it were, vulnerable in a specifically linguistic sense to a social life of language that exceeds the purview of the subject who speaks."[44] Butler's warning can help us see the shaky ground between the utterance of diaspora identity in narrative, the politics of culture, and the material reception of "racially marked" utterances. Black writers are often held unjustly accountable by a community of readers who assume they write a national narrative or represent a national discourse in the sense of speaking for all black people, all African Americans, and so on.[45] For some French readers, for example, Chester Himes becomes a representative of all of Black America, and the Harlem of his novels is consequently imagined as sociologically "true." Himes is held accountable both by European readers, who consider him a native informant on American blackness, and by those critics who see his creation of a lurid Harlem as pandering to French tastes for exoticism. I argue in chapter 3, however, that Himes invests his nostalgic imaginings with trenchant political critique.

At Home in Diaspora interrogates not only the ways that nostalgia for a seamless wholeness, a childhood self, can represent a problematic, ahistorical sense of retreat, but also the ways that social systemic forces act against the acceptance of a diasporic identity. That is, a definition of identity that is singular and exclusive may occasionally be an internal desire betrayed in diasporic literatures, but singular or bounded identities are also externally imposed by the larger social system. In Michelle Cliff's second novel, *No Telephone to Heaven*, Harry/Harriet, a gay male friend of Clare Savage's who cross-dresses, warns Clare, "Cyaan [can't] live split. Not in this world" (131). According to Harry/Harriet, the Jamaican milieu demands that one choose among definitional categories. Clearly, however, the choice is often made for one, by others, dependent on legal definitions and rulings such as *Plessy v. Ferguson* and the counting of "drops of blood." To what extent and in what contexts can Michelle Cliff choose to define herself as black, Jamaican, or lesbian? Audre Lorde illuminates this dilemma when she writes:

> As a black lesbian feminist comfortable with the many different ingredients of my identity, and a woman committed to racial and sexual freedom from oppression, I find I am constantly being encouraged to pluck out some one aspect of myself and present this as the meaningful whole, eclipsing or denying the other parts of myself. But this is a destructive and fragmenting way to live.[46]

At Home in Diaspora explores the sociopolitical dilemma posed by Lorde and Harry/Harriet and addresses the ways that diasporic identifications might exist in tension with discourses of "wholeness." Richard Wright, for example, described himself throughout his life as of the West, yet also not. His papers at Yale contain a manuscript where he writes eighty-five statements, all beginning with "I am an American, but . . ." *At Home in Diaspora* seeks to locate analysis in the space of Wright's comma. I am interested in the process by which writers claim a larger identity, one that becomes neither a seamless wholeness nor a debilitating schizophrenia but perhaps something closer to the fruitfully multiple stagings of identity affirmed by Lorde.

Critical Distances

The displacements of many of the writers discussed in this book seem rather permanent in that no writer seeks a final forever return to her or his homeland, country of origin, or ancestral connection. The nostalgia with which they invest their performances of belonging is often conflicted and uneven.

In *Black Power* (1954), Richard Wright approaches the continent of Africa with both an intense longing and a deep alienation. Despite the fact that Chester Himes repeatedly located his fictions in the United States, he felt that the American reception of his literary work represented a racial injustice emblematic of the larger racism of U.S. culture as a whole; he died in Spain in the first home he ever owned, purchased when he was in his sixties. Michelle Cliff has stated that she will not return to Jamaica because she is a lesbian and "Jamaica is such a repellently homophobic society." "Because I'm gay," she says, "I don't feel like I have a place there."[47] Though Simon Njami was born in Switzerland, Africa functions in his novels as a homeland that his characters both reject and desire. As for himself, Njami has said, "I don't feel like going to live in Africa. Because I just couldn't live there. I could spend one month, two, three maybe, but not more than that."[48] Coextensive, however, with these disavowals are the ways in which these writers' texts inhabit the very sites they reject. Even as they may deny a particular national or continental identity, they use the discursive space of prose narrative to encircle and claim that very identity. Yet what makes these writers so complex and interesting is the political critique of "home" with which they invest their literary visions. These ambivalences form the gist of this study as I attempt to flesh out the ways that physical distance allows these writers to perform the double work of nostalgic longing and political critique. In *Black Power*, for example, Richard Wright is interested both in distancing himself from Africa and in instructing Kwame Nkrumah in the appropriate governance of Ghana. Himes clearly critiques U.S. racism even as he desires both African American community and American literary fame. Cliff's work clearly critiques Jamaican homophobia and color prejudice, even as she views the writing of *Abeng* as her attempt "to construct [herself] as a Jamaican."[49]

What I have been suggesting throughout this introduction is that it is the discursive space of fiction that exiled diasporic writers use to enact their relationships to home. Himes has said that he only felt at home in his detective novels; Cliff writes *Abeng* to construct herself as a Jamaican; Caryl Phillips depicts centuries of diasporic identities and the ways they overlap in his book *Higher Ground*. Perhaps we may say that the condition of exile and distance enables a certain kind of literary creativity. Cliff has said of the United States, "I like writing from here; I like the view from here."[50] But this comment is made in direct response to her previous comment about the ways that Jamaica excludes her because she is a lesbian; Cliff sees the United States as more tolerant of her sexual identification. Both Himes and Njami have represented France as sometimes welcoming to black people. Yet though the space of exile becomes a vantage point from which to view a home country, it never becomes a "home" for these writers. Himes never learned to speak a European language. Njami has said that though he has lived all his life in Europe, "[i]n some other ways I'm not a European."[51] Cliff has stated that no number of years living in the United States will make this "home" for her.[52] Thus, as each diasporic writer rejects, or is rejected by, a home or country of origin, so, too, do they feel that an adopted country will never be "home." Cliff connects this condition of "statelessness" (her word) to notions of race and diaspora. She aligns herself with African Americans, whom she feels "have never been wholeheartedly accepted as Americans in this country. So in a sense that's the kind of American I am." And she also aligns herself with other "children who came out of diaspora . . . people who don't have a country."[53] Exiled South African writer Bessie Head comes immediately to mind, and Cliff dedicates *Abeng* to her.

If in the beginning of this introduction I proposed that these writers use the literary act to construct a home in diaspora, I would now like to put further pressure on the term *home*. Michele Wallace has said that "to be 'black' . . . is not a homeland but a temporary and provisional resting place."[54] By redefining the word *home*, we can retain its power as a desire, yet lose its bounded and exclusionary nature. Perhaps we can think of a coalitional, processual "resting place," temporary and nomadic, that black writers create through fiction. Wallace's definition of blackness as a "resting place" exactly captures what I intend in describing the performance of diaspora in narrative as a home. Perhaps the idea of a resting place is precisely what appeals to people experiencing various forms of racist exclusion.

Diaspora Literacy and Strategies of Reading

The concept of diaspora identity is not new and begins with such texts as Olaudah Equiano's 1789 narrative, in which he details his movements from the time of his kidnapping in Africa to his eventual claiming of an Afro-British identity, describing his many "homes" along this journey.[55] Formulating a method of inquiry about diasporic texts demands that we develop reading strategies that will allow us to hear the doubleness in many of these texts—the critique and the construction. Bhabha describes this textual power as a

> *performative, deformative* structure that does not simply revalue the contents of a cultural tradition, or transpose values "cross-culturally." The cultural

inheritance of slavery or colonialism is brought *before* modernity *not* to resolve its historic differences into a new totality, nor to forego its traditions.
It is to introduce another locus of inscription and intervention.[56]

Reading such diverse textual performances demands that we also employ
a reading strategy of "diaspora literacy." Vè Vè Clark's key critical term,
"diaspora literacy," requires that readers possess "a knowledge of historical,
social, cultural, and political development generated by lived and textual
experience."[57] An attention to historical detail, to geographical specificity,
can help us avoid (mis)using diaspora as an overfull metaphor.

Though *At Home in Diaspora* analyzes the way these writers use fiction to
perform their varied and multiple claims to home, I think their texts also
importantly perform a "rhetoric of refusal," to quote Doris Sommer.[58] There
are spaces in these texts that disrupt whatever impulses a reader may have
to read these books "about" home(s) as national narratives. Michelle Cliff's
recent novel *Free Enterprise* begins with an epigraph from Miles Davis: "I
always listen for what I can leave out." This performative refusal to divulge
all, to present the "perfect oppositional other," is a strategy diasporic narratives employ to remain oppositional, and it is a strategy that implicates the
reader as well. That is, we must learn to listen for what the author has left
out, yet paradoxically without assuming that we can fill it in, master, or
know it. Sommer emphasizes the significant challenge posed by learning to
read resistance as she points to the potentially coalitional political strategies of a reading that respects difference.[59] The suggestion of a coalitional
politics between writer and reader is very hopeful and productive and presents an answer to the question: why literature? Does diasporic literature
present us with a mode of engagement that must be attended, that demands
our participation? Think of Toni Morrison's gorgeous conclusion to her
novel *Jazz*. Consider the interpretive power she signals between the reader
and the book as the (talking) book itself invites us: "Say make me, remake
me. You are free to do it and I am free to let you because look, look. Look
where your hands are. Now" (229). Doris Sommer's warnings also point to
the oppositional interpretation, as well as oppositional pedagogy, which I
hope this book enables. That is, in learning and teaching how to read the
resistance in a text, how to recognize the spaces at least of what is left out,
perhaps we can avoid being guilty of some of the misreadings of Himes, for
example, discussed in chapter 3. Perhaps these texts point not only to a coalitional home in diaspora, but to the potential of coalitional reading and teaching strategies.[60]

Part I
The Fact of Slavery

1

"On the Clifflike Margins of Many Cultures": Richard Wright's Travels

The history of the Negro in America is the history of America written in vivid and bloody terms; it is the history of Western Man writ small. It is the history of men who tried to adjust themselves to a world whose laws, customs, and instruments of force were leveled against them. The Negro is America's metaphor.

—Richard Wright

Words Know No National Boundaries

In an article published in *Ebony* magazine in 1953, Richard Wright tells his interviewer, black American writer William Gardner Smith, about his views on writing and his expatriate life in Paris: "People think . . . that because I'm here, I'm out of touch with the States. I find that the reverse is true. I see the States in better perspective from a distance. The outlines of the Negro struggle, and the shape of the whole society, become more sharply defined."[1] When Smith presses him on his ability to fight in the "Negro struggle," Wright replies, "I fight with words. They know no national boundaries."[2] Richard Wright was at this time perhaps the most famous African American author in the world, having published the best-selling *Native Son* in 1940 and a portion of his autobiography, *Black Boy*, in 1945.[3] He left the United States permanently for Paris in 1948, and spent the rest of his life traveling and writing about multiple locations—among them Spain, Ghana, and Indonesia. Wright's comments to Smith in *Ebony* draw our attention to issues of perspective and distance and the way these intersect with writing and expatriation. Wright describes a sharper focus that geographical distance paradoxically allows. Understanding Wright as a diasporic author, writing from the mobile and multiple locations of expatriate travel, yet ever within the shifting identity spaces of global blackness, enables us to reexamine some of his important and relatively neglected literary works in a new light.

This chapter foregrounds Wright's use of his writing as a forum where he could articulate a space between national and diasporic identities. Two essays by Wright, "Blueprint for Negro Writing" (1937) and "The Literature of the Negro in the U.S." (1957), open up this topic of writing and its relationship to national identity. "The Literature of the Negro in the U.S." is an essay from Wright's collection, *White Man, Listen! Lectures in Europe 1950–1956,* published in 1957. Wright dedicates *White Man, Listen!* to both Eric Williams (prime minister of Trinidad and Tobago from 1962 until his death in 1981, and the author of *Capitalism and Slavery*) and "*the Westernized and tragic elite of Asia, Africa, and the West Indies*—the lonely outsiders who exist on the clifflike margins of many cultures . . . men who . . . seek desperately for a home for their hearts: a home which, if found, could be a home for the hearts of all men." In his characteristically Wrightian introduction to *White Man, Listen!* entitled "Why and Wherefore," he sets out his perspective and angle of vision, stating, "I'm a rootless man, but I'm neither psychologically distraught nor in any wise particularly perturbed because of it. . . . I can make myself at home almost anywhere on this earth" (xxviii–xix). This chapter will explore the tension in Wright's discourse between distance and desire, between alignment and aloneness, as I attempt to show the ways that Wright uses several genres to construct an identity outside the categories of nation and/or race.

Reading *White Man, Listen!* alongside one of Wright's travel narratives, *Black Power,* allows us to see the ways that Wright uses multiple genres to search for a home in the heart.[4] This chapter pursues two lines of argument: first I am interested in framing Wright in the context of "the lonely outsiders" with whom he frequently aligns himself. To do so, I want to turn to the multiple global locations of Wright's traveling to study the ways that these places shape his writing. Wright's constant textual and geographical transit does not result in a fixed notion of home thrown into sharper relief by the vantage point of distance. Rather, Wright uses this movement to redefine home as a more fluid space. In the following telling passage from Wright's essay, "How Bigger Was Born" (appended to most versions of his most famous novel, *Native Son*), he describes both his and his protagonist's status as outsiders: "Bigger was attracted and repelled by the American scene. He was an American, because he was a native son; but he was also a Negro nationalist in a vague sense because he was not allowed to live as an American. Such was his life and mine; neither Bigger nor I resided fully in either camp" (450–51). This ground between what Wright describes as a vague Negro nationalism and a natal, yet prohibited, Americanism, sheds light on the ways that Wright uses writing to articulate an identity that can accommodate this in-betweenness.

The second question this chapter poses is: What is the home in the heart of which Wright speaks in his dedication to *White Man, Listen!*? I am interested in the ways that writing (of the essay and of travel narratives) becomes for Wright a "home in the heart." And yet this home must be read as ambivalent, not definitive, shifting rather than fixed, as we trace Wright's vacillations between connection and disassociation. At various points in his career Wright was considered both the most prominent African American author and a key black expatriate author. There is a triangle represented by Wright's 1937 essay, "Blueprint for Negro Writing"; his travel narrative to Ghana, *Black Power*; and his European lectures collected in *White Man, Listen!* Wright probably would not have called this triangle *diaspora*, but reading these texts together, in a diasporic frame, enables us to see how writing becomes for the diasporic author a way to articulate identity beyond national boundaries. In Wright's life and work we can see the tensions, overlaps, and intersections between various forms of national and "racial" identity. This chapter will analyze Wright's rootlessness; the multiple meanings of his phrase, "I can make myself at home almost anywhere on this earth"; what it would mean for him to be at home; and how the concepts of both rootlessness and being at home are related to his identity and practice as a writer, specifically an expatriate writer. To examine these issues, I turn to writing that Wright produced both in the United States and elsewhere—work in which he analyzed U.S. literature and evaluated African politics as projected by the Ghanaian independence movement.

Writing and National Identity: "The Literature of the Negro in the U.S."

The third chapter of *White Man, Listen!*, "The Literature of the Negro in the U.S.," shows us the place that writing itself occupies in Wright's global thought. It is significant that the central chapter of this book of essays on various global political issues concerns black American literature. Clearly this was a likely topic for Wright to be asked to lecture on in his various European travels. Nina Kressner Cobb identifies this essay as the earliest one in the collection, and she has found a similar speech in the Webb Collection of the Schomburg Collection in New York entitled "Speech for a White Audience," which was written shortly after World War II.[5] As one of the most prominent African American authors of his era, Wright was seen (globally) as a spokesman for the subject of "the literature of the Negro in the U.S." And yet we see Wright's early internationalism, as his topic here quickly extends beyond the boundaries of the United States.

What does the most famous African American author have to say to his European audiences about the literature of the Negro in the United States? Wright, who rejects racial essentialism on many levels of his work, utters the question that any such generalizing title must address: "What is a Negro? What is Negro writing?" In his answer he speaks in national terms, specifically addressing black American identity through the proper noun *Negro:* "Being a Negro has to do with the American scene, with race hate, rejection, ignorance, segregation, discrimination, slavery, murder, fiery crosses, and fear."[6] Wright here describes Negro identity as an American identity that is marked, and even formed, by the experience of racial subjugation and violence. He explains that the centuries of slavery that define the experience of black people in America created "a psychological distance between [the Negro writer] and the land in which he lives."[7] What is this sense of distance between a writer and a geographic space or a politico-juridical idea that is "the land in which he lives"? In this section Wright suggests that "distance" from one's writing subject is not a condition unique to a writer living in exile or expatriation. Rather, he describes a political distance from the meaningful benefits and rewards of full citizenship rights within one's "home" country. For Wright this distance, created by systemic racial discrimination, generates critical consciousness. He sees writing as political and unavoidably fastened on "the land in which he lives." Wright in this chapter is circling around what he sees as a paradoxical conflict between being Western and being a "Negro." It is important to see that Wright rejects an idea of identity based on "race" but acknowledges that the experience of racial discrimination in the United States is constitutive of the identity "Negro."

The distance that Wright describes, the "psychological distance" that exists between the Negro writer and "the land in which he lives," is paradoxically a distance that cannot avoid the closeness of the visual. In fact, distance telescopes quickly and becomes microscopic. Here Wright's prose takes on the vocabularies of the visual, a discourse of the scopic regimes that bind black subjectivity in America. Wright explains this visual focus and how it affects one's writerly attention: "[T]he eyes of the American Negro were fastened in horror upon something from which he could not turn away. The Negro could not take his eyes off the auction block: he never had a chance to; he could not stop thinking of lynching: he never had a chance to."[8] We will later see how the spectacle of the auction block comes to haunt Wright in his visit to Kwame Nkrumah's Gold Coast, as he tours Christianborg Castle and other physical remnants of the slave trade.

Wright's analysis of early black American writers such as George Moses Horton (1797–1883) demonstrates that what makes this literature "Negro" is not a "racial feeling," but rather the "social situation" from which the literature stems, i.e., the "race hate and Jim Crowism" that characterizes American life, "the land in which he lived."[9] I want to argue here that for Wright, racial feeling itself is generated by the persistence of this spectacle of violence, as he compares his own poetry on lynching to that of James Weldon Johnson. Wright invites this comparison of the poetic works of Johnson (whom he calls "as conservative a Negro as ever lived in America") with his own famous poem, "Between the World and Me," and asks, "Did ever in history a race of men have for so long a time the same horror *before their eyes?* . . . The horrors that confront Negroes stay in peace and war, in winter and summer, night and day."[10] In this comparison Wright suggests that the identity "Negro" is constructed across class lines, based on the common visual focus that the material threat of racial violence demands of its victims. In her essay, "'Can You Be BLACK and Look at This?'" Elizabeth Alexander analyzes the display of terroristic images in American culture. She argues that such images as the Rodney King videos and Emmett Till's open casket function to "consolidate group affiliations by making blackness an unavoidable, irreducible sign which despite its abjection leaves creative space for group self-definition and self-knowledge."[11] African diasporic writers frequently engage this creative space, and in doing so they transform a position of abject subjectivity into one of resistant group affiliation.

Trudier Harris's work can help us see the effects of this brutal focus on ritual violence in the African diasporic literary canon. Her book, *Exorcising Blackness: Historical and Literary Lynching and Burning Rituals,* theorizes the black writer's focus on lynching as a ritual exorcism, parallel and counter to the ritualistic nature of lynching itself. Harris includes Wright prominently in her study of black American authors who perform this exorcism, devoting a chapter to Wright because lynching was so prevalent in his aesthetic vision. She explains, "Richard Wright uses the lynching and burning ritual, and historical and social connotations surrounding it, to shape the basis of his aesthetic vision of the world. Metaphoric lynching, along with literal lynching, permeates his works."[12] Harris's analysis of Wright focuses largely on writing undertaken by him while in the United States and may imply that part of the reason for Wright's self-exile was to escape the psychologically violent toll exacted by this focus. Indeed, Wright once wrote out eighty-five statements, each beginning with the words, "I am an American, but—." Statement 2 alludes to his reasons for exile, lest there be any doubt: "I am an American, but—I live in exile for reasons that the tint of my skin should make plain to you without any cataloguing of the racial evils that exist for millions of black, brown, and yellow men on American soil."[13] Perhaps we can say that Wright's move to France was an attempt to escape the socially designated American category, Negro, as delimited by the threat of white violence.

Harris's study shows how literary portrayals of violence against African Americans function to indirectly generate community: "As rituals for whites reinforced their solidarity against blacks, so, too, in a way do black writers' portrayals of such rituals consolidate for their black readers the threats that could originate in the white community."[14] Harris is not saying here that the scenes themselves create community, but that they communalize a sense of the fear of violence. She examines "the function [such scenes] serve for the black writer in relation to his black readers. The black writer becomes a kind of ritual priest in ever keeping before his black audience the essence of one of the forces that have shaped their lives . . . for the sake of racial memory."[15] The term "racial memory" can help us understand the ways that Richard Wright speaks of the specter of lynching that is ever before the black American writer. Wright is a person who would not subscribe to the notion of a "racial memory," implying as it does a genetically inscribed code of reactions, responses, or models of behavior. And yet there is a concrete historical reality that asserts itself when he attempts to talk about Negro literature and Negro writing. Perhaps he would call this reality "nationalism." In working through the concept of diaspora, I have tried to avoid getting stuck between the poles of nation and exile—there is another way of describing identity that comprises both.[16] In its literary focus on lynching, Wright's work demonstrates how experiences of state-sanctioned racial exclusion (1) create a subset nationalist identity within the nation-state; and (2) create the disavowal of belonging to or being accountable to the nation-state. Harris describes this positioning further: "Being historically informed about his or her heritage in blood and violence makes each black writer a member of a club from whose membership he or she cannot be severed."[17] Richard Wright was a person, however, who was often quite critical of any such "clubs."

We can turn to Wright's early essay, "Blueprint for Negro Writing," to see his views on "the nationalism of the Negro." This much-anthologized essay, published in *New Challenge* in 1937 (the same year as Zora Neale Hurston's *Their Eyes Were Watching God*), explains that "the nationalism of the Negro" is born from both a desire and a struggle for freedom and the "lynch rope, bayonet and mob rule."[18] Here Wright describes an identity that is created by both oppression and resistance to oppression. Wright signals this sense of "Negro" as an identity created by the system of racial subordination as practiced in the United States in order to talk about writing. My aim here is to show how diasporic writers use their literary expression to revise and redefine their identity in resistance to this negative space, outside the limiting space of abjection.

Literature enables both the writer and the reader to formulate a positive and oppositional response to a life marked by the threat of potential violence. Harris's discussion of Wright's poem, "Between the World and Me" (originally published in the *Partisan Review* in 1935), sheds light on the role of the artist. The speaker of the poem stumbles across the remains of a lynching in the woods, and the speaker's voiced identity shifts from that of a witness to the scene to that of the next victim of such violence. Harris states, "The speaker is alone, but he is alone with the community of his race. Individual black tragedies become racial tragedies."[19] In the last lines of the poem, the speaker identifies himself with the dry bones of the victim's skull, indicating that

> [t]he speaker defines himself as potential, potential not to rise up recreated in flesh to save a race, but the potential of the artist to become spokesman for that race and to assume a certain amount of responsibility toward it. His are the dry bones of creativity, the skeleton from which his body of works will grow...he moves...from the casual observer of related details to the ordering of details into literature.[20]

It is this ordering of details into literature, and the body of works that they create, that is my topic and focus here. Perhaps diaspora is a way of talking about an international nationalism—it is a linking of these terms, as "diaspora" becomes a way to describe a globally dispersed identity of diverse peoples who share certain similar historical experiences. Harris's point is that the creative exorcising of lynching literature, through the repetition of the

violent scene, affirms the artist's "basic belief in racial survival," thus keeping this belief alive for other readers. Again, if we look to "Blueprint," we
see Wright's thoughts on the role of the writer: "Negro writers must accept
the nationalist implications of their lives, not in order to encourage them,
but in order to change and transcend them. . . . And a nationalist spirit in
Negro writing means a nationalism carrying the highest possible pitch of
social consciousness."[21] Richard Wright's life and work present us with
this ongoing tension between nationalist discourse and antiessentialism as
Wright's intellectual thought twists and turns along the paths of diaspora
and expatriation.

Readers of *Black Boy/American Hunger* know that a young Richard Wright,
growing up in Jim Crow Mississippi, discovered in the "whites only" library
that words could be used as weapons. Wright's autobiography shows us the
ways that he formed his identity as a writer, the ways that writing became a
response to the oppressive social situation in which he was raised. In "The
Literature of the Negro in the U.S.," Wright explains that literature is what
enables "the Negro" to "launch criticism upon his native land, which made
him feel a sense of estrangement that he never wanted" (109). Wright's essay
moves his discussion of black American literature from a reactive stance to
a proactive one, as he explains the international role of black American
writing: "The American Negro is the only group in our nation that consistently and passionately raises the question of freedom. . . . This is a service
to America and to the world. More than this: The voice of the American
Negro is rapidly becoming the most representative voice of America and of
oppressed people anywhere in the world today" (105). Wright further unites
black American writers with a global coalition when he states that oppressed
people in the world "want our testimony." Here the political role of writing
is explicitly international, and we see the ways that writing becomes a home
for the diasporic author when he states, "So, the voice that America rejected
is finding a home at last, a home such as was never dreamed of" (106). Thus
in this early essay/lecture, he circles back to the international importance of
a voice for freedom, as well as to the ability of this literary voice to carve
out a political space called home.

Black Power and the Myth of a "Return" to Africa

Wright also used the genre of the travel narrative to articulate a politics of
nationalism, diaspora, and identity. In Wright's final chapter of *White Man,
Listen!*, "The Miracle of Nationalism in the African Gold Coast," he fol-

lows on his travels to Ghana, describing a nationalism different from the nationalism he associated with Negro literature. Kwame Nkrumah's nationalism grows out of the rise of a formerly colonized people into a state of independence and international recognition known as Ghana, not the British-ruled Gold Coast. In *Black Power*, however, Wright approaches his trip to Ghana with perhaps much more personal issues in mind than the role of nationalism in this early and important African independence movement. Reading Wright's travel narrative, *Black Power*, expands and complicates our analysis of Wright's discourse on global black identities.

As a black American expatriate author pondering why a journey to Africa would be significant for him, Richard Wright explains,

> The fortuity of my birth had cast me in the "racial" role of being of African descent, and that fact now resounded in my mind with associations of hatred, violence, and death. Phrases from my childhood rang in my memory: one-half Negro, one-quarter Negro, one-eighth Negro, one-sixteenth Negro, one thirty-second Negro. . . . In thirty-eight out of the forty-eight states of the American Federal Union, marriage between a white person and a person of African descent was a criminal offense. To be of "black" blood meant being consigned to a lower plane in the social scheme of American life, and if one violated that scheme, one risked danger, even death sometimes. And all of this was predicated upon the presence of *African* blood in one's veins. How much of me was *African*?[22]

In this quote from the early pages of *Black Power*, the designation "Negro" signifies for Wright "associations of hatred, violence, and death." We have also seen Wright evoke these significations in his discussion of Negro literature and its focus on lynching and the auction block. But in this paragraph Wright moves beyond seeing the Negro as America's metaphor, instead linking the violence of his American past directly to the "presence of *African* blood." This section will examine how Wright uses the travel narrative genre to make sense of the presence of (something he calls) Africa, in America and in himself. Running through the above passage, and indeed throughout the text, is a tension between the genealogical and the political. Wright talks about his own blood, evoking tropes of kinship, yet he also retains his focus on the political, on an almost social-scientific analysis of the slave trade, for example, mediated through Eric Williams's classic volume, *Capitalism and Slavery*. Though Wright, living in exile in Paris, felt bitterly excluded from any kind of "American dream," the idea that Africa represented a potential "home" to which he could "return" was for him a myth. He did not journey to the continent expecting to find his lost home. Having dismantled the concept of "race" in his own intellectual work, Wright early on in the narrative also denies and deconstructs the notion of a biological blackness that would connect him to the people he would meet in Ghana (then the Gold Coast). In the early pages of his text, Wright introduces himself as "an American Negro whose life is governed by racial codes written into law," an "uneasy member" of the Western world.[23] Throughout *Black Power* we see Wright caught up in anthropological discourses about "the native" as, bound perhaps by his own ideas of travel narrative conventions, he attempts to catalogue and describe what he calls "the African mind."

It is important to see that Wright's cataloging impulse is connected to his articulation of his own identity as Western. As an African American born and raised in the virulent racism of the mid-twentieth-century American South, Wright never did feel "at home" in the United States. And yet he also admits early in *Black Power*, "When I'd come to Africa, I didn't know what I'd find, what I'd see; the only prepossession I'd had was that I'd doubted that I'd be able to walk into the African's cultural house and feel at home and know my way around" (62).[24] Yet the sense of displacement produced by U.S. racism causes Wright to display a double-sided desire. On the one hand, he wants to claim an identity he considers modern and rational, rather than primitive. To that end he relies on false binaries, such as pagan/Christian, ancient/technological, and so on as he dangerously ascribes concepts of cultural purity and essential "Africanness" to those from whom he would distance himself.

The other side of Wright's desire is his very ambivalence about diasporic subjectivity and connection. Though Wright denies seeking racial essence, the fact that "race" neither enables nor facilitates cross-cultural communication always frustrates him. For example, he makes such statements as, "I'm of African descent and I'm in the midst of Africans, yet I cannot tell what they are thinking and feeling" (151). Wright thus reveals that he perhaps cannot avoid seeking a cultural home in Africa, even as he intellectually denies that he *should* seek one. When George Padmore's wife, Dorothy, suggests that Wright visit the Gold Coast in the midst of Kwame Nkrumah's rise to political power as "the first black Prime Minister in history," Wright thinks,

> *Africa!* Being of African descent, would I be able to feel and know something about Africa on the basis of a common "racial" heritage? Africa was a vast continent full of "my people."... Or had 300 years imposed a psychological distance between me and the "racial stock" from which I had sprung? (4)

It is helpful here to recall Wright's essay, "The Literature of the Negro in the U.S.," where he describes another form of "psychological distance," that between the black American writer and "the land in which he lives" (81). In that text, the psychological distance was figured as a political distance resulting from racial discrimination and white supremacist ideology. In *Black Power*, however, Wright figures Africa, the source of "racial stock," as that from which he is psychologically distant.[25] Diaspora identity is indirectly articulated in this spatial conception of a (global) black identity that is psychologically distant from both America and Africa. Between these two poles, black international writers formulate an alternative political space. Wright's initial consideration of travel to Africa is marked by these questions about distance and diasporic subjectivity, the meaning of his own "racial" identity, and his identity as Western.

In his analysis of *Black Power*, "A Long Way from Home: Wright in the Gold Coast," Kwame Anthony Appiah argues that Wright's central dilemma in Africa could be summed up by the question "What am I doing here?" Appiah says, "His materialist analyses could offer him the shared experience of racial exploitation as an answer, but that could give him no special reason to be in Africa rather than anywhere else in the non-white colonized world" (180). Clearly Wright did not see "race" as a particular bond that would tie him to Africa. I want to take the argument in another direction, though, and assert that throughout *Black Power*, in which Wright repeatedly makes elaborate moves to emphasize his difference from the Africans among whom he travels, it is not solely "the shared experience of racial exploitation" that triggers a sense of diasporic connection for him. Rather, I argue that it is more specifically Wright's focus on the experience of racial slavery that structures his physical voyage and narrative, as much as it signals his diasporic connection. The image ever before Wright's eyes is not the lynching, but the auction block. And before the New World auction block, Wright sees the slave castles of Elmina, Cape Coast, and Christianborg. What becomes crucial are the different ways that Wright imagines that he and the Africans he meets share in the transatlantic history of slavery and the auction block.

The history of slavery begins and ends Wright's journey to Africa. He writes, "Over the Easter Sunday luncheon table, I mapped out my voyage. I wanted to see this Africa that was posing such acute questions for me and was conjuring up in my mind notions of the fabulous and remote: heat, jungle, rain, strange place names like Cape Coast, Elmina, Accra, Kumasi. . . .

I wanted to see the crumbling slave castles where my ancestors had lain panting in hot despair. The more I thought of it, the more excited I became."[26]
It is this melancholic poetic connection—between an African American
expatriate in mid-twentieth-century Europe, planning over an Easter Sunday luncheon table a journey to the dungeon of a slave castle, and the affective "idea" that this person has of his ancestors "panting in hot despair"—
that I want to explore. In other words, I want to show how the fact of slavery
becomes for Wright (and other black international writers) the very sign of
diasporic subjectivity. Wright approaches Africa via the transatlantic history of the slave trade; his point of embarkation for this journey is, in fact,
Liverpool, "the city that had been the center and focal point of the slave
trade" (8). He titles part 1 "Approaching Africa," quoting and drawing from
Eric Williams's text as he presents this history and its connection to the city
of Liverpool. I want to call attention here to the very material terms in
which the history of slavery is experienced by Wright: "Profits from the
slave trade built Liverpool docks; the foundations of the city were built of
human flesh and blood"(14). After the statistics and economic analyses,
Wright's view circles back to the physical remnants, as his poem on lynching, "Between the World and Me," also circles around "a scorched coil of
greasy hemp," "a whore's lipstick," and "a stony skull." In both texts, Wright's
speaker cannot avoid this close visceral identification with the historical
violence that has preceded his entry into the scene, which has perhaps even
formed the subjectivity that his discourse enunciates. *Black Power* as a text
is most resonant in those passages where Wright repeatedly returns to these
material traces of stolen slaves, to "the iron rings and chains which had fastened their black bodies to the masonry," and which were, at Wright's visit,
"still intact" (46). These images recall Wright's use of the visual terms that
structure his discussion of "The Literature of the Negro in the U.S." and the
way that he characterizes black American literature as being unavoidably
focused on lynching.

    After discussing the flesh and blood that built the very foundations of
the city of Liverpool, Wright goes on to write, "Yet, how calm, innocent,
how staid Liverpool looked in the June sunshine! . . . Along the sidewalks
men and women moved unhurriedly. Did they ever think of their city's history?" (14). In this passage, Wright sets up his oppositional other as the
(white) contemporary residents of Liverpool, calmly and (not so) innocently
residing in a criminal city built on the flesh and blood of the slave trade.
Perhaps Wright's next, unspoken question would be, "Can I ever *not* think
of it?" Here Wright's identity as an African diasporic person marks him as

opposite to the white British person, who thinks he has the choice of not thinking of history. But diasporic identity is not built on such tidy binarisms, and Wright's work, perhaps more than that of many midcentury diasporic writers, seems to unsettle these binarisms at every turn. Though the history of slavery continues to be the fulcrum around which Wright enunciates his diasporic subjectivity, the terms of this enunciation shift quite significantly from the white Britisher as oppositional subject to the black African as oppositional subject.

Wright's image of slavery and Africa includes more than the physical scene of his ancestors' despair. Throughout *Black Power*, the other ancestor peopling Wright's thoughts about slavery is configured by him as guilty: this is the ancestor of the African, not the African American. The following quote, from the beginning of Wright's narrative, lays out the paradox of attempting to describe Wright's concept of diaspora: "What would my feelings be when I looked into the black face of an African, feeling that maybe his great-great-great-grandfather had sold my great-great-great-grandfather into slavery?" (4). This question introduces a dynamic of oppositional identities between Africans and African Americans that continues throughout Wright's travel narrative: this binary is not configured in terms of black versus white, but rather in terms of black sellers versus black sold. At this early point in the narrative, however, Wright is hopeful of finding a way to bridge this opposition. Wright's questions continue almost wistfully: "Was there something in Africa that my feelings could latch onto to make all of this dark past clear and meaningful? Would the Africans regard me as a lost brother who had returned?" (4). Here, then, we see Wright's desire to find in Africa a potential homecoming, even as he intellectually denies that this is possible. For Appiah, this represents Wright's "African dream," which when revealed as illusion causes Wright to respond to Africa "with the fury of a lover spurned."[27]

Many other black Western writers have recorded their surprise, and/or frustration when, in journeying to Africa, they are not immediately seen as brothers (or sisters) by Africans. We see this in texts by Langston Hughes, Marita Golden, Eddy Harris, and many more.[28] Wright's text, however, provides many clues about why he is not regarded as a "lost brother who has returned." Throughout *Black Power*, Wright depicts Africans as childlike, superstitious, outside the realm of the rational, which he claims solely for himself as a Westerner. To give one example, he shows what he must have looked like as a tourist when he explains how he attempted to "catch the native African without warning; he would have no chance to dress up or pretend; the chiefs would have no opportunity to get out those big and ridiculous umbrellas.... Wearing a sun helmet and a T-shirt, with a camera slung over my shoulder, I ambled out to a line of waiting taxis at the hotel entrance" (156). It is hard to believe that Wright is here unselfconscious about his assumption that he can have an unmediated experience in an African village, arriving in a taxicab and accessorized with a sun helmet and camera. But it is worth quoting the scene further. As he approaches the taxis, he says, "The drivers began honking their horns, trying to attract my attention. I went to an elderly man, feeling that he would think twice before trying any tricks or cheating.... 'What's the nearest village that's worth look-ing at?' 'Don't know, Massa'" (156). The taxi arrives in Labadi and Wright quotes himself as saying to his driver, "'Lock your car and come with me,' I ordered him, expecting him to demur. But he didn't. I found that that was the only way to get any consideration out of a native; he'd been condi-tioned by the British to being ordered and would obey only when ordered" (156–57). Notice how Wright has again shifted his position, aligning his own behavior with that of the British colonizer against the African driver, suggesting that his skin color does not exempt him from stepping into a colonialist touristic mode.[29]

Wright's oppositional relationship to Africa, in general, turns on the issue of slavery. Here we see Wright's relationship to the larger metonym of Africa, played out in a focused interaction with individual Africans. Early in Wright's trip he accompanies one of Nkrumah's aides to a supermarket. This scene is very important for analyzing Wright's distance from, and his desire for, Africa. He meets a salesman who is quickly able to identify him as American. The man is joined by a coworker who asks Wright, "What part of Africa did you come from, sar?" Wright says, "I stared at him and then laughed. I felt uneasy. 'I don't know.' 'Didn't your mother or grand-mother ever tell you what part of Africa you came from, sar?'" (39). Here Wright is addressed as the long-lost brother returning home, an identification that part of him had wished to experience. And yet for Wright, the histori-cal gap represented by the question of slavery, in fact the very rupture of clear lines of ancestry and genealogy, produces unease and anxiety. Repeat-edly in *Black Power*, Wright resolves this anxiety by underlining distance. When the men press, "Haven't you tried to find out where in Africa you came from, sar?" Wright answers, "'You know, you fellows who sold us and the white men who bought us didn't keep any records,' Silence stood be-tween us. We avoided each other's eyes" (140). Slavery, for Wright, becomes the silence in the history of diaspora, the space where speech fails. The supermarket scene shows how Wright sees his relationship with Africans in terms that cement an opposition between sellers and sold, with white men in the middle. Later Wright describes African Americans' troubled conceptualizations of Africa as due to its description as "a land in which his ancestors had sold their kith and kin as slaves," here eliminating direct reference to white men (73). The selling of "kith and kin" becomes for Wright the inaugural trauma of slavery. Hence, any attempt to consider himself a part of a "family" relationship to Africa must contend with this trauma. For Wright, the roles are most commonly fixed with Africans as descendants of those guilty of selling their "brethren," hence the criminals, and African Americans as descendants of those who were sold, hence the victims. Wright assumes that black people existing in Africa postslavery never had ancestors who were slaves, whereas all African Americans can assume a slave ancestor.

It is also important to examine how "race" figures into Wright's concepts of oppositional identities. When Wright says that Africans had sold "many millions of their black brothers into slavery," he is constructing a (continental) identity based on race, which he has denied throughout *Black Power* and indeed his entire oeuvre. We know that Africans were captured in many widely separated areas of the African continent and that American slaves were the descendants of diverse African peoples. What then makes these ancestors "brothers" or "kith and kin" if it is not a kind of biological blackness, which Wright otherwise denies? Wright's text is filled with passages in which he disproves and contests any kind of racial connection between Africans and African Americans. Why, then, does he consider diverse African peoples brothers? The answer is somewhere in the difficult conceptualization of diaspora identifications traversed by his texts.

The end of this long text, and the end of Wright's trip to Africa, is the originary scene of diasporic departure. Wright visits several prominent and ancient slave castles in the final chapter of *Black Power*. These sites of the initial rupture in identity stand, as they have throughout the text for Wright, for the very moment of rupture in any relationship that could be called familial. As Wright tours the inner depths of Christianborg castle, he again calls upon the metaphors of vision as he identifies with historical slaves, asking questions such as, "Are these the same windows that the slaves looked out of?" aligning his own traveler's visual perspective with that of the slaves. Fastening his own skin, as well as his language, to the material artifact, he writes, "[T]he same iron bolts which secured the doors to keep the slaves imprisoned were the ones that my fingers now touched" (382). Then Wright disrupts this intimacy and exits the castle to gaze at the walls from the outside. His perspective shifts and he writes, "I tried to picture in my mind a chief, decked out in cowrie shells, leopard skin, golden bracelets, leading a string of black prisoners of war to the castle to be sold. . . . My mind refused to function" (383). This passage at the end of Wright's text, which circles back to slavery as the initiation of Wright's exploration of diaspora identity, records the perceptual breakdown—the limit of identification that keeps Wright at such a remove from the individual Africans he meets.

Indeed the most intensely moving passage of the text comes as Wright then reconstructs a notion of family based in a different way, identifying a singular (metonymic) black woman's sorrow as the mother of diaspora:

> If there is any treasure hidden in these vast walls, I'm sure that it has a sheen that outshines gold—a tiny, pear-shaped tear that formed on the cheek of some black woman torn away from her children . . . there on that black cheek, unredeemed, unappeased—a tear that was hastily brushed off when her arm was grabbed and she was led toward those narrow, dank steps that guided her to the tunnel that directed her feet to the waiting ship that would bear her across the heaving, mist-shrouded Atlantic. (384)

The woman's tear bears the symbolic trace and the weight of the passage, as it is significantly ephemeral, rather than material. Unlike the iron rings, still intact, this tear is only accessible to Wright *via language*. It is his poetic evocation of the tear that resonates for Wright and his readers, creating the poignancy of diaspora identification. Wright does not describe this woman as African, but black. And it is her suffering, which he so keenly evokes, that I think best represents his attachment to a kind of identity in diaspora. Though he regards chiefs and kings (and other male Africans) with a distance marked by the relations of slave sellers to slaves themselves, he closes the distance here and vividly identifies with the suffering of this black woman as mother. This is a significant moment in Wright's work because it is rare in his oeuvre to see him so strongly identify with the suffering of black women.[30] Wright's record of his visit to the castles then becomes the scene of the rupture of African identity and the inauguration of diasporic and African American identity, via the body and tears of the black woman as mother. The symbol of the tear later crosses the Atlantic, when Kwame Nkrumah visits Harlem in 1958, addressing a crowd of almost ten thousand people gathered at the U.S. Armory. St. Clair Drake relates that Nkrumah invited the crowd to come to Africa as teachers and technicians, and in return the African leader "was presented with a silver bowl on behalf of the people of Harlem as a symbol: 'the vessel that has caught the tears of all the mothers of Africa weeping as their children were torn from them and sent across the ocean.'"[31]

Wright's approach to Africa is marked by the interference of history — that is, the conclusions that Wright reaches about the meanings of "kinship" cannot be considered outside of the history of slavery and the material remnants and embodiments of that history. I think it is, in fact, the conjunction of these notions of kinship and the history of slavery that compose what we might call diaspora identity. I am arguing, however, that this conjunction was not seamless for Wright himself, that he was perhaps quite understandably unable to unite these concepts in his own discourse about identity. These moments of tension, ambivalence, and even contradiction sketch out for us the complex constellation of responses that various diasporic writers have brought to the question of identity in their literary practices.

One of the things I have been trying to show in this chapter is how an understanding of slavery or what it means to be the descendant of slaves is, for Richard Wright, a critical moment in the journey of diaspora identity. The fact of slavery locks Wright into an opposition between Western and African — and he chooses to identify himself as the descendant of the black woman slave, not the male African chief(s) who may have sold her. When we turn to a slightly later text, however, we can see the ways that Wright delineates a third space, a critical position between the binaries that seem to repeatedly capture him in *Black Power*.

Between the West and the Rest

Wright's essays in *White Man, Listen!* shed light on his sense of what it means to be "Western," as he describes the split vision that makes him both "of the West" and somewhat outside it. This volume also turns to Africa and other global locations where "Westernized elites" are engaged in freedom struggles. Because of these intersections, *White Man, Listen!* is an important text to read alongside *Black Power*. Wright's intellectual work forms an arc, circling from experience to ontology as he tries to describe identity in nonracial terms while simultaneously accounting for the effects of history. These texts, taken together, are important pieces of Wright's oeuvre, demonstrating his complex understandings of race and identity. *White Man, Listen!* represents a critical early definition of whiteness as a social category deployed with dire consequences. Wright's midcentury text intersects with late twentieth-century scholarly inroads in postcolonial studies, whiteness studies, and travel literature. How is Wright's self-proclaimed rootlessness related to the global politics he describes? In *Black Power* we see the pressures that Wright's conception of rootlessness creates as he travels to Ghana. In the remainder of this chapter, I examine several of Wright's essays from *White Man, Listen!* showing how Wright makes rootlessness and restlessness integral parts of his identity as a black person in "Western" society and exploring how these conditions of intellectual and political "restlessness" are in turn constitutive elements of diaspora identity. How can Wright wrench himself free from the iron rings, the blood and flesh of the history of slavery? Perhaps one answer is via language, via the discursive reference to the black woman's tear and its engendering of diasporic subjectivity.

Since Wright was adept at so many genres, we must retain sight of the particulars of the multiple sites of Wright's articulations of diaspora identity. That is, his passage at the end of *Black Power,* which so poetically evokes the suffering of captured Africans, is perhaps linked to the poetic voice of "Between the World and Me." But Wright also wrote (and indeed lectured) in another political register, and it is the analysis of colonialism and the status of postcolonial intellectuals that draw our attention in other chapters of *White Man, Listen!* The important first chapter, "The Psychological Reactions of Oppressed People," presents a critique of colonialism in which Wright describes imperial travelers as "human debris anxious for any adventures" (1). Wright's writing in this collection traces a critical textual journey among topics of colonialism, travel, identity, and literature, and thus *White Man, Listen!* is a key component of Wright's own lifework as an expatriate African American author who traveled widely and associated with political leaders of various postcolonial struggles. In *The Unfinished Quest of Richard Wright*, Michel Fabre cites an October 9, 1950, letter from Wright to Jawaharlal Nehru in which Wright states, "The situation of oppressed people the world over is universally the same and their solidarity is essential, not only in opposing oppression but also in fighting for human progress" (387). In the spring of 1955, Wright traveled to Jakarta, Indonesia, to take part in the Bandung Conference of Third World Peoples, publishing *The Color Curtain* in 1955 as a record of this trip. Wright also spoke before the Congress of Negro-African Writers and Artists in 1956 in Paris. This conference was sponsored by the Pan-Africanist Paris-based journal *Présence Africaine,* and Wright published a version of his speech in *White Man, Listen!* entitled "Tradition and Industrialization."[32] Wright's position on colonialism is complicated by statements he makes about what he perceives to be the merits of industrialization, and the detriments of what he calls magic and superstition on the part of "traditional" peoples. We see, then, a frequent dynamic in Wright's midcentury writing on "race" and culture: he repeatedly shifts from a position of denying "race" as an essence to generalizing "racial" traits. A closer look at some of these essays can show us why and how it is possible (and perhaps even inevitable) to simultaneously hold these multiple positions.

"Like a sleepwalker, Europe blundered into the house of mankind."

In his essay, "The Psychological Reactions of Oppressed People," Wright entitles one section "The 'Whiteness' of the White World." Wright's work here is a precursor to the contemporary articulation of whiteness studies, which aims to study the ideological and material effects of white supremacist sociopolitical arrangements.[33] Wright states, "It would take an effort of imagination on the part of whites to appreciate what I term 'the reality of whiteness' as it is reflected in the colored mind" (8). On the other hand, Wright speaks here of a unified "colored mind," and at the same time he explains quite clearly why he is also speaking of a consolidated concept of whiteness—this is always tied to global politics. Wright explains that Africans and Asians (who represent, in Wright's discourse, "colored people") make no distinctions between various European national entities in terms of race "because the 'whiteness' of Europe is an old reality, stemming from some five hundred years of European history. It has become a tradition, a psychological reality in the minds of Asians and Africans" (8). Let us put aside for the moment the problematic nature of such undifferentiated categories as Asians and Africans, subsuming as they do entire continents of diverse peoples. What Wright is trying to achieve politically is to posit an international solidarity of peoples of color (as did Du Bois and others before him), if only in their understanding of whiteness as a social force, an aggregate political hegemony that "has been reinforced by a 'gentleman's agreement' (of centuries standing) implemented by treaties and other forms of aid between big colony-owning powers to support one another in their colonial difficulties"(8). In a key section entitled "What is a 'White Man'?" Wright clarifies this position, which is neither essentialist, nor biological, but political:

> The "white man" is a distinct image in Asian-African minds. This image
> has nothing to do with biology, for, from a biological point of view, what a
> "white man" is is not interesting. Scientifically speaking the leaders of Asia

and Africa know that there is no such thing as race. It is, therefore, only from a historical or sociological point of view that the image of "white man" means anything. (15)

In answer to the charge of homogenizing or essentializing Asian and African peoples, he explains at the end of this section, "What I've called Asian and African psychological facts are such only in a contingent sense. They are human reactions, and, as such, they belong to everybody. White men under the conditions I've described would have reacted more or less the same" (41). It is this sense of the contingency of historical facts that Wright returns to again and again and which anchors his discourse on "race" throughout these talks.[34]

Appropriating the Vocabulary of History:
Wright and Postcolonial Studies

Wright's critique of colonialism circles around two larger questions that characterize much of his work: what is the role of the writer and/or intellectual? And what is the position of the person of African descent in the United States? Two sections of "The Psychological Reactions of Oppressed People" bring these questions into focus with their attention to voice. These sections, "Men without Language" and "The Zone of Silence," speak of European-educated elites of Asia and Africa not simply as men deprived of their native language, but more cogently as men deprived of the language of historical interpretation. Here Wright identifies colonialism's greatest psychological rupture as the rupture produced by the colonizer's version of history. Wright explains,

> For these men there is a "hole" in history, a storm in their hearts that they cannot describe, a stretch of centuries whose content has been interpreted only by white westerners. The seizure of his country, its subjugation, the introduction of military rule, another language, another religion—all of these events existed without his interpretation of them. . . . Put differently, one can say that at this point the elite has no *vocabulary of history*. What has happened to him is something about which he has *yet to speak*. (36)

Wright here underscores the need to speak the truth of history, to rewrite the colonial drama from the perspective of the colonized. Clearly postcolonial writers, since at least the 1950s, have been engaged in this literary and political project, and postcolonial studies has emphasized its importance as well.[35] Wright, referring in the mid-1950s to this interpretive vocabulary of history, is also speaking as a writer. Wright's identity as a writer is important as he recounts a conversation held with an Indonesian educator and writer who envies him the English language, saying, "[Y]ou can appeal, as a writer, to a vast, world-wide audience" (37). Wright's conversation with the Indonesian educator calls to mind the well-known debate between Chinua Achebe and Ngũgĩ wa Thiong'o over what is the proper language for African writers to publish in.[36] Postcolonial writers have shown us that English may be a worldwide language, and therefore a widely recognized method of communication, but it is also a "foreign anguish."[37]

Language is also not the only factor affecting a writer's ability to reach a wide audience and therefore use "words as weapons," as Wright envisions in *Black Boy*. We know that as an expatriate writer and former member of the Communist Party, Wright's movements throughout his career were closely followed by the CIA and the state department.[38] Indeed these bureaus also read the work of other diasporic writers, such as James Baldwin, Chester Himes, and Claude McKay, to name a few.[39] Beyond this (not always covert) surveillance is another type of literary monitoring as well. In *The Unfinished Quest of Richard Wright*, Michel Fabre states, "On May 24, 1954, Paul Reynolds [Wright's U.S. literary agent] had repeated his opinion that Wright had been absent [from the United States] too long to make present-day America the setting for a novel" (407). Reynolds's letter to Wright raises questions not only about Wright's topic choice, but about his choice of genre. Wright's agent feels, perhaps, that Wright's exile limits his literary influence on the American scene. And yet, paradoxically, the security arms of the U.S. government consider him to have enough political influence to warrant shadowing him closely. Reynolds's letter points to a tension between what Wright can say, is encouraged to say, and cannot say because it will not be published. In these spaces, determined and defined in part by the literary marketplace and in part by the U.S. publishing industry, black international writers resist the pressure and define their own literary topics. Clearly Wright himself was very interested in the international political scene; we should not assume that his agent controlled his writing decisions. In fact, Fabre quotes the following letter, dated May 30, 1954, in which Wright replies to Reynolds:

> I'm inclined to feel that I ought not to work right now on a novel. This does not mean that I'm giving up writing fiction, but, really, there are so many more exciting and interesting things happening now in the world that I feel sort of dodging them if I don't say something about them.[40]

I suggest that we can read this exchange between Wright and his agent in the context of diasporic authors residing in "adopted" countries. When we place Reynolds's letter alongside documentation of CIA and FBI surveillance of Wright, we witness the competing claims made on the body (and body of work) of the writer. Wright is the quintessential expert on black American literature at the same time that he is considered too distant from the precise geographies of American political life to further comment on U.S. affairs through the medium of literature.

Similar tensions arise in the lives and works of Chester Himes and Michelle Cliff, writers whose residence outside their "homelands" makes them sometimes "suspects,"other times experts and exemplars. This is the tension between diasporic identities and national identities as played out in the cultural politics of literature and publishing. It is this tension that allows Wright to be both "the" black American writer and "not American enough." Affinities exist, then, between Wright and "the tragic elite" he writes about, men he characterizes as "lonely outsiders who exist on the clifflike margins of many cultures." We can make sense of this paradox by understanding Wright as a diasporic writer. It is both Wright's internationalism and his "blackness" that create this paradox of belonging.

Though Wright describes himself in the introduction to *White Man, Listen!* as "rootless," it is important to see that the rootlessness that Wright describes as part of his background is neither an ontological, nor a particularly "postmodern" characteristic; rather, it is one born of the experiences of racial exclusion. He says, "I've been shaped to this mental state by the kind of experiences that I have fallen heir to" (xxix). Readers of *Black Boy* know what Wright later explains in *White Man, Listen!*: "I was born a black Protestant in that most racist of all the American states: Mississippi. I lived my childhood under a racial code, brutal and bloody, that white men proclaimed was ordained of God" (55). Wright thus locates the very source of his global wandering in the psychological distance, the political exclusion, and the racial violence he experienced growing up in the United States. In an unpublished manuscript entitled, "The Position of the Negro Artist and Intellectual in American Society," Wright relates the story of a *Time* magazine journalist coming to Paris to ask "American Negro artists" why they were living abroad. Wright says, "I, upon hearing about this journalistic venture, decided not to cooperate, for I was certain that any white man in America above the mental level of a nitwit knew only too well why we were living in France."[41] Is Wright then able to construct a "home in the heart" via his writing, in his African travel narrative or his essay/lectures in *White Man, Listen!?*

Like the Western-educated elites and postcolonial intellectuals that Wright mentions in *White Man, Listen!* who must repossess the vocabularies of history and the languages of historical interpretation, Wright, too, attempts in his work to overcome a silence—the space where his "mind refuses to function." For Wright to conceive of himself as a diasporic intellectual, he must contend with the silences surrounding the histories of slavery. In *Black Power,* we see Wright recoil from these histories, retreating into an opposition between himself and the Africans he meets. And yet he is also drawn to the eloquent materiality of these histories. Perhaps the central place where both an intellectual and a material reckoning with the history of slavery occurs for Wright is in his moving elegy on the black woman's tear. The journeying back and forth between positions of affiliation and repudiation, however, the constant tension between distance and desire that structures *Black Power,* leaves Wright where he began: in the middle. Wright describes this sense of in-betweenness as he turns from America, to Africa, via Europe: "If you are a tribal stranger, you seek out your tribe and you are taken care of. If you are a European, you seek the shelter of the European community. But an American Negro is an oddity; he has one foot in both worlds and he pays through the nose for what he gets from each" (353). In his profession as a writer, Wright found the space to claim a critical identity that would straddle these worlds. In an unpublished interview, Wright locates this freedom in the space of writing when he says,

> Writing is my way of being a free man, of expressing my relationship to the world and to the society in which I live. My relationship to the society of the Western world is dubious because of my race and color. My writing is therefore charged with the burden of my concern about my relation to that society. The accident of race and color has placed me on both sides: the Western world and its enemies.[42]

In "Tradition and Industrialization," a chapter of *White Man, Listen!* we see how Wright defines himself as Western. Though he mobilizes this self-definition in direct opposition to what he sees as a backward "traditionalism" among African peoples, he also clearly explains how he can be both a critic of colonialism and a (black) Westerner. Wright defines his critical consciousness as *part of* his Western identity. He explains, "I'm black. I'm a man of the West. . . . Though Western, I'm inevitably critical of the West. Indeed, a vital element of my Westernness resides in this chronically skeptical, this irredeemably critical, outlook. I'm restless. . . . I see both worlds from another and third point of view" (48–49). Perhaps we can call this third point of view "diaspora identity." For Wright, diaspora identity becomes a restless, critical black Western identity.

2

The Postcolonial as Post-Enlightenment: Michelle Cliff and the Genealogies of History

> The Caribbean doesn't exist as an entity; it exists all over the world. It started in diaspora and it continues in diaspora.
>
> —*Michelle Cliff*

> Movement and multiplicity frustrate any logic that seeks to reduce everything... to the apparently transparent discourse of "history" or "knowledge."
>
> —*Iain Chambers*

Richard Wright's travel writing about Africa, when read against his essays on "Negro" national literature, shows us how the author sought in his writing a place free from both the romanticization of Africa as homeland and as the space of suffering for a descendant of slaves. Wright emerges as an international black writer, poised "on the clifflike margins of many cultures," a result of both his physical journeying and his journeying across the page and across genres. The double displacement of expatriate diasporic writers like Richard Wright, as well as Michelle Cliff, denies an easy nostalgia for an irretrievable homeland present in some diasporic discourses. In the Gold Coast, the specter of slavery becomes one of the ghosts arresting Wright's conflicted hopes for a familial reconciliation in Africa. Across the Atlantic,

Michelle Cliff's novels move us to a middle ground in the history of slavery, the island of Jamaica.

Like Wright, Cliff is a writer whose work embraces many genres, from the semiautobiographical novel to poetry, essays, and short stories, and all of her writing articulates diasporic perspectives. Though they trace the "return" of a migrating authorial subjectivity back to the originary site of the island, Cliff's novels refuse to romanticize this space outside of history or politics. Instead, her work consistently traces out the genealogies of slavery, the complicated connections between the multiple national identities at play in Jamaican politics, and the intersections in the lives of individuals occupying multiple class, race, and national social locations. She most frequently uses the genres of fiction (novels and short stories) to flesh out these individual stories, but the narratives of history as recorded in official doctrines are also her subjects. Thus her work entails multiple perspectives as she develops characters like Clare Savage, characters who trace their lineage to both slaves and slaveholders. Cliff both narrates forgotten histories of struggle and constructs a contemporary literary politics of resistance.

This chapter focuses on Cliff's first novel, *Abeng*, because this novel foregrounds Cliff's revisions of Jamaican history. The semiautobiographical aspect of *Abeng* allows us to see the ways that Cliff inserts herself and her family into the complex narratives that compose the various histories of Jamaican identities. Clare Savage, the protagonist of this novel, is a light-skinned adolescent girl.[1] Clare is thereby positioned in the interstices of a genealogy that includes slave and slaveholder, black and white, upper class and middle class. This coming-of-age story does not end with Clare's resolution into a full Self; instead the novel works to show that such a subjectivity is a defunct Enlightenment fantasy. *Abeng* can, in fact, be read as an *antibildungsroman* because the type of education Clare receives is fragmented and multiple and does not progress toward a stable whole at the end of the novel. Though Cliff has said that she wrote *Abeng* to claim herself as Jamaican, her novel puts pressure on this island/national identity so the claim is not seamless. By focusing on liminal states between childhood and adulthood, white and black, colonizer and colonized, Cliff accomplishes complex analyses of language, history, race, and identity. Her novel shows the way that these categories are also discursive constructs that are unsettled by "the dispersal attendant on migrancy that disrupts and interrogates the overarching themes of modernity."[2] These overarching themes can be seen as part of the Euro-American intellectual heritage of modernity, which propels the subject "to acquire a supposedly authentic, natural and stable 'rooted' identity" contigu-

ous with a unified racial or national self.[3] Juxtaposed to this imagined stable
identity, the passage of Clare's physical (embodied) self from child to adult
can be seen as a microcosmic mirror of the larger movements and passages
that have created the Caribbean, both as region and as diaspora.

Cliff's account of Clare's fractured and multiple educational and physical
developments demonstrates how many "received truths" about the Caribbean are in fact representational fictions. This indeterminacy troubles the
epistemology of historiographic projects that rely on a linear narrative of
progress or development. While "the representational systems of the West . . .
posit the subject of representation as absolutely centered, unitary, mascu-
line, [and white]," Cliff's work can be considered postmodern in the way
that it "upset[s] the reassuring stability of that mastering position."[4] Further,
this chapter will show that in its refusal to stage an exotic or Edenic Caribbean scene, Cliff's semiautobiographical novel also denies its *own* representation as an authentic oppositional other to an imagined Western reader.
Cliff provides no easy resting place for a reader to situate her- or himself
outside the webbed networks of colonialism and diaspora.

Clare Savage is the daughter of Boy Savage, descended from both slaves
and slaveholders, and Kitty Freeman Savage, descended from property-
owning Jamaican small farmers. Due to his light skin, Boy claims whiteness
as his (and his daughter's) racial identification, but the rape of slave women
is also a part of his ancestors' family history. Cliff writes, "The definition of
what a Savage was like was fixed by color, class, and religion, and over the
years a carefully contrived mythology was constructed, which they used to
protect their identities. When they were poor, and not all of them white,
the mythology persisted."[5] Clare's mother, Kitty, claims allegiance not only
to the black middle-class members of her family, but to the island's poor
black people as well. Clare's very genealogy, therefore, is complexly hybrid,
a condition the narrator indicates is prevalent on the island and that paral-
lels the varieties and mixings of mangoes on the first page of the novel:
"The fruit was all over and each variety was unto itself—with its own taste,
its own distinction of shade and highlight, its own occasion and use" (3).
The narrative structure of *Abeng* shifts between descriptions of island landscape, tracings of colonial history, the detailing of Savage or Freeman familial genealogy, and particular events in the life of Clare Savage (events that
are less "formative" than they are deconstructive).

Françoise Lionnet describes a parallel between a multiplicity of flora (like
the mangoes) and a proliferation of discourses, describing what she calls a
"Darwinian divergence." Echoing Bakhtin, she states, "a given space (text)

will support more life (generate more meanings) if occupied by diverse forms of life (languages)."[6] To expose this multiplicity of meanings as a defining characteristic of the Caribbean is one of the aims of Cliff's own autobiographical discourses. She has described this process as an unraveling of intertwined histories. *Abeng* is nonlinear and presents the reader with filaments and segments that do not weave themselves together to resemble a whole or unfractured self or narrative. Writing about the ways that women's autobiographical practices address issues of decolonization, Sidonie Smith and Julia Watson state that "autobiographical performances, drawing upon exogenous and indigenous cultural practices, signal the heterogeneity of the subject and her narrative itinerary."[7] This chapter will show how Cliff's novel signals more than the heterogeneity of the migrating autobiographical subject.

Clearly part of Cliff's project is to present colonial history (the exogenous) and to critique it through the lens of "indigenous" knowledge(s). The conflicts arising from the seemingly binary opposition between indigenous and exogenous represent part of the heterogeneity of Cliff's "narrative itinerary." *Abeng* radically disrupts the two categories mentioned by Smith and Watson: I argue that *Abeng* shows exogenous and indigenous to be porous and mutually constitutive. Cliff shows how the exogenous (Europeanness) is constructed by a reliance on colonialism, for example relying on the indigenous nature of sugarcane to Jamaica. What it means to be British, part of British national cultural identity, in fact, is expressed in the social consumption of afternoon tea. Jamaican-born theorist Stuart Hall points to the same interconnectedness between the British empire and its "Others" when he writes,

> I am the sugar at the bottom of the English cup of tea. . . . There are thousands of others besides me that are, you know, the cup of tea itself. Because they don't grow it in Lancashire, you know. . . . Where does it come from? Ceylon—Sri Lanka, India. That is the outside history that is inside the history of the English. There is no English history without that other history.[8]

Hall here explicitly conflates and complicates notions of outside/inside, exogenous/indigenous. And Cliff shows us not only that inside and outside do not exist without influencing or interweaving each other, but that they were never stable categories within themselves. She writes,

> [S]ugar was a necessity of Western civilization—to the tea-drinkers of England and the coffee-drinkers on the Continent, those who used it to sweeten their beverage, or who laced these beverages with rum. Those who took these products at their leisure—to finish a meal, begin a day, to stimulate

them, keep them awake, as they considered fashion or poetry or politics or
family, sitting around their cherrywood tables or relaxing in their wing-back
chairs. (27)

This clear image of privilege may allow the reader to imagine, for a moment,
that the "exogenous," these Continental café-goers, are a category at once
recognizable and, importantly, also unlike him- or herself. But Cliff's following sentences disperse both this image of unified privilege and the easy identification of political sentiment or allegiance that might attend it. Her cata-
log of those who enjoy tea with sugar continues:

> People who spent afternoons in the clubs of Mayfair or evenings in the cafés
> on the rue de la Paix. People holding forth in Parliament. The Rathaus.
> The Comédie Française. People who talked revolution or who worried about
> revolution. . . . The fabric of their society, their civilization, their culture, was
> an intricate weave, at the heart of which was enforced labor of one kind or
> another. (27–28)

Both revolutionaries and reactionaries are here included in Cliff's picture of
the "exogenous," which therefore cannot stand as a stable or unified political category. Exposing this weave of complicity is part of *Abeng*'s project,
and thus the novel can be called a biomythography in the sense used by
Caren Kaplan, after Avdre Lorde, who has said, "Making 'maps' of changing
affiliations and coalitions is part of the 'work' of biomythography as text."[9]
The cartographic quality of Cliff's narrative, however, may not yield a map
that can comfortably be read or even followed with repetition. As her novel
is an antibildungsroman, then, perhaps it is also an anticartography. The
reading is different each time because one of the purposes of the novel is to
cast doubt on the mastering impulse that accompanies mapping.

Connecting cartography to discourses of domination, Geoffrey Galt
Harpham states that "the Enlightenment has been historically implicated in
a practice of imperial/colonial world mapping, a moral crusade with racist
overtones undertaken by a privileged hegemonic culture with the power to
impose its own values and beliefs on a well-nigh global scale."[10] Cliff's charting of unease among exogenous consumers of sugar and her further unsettling of any easily oppositional political position for the reader to facilely
assume, continues:

> Slavery was not an aberration—it was an extreme. Consider the tea
> plantations of Ceylon and China. The coffee plantations of Sumatra and
> Colombia. The tobacco plantations of Pakistan and the Philippines.
> The mills of Lowell. Manchester. Leeds. Marseilles. The mines of Wales.

Alsace-Lorraine. The railroads of the Union-Pacific. Cape-to-Cairo. All worked by captive labor.... Slavery-in-fact—which was distasteful to some of the coffee-drinkers and tea-drinkers, who might have read about these things or saw them illustrated in the newspapers the clubs and cafés provided for their patrons, neatly hung on a rack from dowel sticks—slavery-in-fact was abolished, and the freedom which followed on abolition turned into veiled slavery, the model of the rest of the western world. (28)

Hence, the "western world" does not represent a unified, homogeneous entity, but clearly entails both abolitionists and slaveowners, radicals and conservatives. Where Richard Wright's travel writing about Africa was caught by such binarisms as traditional/modern, African/Western, slave/slaveseller, Cliff tries to construct a novel of Jamaica that revises these oppositions. The fact of (first slavery, and then) colonialism has complexly worked to implicate the histories of the "western world" in the histories of the "indigenous" peoples of the Caribbean, among other areas where labor is exploited, including Leeds, Manchester, and Marseilles, within the so-called western world. Cliff's reminder of slavery is a central aspect of her own and other Caribbean writers' narrative projects, whose mode of seeing from the "slaves' perspectives" enables a questioning of central Enlightenment categories, such as "universality, the fixity of meaning, the coherence of the subject, and of course the foundational ethnocentrism in which these have all tended to be anchored."[11] Cliff's work, however, shows that "the slaves' perspectives" themselves are often nonrecoverable in some fixed or pure sense, and are, in fact, also always narrativized. Cliff's fiction here calls attention to the very complicated process of writing diaspora.

In its operation of deconstructing the totalizing tendencies of historical narratives, the truly radical aspect of *Abeng* is its offering of an antirepresentational history of the West's "other" as well. That is, the novel refuses to present a unified Caribbean subject who could stand as an authentic oppositional "other." Nor is there a singular oppositional Caribbean history. Rey Chow's work on postcolonial cultural studies calls attention to the way that "the production of the West's 'others' depends on a logic of visuality that bifurcates 'subjects' and 'objects' into the incompatible positions of intellectuality and spectacularity." Chow asks, "Is there a way of conceiving of the native beyond imagistic resemblance?" My argument is that *Abeng* refuses "to uphold the other as the non-duped—the site of authenticity and true knowledge," just as it shows how "the West" is marked by gaps or intersections.[12] Much scholarship on diasporic literature betrays a desire or an attempt to chart a path from fragmented subject to whole self. Clearly

such critical moves are made in response to centuries of denial of the selfhood of oppressed groups by dominating cultures. The danger inherent in
such charting, however, is that "the search for such a 'full' and total position
is the search for the fetishized perfect subject of oppositional history, sometimes appearing in feminist theory as the essentialized Third World Woman,"
as Donna Haraway argues.[13] Against such essentialism, Cliff's antibildungsroman refuses to represent this perfect oppositional subject.

Françoise Lionnet sees *Abeng* as a site where Cliff uses "the broken threads
of the colonial diaspora to weave a different narrative of belonging, inclusion, and kinship."[14] I would extend the critique and say that rather than
reweaving, *Abeng* complicates or destabilizes notions of belonging, inclusion, and kinship, disrupting rather than refiguring the "real." In *Writing in
Limbo*, Simon Gikandi sees postcolonial novelists as affirming "the continuing urgency of an oppositional history and discourse that strive for the status
of a grand narrative" (232–33), but I think Cliff's novels explicitly refuse to
participate in this striving for grand narratives. Though Gikandi rightly sees
Abeng as "dispersing the historical narratives of colonialism," his claim that
in so doing "Cliff recenters, and gives value, to margins and edges" (236)
bespeaks a wish to maintain grand narratives and stable centers that feminist reading practices often reject. Bell hooks, for example, locates the margin itself as the productive location for counterhegemonic discourse. Denying a desire to "recenter" the margin, hooks rejects totalizing gestures when
she states that "margins have been both sites of repression and resistance."[15]
Cliff, too, shows us that repression and resistance can come from multiple
directions.

"They [Who] Did Not Know": Complicating the Colonized

Much of *Abeng* is concerned with revising the history presented by the colonizer and impressed upon Clare and other Jamaicans via the colonial education system. Part of Cliff's narrative aim is to restore certain histories of
resistance that have been erased from "official accounts." She writes,

> Clare had been taught at St. Catherine's School for Girls that Jamaica had
> been a slave society. The white and creole mistresses hastened to say that
> England was the first country to free its slaves. They also taught her about
> Anne Bonney and Mary Reade, the pirates. . . . She learned that there had
> been a freedman's uprising at Morant Bay in 1865, led by Paul Bogle; but
> that this rebellion had been unwarranted and of little consequence, and that
> Bogle had been rightfully executed by the governor. She knew that there

had been Maroons, and that many of them still existed in the towns of the
Cockpit Country. But she learned that these towns had been a gift from
England in compensation for slavery. Slaves mixed with pirates. Revolution
with reward. And a sense of history was lost in romance. This history was
slight compared to the history of Empire. (30)

Abeng's use of montage techniques helps to "articulate an alternative 'archae-
ological' account. . . . to excavate and reclaim a creole counter-memory of
black struggle, itself always repressed, erased and made invisible in the dominant 'popular memory.'"[16] The dominant popular memory Kobena Mercer
refers to here is British film and media, and in terms of *Abeng* we could see
this popular memory as represented by several different ideologies. Cliff's
novel, in fact, troubles the potential homogeneity of the concept "popular
memory." For instance, one form of popular memory may represent neocolonial Jamaican bourgeois ideologies of Britishness. Against this ruling-
class culture, Cliff's narrative repeatedly invokes another group, referred to
as "they" who "did not know" because they had not been told of various histories of resistance and rebellion in Jamaica.

I would like to take a moment to consider the ideological and social location of this "they." Cliff commonly uses the pronoun to refer to "the people"
and seems most often to imply middle- or working-class Jamaicans. For
example:

The people in the Tabernacle could trace their bloodlines back to a past of
slavery. But this was not something they talked about much, or knew much
about. In school they were told that their ancestors had been pagan. . . . No
one had told the people in the Tabernacle that of all the slave societies in
the New World, Jamaica was considered among the most brutal. . . . They
did not know about the Kingdom of the Ashanti or the Kingdom of the
Dahomey, where most of their ancestors had come from. They did not
imagine that Black Africans had commanded thousands of warriors. Built
universities. Created systems of law. Devised language. Wrote history.
Poetry. Were traders. Artists. Diplomats. (18, 20)

In her repeated use of the phrasing, "no one had told," "they did not know,"
"they did not imagine," Cliff's narrator denies the existence of particular
local knowledges. Cliff here presents a popular memory marked by gaps both
in knowing and in telling. And she most explicitly indicts an ideologically
biased colonial education system for enforcing such gaps, for mis-telling
these histories. As Lemuel Johnson has noted, Cliff's writing here "contextu-
alize[s] the problem of consciousness and being in the island in-between."[17]

It is important to note, however, the way that Cliff's narrative process indicts the very popular memory that in some ways may have informed and enabled her novel's own existence. The repetition of "they did not know" clearly points to the hegemony of the oppressor's version of history. But it also denies verbal or epistemological resistance, which undoubtedly resides (and resided) in an oral culture maintaining various oppositional historical narratives. What is the relationship of Cliff, postcolonial novelist residing in an imperialist center (the United States) to potentially marginalized cultures of resistance in Jamaica?[18] Sections of the novel dominated by "they did not know" are often followed by a statement of historical "facts" purposely filling in what is assumed to be a missing narrative:

> The capture of the island from the Spanish had been an afterthought. The British fleet, under the command of Penn and Venables, following the orders of the Lord Protector Oliver Cromwell, was unable to take Santo Domingo, and so moved on Jamaica. This took place in 1655. Over the course of the next 180 years, until freedom was obtained in 1834, there was armed, sustained guerilla warfare against the forces of enslavement. (20)

The narrator here speaks the language of a textbook, yet supplies a rebel consciousness to the text. The narrator both speaks the colonizer's language and rewrites a sanctioned historical discourse. Yet what is the source of her own knowledge? Cliff's epigrammatical acknowledgments state, "For some of the details of this book I am indebted to the work of Zora Neale Hurston, Jervis Anderson, and Orlando Patterson." At some point there are local sources, local knowledges, and oppositional consciousnesses maintaining and revising countermemories of resistance, the very memories that clearly inform Cliff's own narrative act. Lucille Mathurin Mair reminds us that "[t]he militant acts and words of Afro-Jamaican women were neither isolated nor inadvertent. They constituted a political strategy that took different forms at different times but at all times expressed the conscious resolve of the African enslaved to confront the New World plantation's assault on their person and their culture."[19] Cliff's own words reinstate the specific militant acts of Afro-Jamaican women as she relates the revolutionary strategies of Maroon Nanny and details her guerrilla tactics and organizational/ leadership skills (19–22). And yet Cliff's repeated reminders of gaps in popular knowledge work in some ways to deemphasize the power of the militant *words* of Afro-Jamaican women. This move exists in tension with Cliff's conscious purpose to remind us of the hegemonic power of those discourses that would repress, erase, and make invisible (to recall Mercer) popular counter-memories of struggle.

The gap between the novelist's knowledge and her portrayal of an absence of popular knowledge points to the complex dialogism within not only Caribbean historical representation, but all historical representation in general. Kobena Mercer succinctly states, "Diaspora perspective disrupts monologic dominant discourses via heterogeneity," and Vè Vè Clark cites "the environment of continuous change" in Caribbean culture, enabling a spiralist "*Marasa* conciousness" that "invites us to imagine beyond the binary."[20] *Abeng* invites (and indeed demands) this kind of spiralist reading strategy, traversing the seemingly stable categories that so often are used to define identity. Perhaps this "environment of continuous change" is why Cliff repeatedly denies the existence of a *retrievable* oppositional counter-memory by restating "they did not know." For as Stuart Hall reminds us, there is no guaranteed authenticity in oral narratives of dispossessed peoples: "The past is not waiting for us back there to recoup our identities against. It is always retold, rediscovered, reinvented. It has to be narrativized. We go to our own pasts through history, through memory, through desire, not as a lit-eral fact."[21] These strains of history, memory, and desire mark Cliff's narra-tion of Clare Savage's past and her movement through adolescence.

The novel's refusal to fetishize oral narratives is one of the ways it suc-cessfully avoids the danger of reifying the other in an image about which the reader might like to fantasize. Contemporary postcolonial (multi)cultural production disperses the binary "dialectic of subordinate reply and reaction to power and hegemony. Subordinate subjects have invariably been ordained to the stereotyped immobilism of an essential 'authenticity,' in which they are expected to play out roles, designated for them by others...for ever."[22] It is this immobilism that Cliff avoids, at times perhaps by presenting an absence rather than an "essential authenticity." That is, rather than locate and represent a consistent, unified oppositional discourse, she depicts the shifting, heteroglossic nature of Jamaican popular memories, which disrupts a binary logic of subordination and hegemony. This heteroglossia is born of diaspora, and creolité. Edouard Glissant states that creolization represents a return not to lost origins, but to the point of entanglement. Cliff's feminist viewpoint would emphasize *multiple* points of entanglement(s). In *Caribbean Discourse*, Glissant writes, "In my case, for some time I have tried to master a time that keeps slipping away, to live a landscape that is constantly chang-ing, to celebrate a history that is documented nowhere."[23] Clearly these, too, are some of Cliff's entanglements and desires, and her work vacillates between mastering facts and denying any kind of monolithic perspective. Her writing continually questions the real and emphasizes slippages in temporality as well as in representation. Neither the narrator nor the reader is allowed to be for long the "master" of a Jamaican time or identity.[24]

In Cliff's writing this tension exists within single novels like *Abeng* and *No Telephone to Heaven*. One example of how the narrative of *Abeng* disturbs a reader's potential voyeuristic pleasure in a scene of tropical adolescent eroticism occurs when Clare and her friend, Zoe, bathe together in a river:

> Zoe's naked body was lean and muscled. Her hips were narrow and her thighs long. The patch of tight curly hair between her legs glistened in the riverwater and the sun. Clare's own body was also long. The gold of her legs and arms met the brown of Zoe as the water cascaded between them, creating a shield which served their modesty. They found a piece of Golden Guinea soap in a crevice of rock left by last week's washerwomen, and soaped their skin and hair and splashed each other all over until the piece of soap disappeared and the bubbles and foam from their clean selves ran to another part of the river below them. They didn't stop to think that the soap had been hidden by a particular washerwoman who would have need of it next week, and would have to beg a sliver from the washerwoman at the next rock. (120)

The idyllic nature of the scene is disrupted not only by the allusion to social class disjunctures between the girls and the washerwomen whose soap they steal, but also by the difference (here marked by the colors brown and gold) in Clare and Zoe's Jamaican social status as codified by skin shade stratifications. The river itself is on the property of Clare's grandmother, Miss Mattie. This fact gives Clare a sense of proprietorship that ultimately imperils both her and Zoe. Zoe, too, is an "arranged friend" for Clare, since Zoe and her mother are squatters on Miss Mattie's property. Rights of ownership, privilege, labor, leisure, and skin color all assert themselves as complicating interferences in what might otherwise have been read as an "exotic" erotic moment in idyllic nature.

Refusing Romanticism

There is nowhere readers can uncritically situate themselves in relation to the scenes and events Cliff describes. In addition to presenting the gaps in colonial history and the gaps in popular knowledge, Cliff's novel further troubles an image of a unified oppositional solidarity among contemporary or historical island dwellers even of the same social class. Cliff implicates both colonialism and neocolonialism as the sources for much of this fracturing, but this insistence on fracture is also part of her antirepresentational project, which denies the reader's voyeurism. Among the categories like exogenous/indigenous, black/white, and Jamaican/British, which are shown by the novel to be porous and shifting, is the category of sexuality. Cliff's own lesbian identification is in many ways absent from her writing, due, she has said, to the internalized homophobia she has suffered "having grown up in a society that is enormously homophobic."[25] It is around this fulcrum of homophobia that the narrator of *Abeng* disturbs a romanticized portrayal of an indigenous tradition surrounding burial. Cliff introduces the ritual as the Savage family drives away from Clare's grandmother's house in the country, back toward Kingston:

> Ahead of them now, winding down the road, was a procession of people dressed in white, their presences lit by the torches they all carried. Soft drink and Red Stripe beer bottles had been filled with kerosene and lit from a rag wick stuffed inside.... The procession moved forward underneath a steady hum, which at first seemed of the same key and pitch, but soon differentiated into harmony, led by the high falsetto of a man, whose voice circled the hum and turned it into a mourning chant. The words of the chant were strange, unrecognizable. (50)

The child Clare questions her parents about the actions of the people and the words of the song; she is answered by her mother, who says that it is a funeral procession and that "[t]hey are singing in an old language; it is an ancient song, which the slaves carried with them from Africa" (50). The scene immediately fissures when Cliff describes Clare's father's interjection: "'Some sort of pocomania song,' Mr. Savage added, a bit smugly, as if to contradict the tone of his wife's voice, which had a reverence, even a belief to it" (50). The fissure registered by Boy Savage's disdain can easily be explained along predictable lines of colonizer/colonized: Kitty Savage, who aligns her sympathies with the dark-skinned people of the island, speaks with reverence of the traditional African practices retained by "country people," while her "whiter" husband, who claims to be the descendant primarily of slaveowners, deprecates the language as nonsensical. This picture is further complicated, however, when "the words of 'Lead, Kindly Light, within the Encircling Gloom' reached them, and the voices of the people in the procession moved from the complexity of an African chant into the simplicity of an English hymn. 'The night is dark and I am far from home'—these words sounded faintly as the line of mourners turned into a yard" (50).[26] The New World diasporic cultural space is hybrid by nature—there is no recoverable "pure" African practice, but instead a funeral tradition that contains elements of both the colonizers' and the slaves' multiple cultures. Note also how Cliff's narrator reverses Boy's colonizing discourse by labeling the African chant complex and the English hymn simplistic. This scene, however, still sets up the indigenous peasant funeral procession in ways that allow it to be romanticized by the reader and by Kitty Savage. We are invited to see this ritual as a healing practice, as a way in which a seemingly stable community honors and mourns its deceased members, as an eternal or at least very long-lasting tradition that has survived centuries of repression, exile, and up-heaval. To Clare's wistful mother, the funeral group has an internal coherence, representing a vision of community and solidarity that she has, to some extent, lost in her marital alliance with the white-identified Savage family.

Abeng, however, ultimately refuses romanticized representations and calls many seemingly "natural" solidarities and affiliations into question. Ten pages after the description of the aforementioned funeral procession, we encounter another version of ritual surrounding death, and this depiction fractures the solidarity of "the community" by exposing homophobic oppression. This story concerns "Mad Hannah," an *obeah*-woman turned "mad-woman" following the death by drowning of her son, Clinton. The first gap in community solidarity occurs at the time of Clinton's death itself: "There was a rumor around the place that he was being taunted by some of the other men and boys, and they had left him floundering in the water and gone about their business, while their shouts of 'battyman, battyman' echoed off the rocks and across the water of the swimming hole" (63). Because he is gay, Clinton is excluded from the fraternal sympathies of Cliff's oft-repeated group, "people" or "they." But what is represented as a further tragedy of exclusion is the denial of a community of mourning to Clinton's mother, Hannah. We learn that,

> After his death, no one came forward to assist her in the rite of laying the duppy at peace—no one came to chant that "the living have no right with the dead." There had been no arcade of palm, no white room with a white deathbed, no white rum or white fowl or white rice laid on banana leaves for the duppy to have his final feast—all was white because white was the color of death. . . . No one to create the pillow filled with dried gunga peas, Indian corn, coffee beans, or to sprinkle salt into the coffin and make a trail of salt from the house to the grave. (63)

Cliff's next paragraph details slave-era (and beyond) beliefs in salt, flying Africans, and fears of duppies (or ghosts), thereby anchoring these funeral practices in patterns of cultural retention similar to her earlier funeral description marked by chanted African songs.[27] But because no community of mourners comes forward to assist Hannah in properly burying her son, his duppy gets loose and she becomes obsessed with trying to lay it to rest. Here the narrator's critique of "the people" becomes more overt. Before turning to this critique, however, I want to focus again on Cliff's narration of cultural practices and beliefs. These specific funeral rites are represented as anti-event; that is, they did *not* take place, and the narrative action concerns their absence. Cliff's portrayal of this absence mirrors the rhetorical structure behind her repetition of "they did not know"—the people are claimed as ignorant and the narrator displays her knowledge of traditional burial practices, the significance of the color white, and so forth, while paradoxically depicting the absence of these practices. In this second funeral scene, an image of potentially romanticized ritual is still presented, and the narrator links the rituals to indigenous African practices.

By its exclusions and absences, however, this second funeral depiction appears cruel and damaging, as opposed to healing and restorative. This multilayered, both/and quality is prevalent throughout Cliff's novel. (In fact the abeng of the title is an instrument of both oppression and resistance as it is used by slaveholders to call the slaves to the canefields and by Maroon armies to pass messages to one another.) Cliff repeatedly blurs the categories of oppressor and resister, as her text works to trouble the historiographic project. *Abeng,* like many Caribbean novels, questions and disrupts the historiographies of the colonizer as promoted through the colonial education system; but in the section on "Mad Hannah," Cliff's narrator critiques a very different historical project—one that is oral, "indigenous," and local. Examining this critique will help us to see how Cliff's novel begins to question all representation as exclusionary, all images as violent and partial:

> People made fun of Mad Hannah all around and all the time. They talked as she stood in front of them and they talked behind her back. They traced what they thought was her insanity. They mocked her dead son Clinton and said "him favor gal." They laughed at her journeys and her attempts to lay his soul to rest. And yet when they buried their dead they themselves took all the precautions she had been unable to take. (65)

In pointing out "the people's" hypocrisy or cruelty in not allowing Hannah the same treatment they sought, the narrator clearly condemns them as unneighborly. Not only are the colonizers' histories half-truths, but indigenous versions of history are also shown as partial. The critique gains force by its emphasis on these people as social narrators, authors of a powerful verbal script:

These were men and women who had known Mad Hannah for donkey's years. They didn't stop to consider their actions. To ponder her relationship to magic. Or to think about her journeys as ceremonies of mourning, as expressions of her faith. They thought her foolish and crazy. . . . *They extended their explanation:* If she had not been fool-fool her son would not have been sissy-sissy. Because he was a sissy he was drowned. *They forged a new chain of cause and effect by which her actions were bound.* They removed themselves from any responsibility to Mad Hannah and her son Clinton— two people once in their midst. (65–66, italics added)

The narrator questions the privileges of authorizing by showing "the people" as cruel authors. This passage displays Cliff's ongoing engagement throughout the novel with issues of cause and effect, with forces of rationalization within popular as well as recorded and/or "official" memory. Her novel consistently asks us to interrogate notions of responsibility in our relationship to historical narratives, to recognize the violence that often accompanies acts of "forging" new "chains" of cause and effect and "extending" explanations. We see the ways that "all narrative, by virtue of 'its power to master the dispiriting effects of the corrosive force of the temporal process,' may be a narrative of mastery."[28]

Mastering Histories

This attempt to seek explanation and rationalization in an understanding of history marks Clare Savage's adolescent questions and pursuits. Through Clare's pursuit of the "why" behind the stories she is told and taught, Cliff questions not only the violent ways in which oppressors rationalize their deeds, but the weight of the term "rational" as a judgment. As an example, Cliff presents the history of Boy Savage's great-grandfather, Justice J. E. C. Savage, an infamously cruel slaveholder who set fire to a hundred of his slaves months before Jamaican emancipation. In the fact that J. E. C. Savage is a judge, Cliff explicitly questions the weight of historical judgments and "rationalizations." She shows how even the vilest of judgments are supported by discourses of the Enlightenment as we witness Savage's ruminations before his act, metaphorically weighing and attempting to balance the violence he contemplates:

The justice worried what would happen to the island when it swarmed with free Africans, some only a few years out of the bush. Who would have conceived that the empire would see fit to unleash these people. The justice was not thinking about his crops or even the future of his properties. His mind was on a "higher" plane—he was concerned about the survival of his race. (38)

He then ponders the words (represented in the text) of Enlightenment thinkers Thomas Jefferson and Benjamin Franklin regarding race mixing. Cliff firmly anchors the judge's thoughts, actions, historical precedents, and ideological framework within a discourse of "Enlightened" rationality informed by "higher" notions of justice, freedom, and equality in order to demonstrate the extreme violence possible within these paradigms, the ways in which these very ideologies support excesses of violence and terror.[29] The narrator tells us,

> It is very important to note here that although the judge had had a drink of rum, he was cold sober. His mind was moving through a *logical* series of suppositions and conclusions informed by his beliefs and his assessment of experience.... He was a justice: He had been trained to assess the alternatives available to human beings, and their actions within the limits of these alternatives. These people were not equipped to cope with the responsibilities of freedom. These people were Africans. Their parameters of behavior were out of the range of civilized men. (38, 39)

Clearly the justice's name, Savage, in addition to his actions, clouds the supposed opposition between savage and civilized. So, too, does the description of his behavior, as propelled by centuries of "higher" reasoning, European and American philosophizing, and Enlightenment ideology. His murderous actions show him to be ill-"equipped to cope with the responsibilities of freedom" in his signally unjust acts toward people he deems "only a few years out of the bush." The savage justice enacted by Clare's ancestor depends on the *grands récits* of Enlightenment modernity, which "functioned to legitimize Western man's self-appointed mission of transforming the entire planet in his own image," as the judge assumes the role of "that particular being who gives the measure and draws up the guidelines for everything that is."[30] Because free Africans are not a part of the world picture Savage envisions, he burns their existence from the frame of his mental image.

The narrative of J. E. C. Savage's actions, which composes part of Clare's diasporic genealogy, is told only to the reader, not to Clare. Another historical narrative that does enter Clare's adolescent consciousness, however, is that of the Holocaust. An implicit link is made in the novel between the Holocaust and racial slavery in understanding diaspora. Clare's introduction to the history of the Holocaust comes through her avid reading, which leads her to *The Diary of Anne Frank*. Clare's need for explanation and rationalization spurs her further investigation into the stories told about the Holocaust: "Why did they kill her? That was a question whose answer was always out of reach" (68). Repeatedly Clare's inquiries are met with evasion: "When

Clare asked her teachers to explain this fact of the history of the modern world, this overwhelming fact of the murder of six million Jewish people, the death of this one Jewish girl, the teachers hemmed and hawed" (70). Cliff's novel again questions Enlightenment definitions of reason and justice as young Clare seeks an explanation for something her teachers stumble to rationalize. Iain Chambers writes that "the full impact of the Holocaust—not as an accidental aberration but as something intrinsic to the sense of modernity and the West: 'the terrible revelation of its essence'—has yet to be fully inscribed in the body of contemporary history, culture and critical thought."[31] Clare seeks rationalization for the Holocaust within a Christian explanatory system:

> [T]he teachers insisted: In the hot afternoon sun in a private girls' school built according to the principles of Victorian architecture—they insisted. No one in the world had any idea of what was going on in Germany—and the teachers always limited the swathe of the Holocaust to Germany—as if to isolate the enemy and fix the time when the barbarism of Attila overcame the rationalism of the Lutheran. (71)

Cliff's choice of the Holocaust as a companion narrative to the history of racial slavery furthers her critique of the totalizing paradigms of Christian Enlightenment modernity. In Clare's formal education, these paradigms work to both incorporate and rationalize a horror Clare cannot comprehend. Clare's teachers contrast "the barbarism of Attila" with the "rationalism of the Lutheran," and this dichotomy between rational and barbaric (Clare versus Savage?) confronts Clare as she struggles to reconcile what it might entail to rationalize barbaric acts. Dissatisfied with her teachers' explanations, Clare turns to her father, who "reverted to Christian dogma that the Jews had willfully, his word, turned their backs on salvation" (72). Finally she seeks answers in books in the library's "ADULT" section, "trying to figure out *why* these events had happened. Not knowing that for her at this moment the why would be incomprehensible, always beyond reach, because to understand would be to judge her father capable of the acts which had formed and sustained the Holocaust" (75). The novel thus deconstructs the claims to rationality made by such totalizing discourses of modernity as Enlightenment philosophy and Christian morality by unsettling the notions of barbarism and savagery, saved and infidel, human and inhuman, on which these discourses are based. Cliff questions the judges, asking who may safely or innocently author such judgments and rationalizations. Yet Cliff's writing does not seek simply to change hands, to offer the position of judge to the formerly dispossessed, since this would allow the totalizing paradigm to remain in place—to move the so-called margin to the center, to construct a differently authored master-narrative.

Rather, Cliff's feminist, antirepresentational project interrogates the act of judgment itself, showing this act as potentially violent in any hands, as we see with the example of Mad Hannah's neighbors. The narrator relates another incident, in novelistic time immediately following the section on the Holocaust (which Clare knows about and studies), following the section on Justice Savage's acts (which Clare does not know about). This third incident involves Clare directly and in fact positions her as author of a script about who is human and who is inhuman. True to Cliff's writing, however, this is no easy reversal of terms or of positions. Clare's role is not seamless: she is neither just a privileged light-skinned Jamaican nor an encul- turated Jamaican school child oppressed by the educational values of "the center." Instead her position is much more complex. Clare sees two of her darker-skinned classmates cruelly snub a "dark-skinned," "shabby-looking," "old Black woman" at a bus stop who asks them the time. "Clare watched this and went over to the old lady, gave her the time and the threepence busfare she begged, and turned to hiss a question at her classmates: 'How could you be so inhuman?'" (77). The narrator chastises Clare's naïveté in failing to see both why the darker-skinned students responded as they did and the privilege that upholds her own "right" to judge their actions. Cliff writes,

> [S]he did not analyze; she observed. And after that she made her judgment. "Inhuman" was a horrible word to call anyone. It could mean that you were behaving in an "uncivilized" way. That you were being cruel beyond the bounds of expected human cruelty. Or that you were a "dirty dog," and therefore not human at all. The question of humanness or the lack of it had been purified in the crucible responsible for the society in which this girl now found herself. The society had been built around an absolute definition of who was human and who was not. It really was that simple—except some people were not quite one thing or the other. When clarity diminished, one thing remained. The sufferer was not expected to be human. (78)

In this scene the person most closely aligned with "the oppressor" in terms of privilege is Clare; yet the common scenario is reversed in that it is she who condemns an act of cruelty toward the sufferer, whom she sees as human, as against her classmates, who are labeled as inhuman. But the narrator dis- turbs even our potential identification with Clare's act, linking our identifi- cation and the act as forms of a recognizable liberal response wielding the power of unanalyzed words and labels. The novel subtly indicts such a response for being blind to local complexities and the weight of its own privilege: "Clare had called her classmates 'inhuman'—and it would take her years to recognize the source of this word—to understand that while their act toward the old woman was a sad act, it had a foundation" (79). This scene, and the narrator's analysis of it, shows that all stories are contingent, all definitions exclusionary. Clare's ability to define her classmates as inhuman, while it protects the humanity of the sufferer, is also a power based in her relative class privilege and skin color, perhaps not unconnected to her own ancestor's claiming the right to judge. How would the scene be read if Clare were dark skinned and her classmates light skinned? What are the connections between Clare's use of the word "inhuman" and her great-great-grandfather's own definition of who was civilized and who was not? These are some of the complicated questions posed by the novel and part of the tangled social field that adolescent Clare Savage must negotiate. The narrator's tracing of Clare's diasporic consciousness takes account of these multiple inheritances.

Memory and History

How does the period of adolescence, with its exaggerated physical, mental, and emotional flux, condition Clare's response to the unstable ground of her social environment? Though *Abeng* resists representation by calling the "real" into question, Clare's desire for rationalization is partly a desire for "the real" to remain stable and identifiable, locatable (and mapped?). On a visit with her father to vacation homes at Runaway Bay, the former property of her ancestor, Justice Savage, Clare ponders European-styled wallpaper in the former "great house," designed with pictures of parasoled white women strolling through a park: "The pattern on the wallpaper was only a small glimpse of the background against which this part of her family had once existed. These images surrounded them as they sat in their parlor. The danger to Clare was that the background could slide so easily into the foreground" (25). Antiguan-born writer Jamaica Kincaid also speaks of a slippage between the background and the foreground, describing this as a particularly Caribbean aesthetic, one perhaps linked to *obeah*: "For a while I lived in utter fear when I was little, of just not being sure that anything I saw was itself. . . . I never knew whether the ground would hold, whether the thing next to me was real or not. . . . I want for there to be just one true thing that doesn't come and go."[32] We have seen the ways that Clare's adolescent inquiries seek meaning and rationalization and are frustrated by the multiplicity of contradictions present, for example, in her father's belief system and in her own genealogy. Inderpal Grewal's definition of transnational feminist practices suggests that narratives by women of color around the world propose subjectivities that are "both oppositional and nonessentialist, and confront and fracture the self-other opposition in the name of inclusions, multiple identities, and diasporic subject positions."[33] *Abeng* begins to sketch out some of the complications faced by one Jamaican girl occupying these various subject positions.

Clare Savage's desire for a grounded, nonshifting reality is both complex and contradictory. Thinking back to the wallpaper at Runaway Bay,

> Clare sometimes imagined that the walls of certain places were the records of those places—the events which happened there. More accurate than the stories of the people who had lived within the walls.... The walls might not be able to reveal exactly what they had seen, but perhaps they could indicate to a visitor something, if only a clue, about the time which had passed through them. Maybe there were signs marked on the walls each time they heard a shout—like the slashes on the Rosetta Stone, which she had learned about in school. (32–33)

Just as Richard Wright stops at the walls of Christianborg Castle, struck by his identification with the history of slavery, so, too, does Cliff's protagonist seek a story from the walls at Runaway Bay, on the Atlantic's other side. Clare Savage, avid reader of diaries and a questioning child, distrusts the stories that people tell about their pasts because the stories she has so far encountered crumble against her desire to know. Like Kincaid, perhaps, she longs for a rock-solid history, etched permanently in stone, not a story that is constantly reauthored. And yet only three pages later, the narrator presents another of Clare's historical longings: "The great house had seemed so small, Clare thought. Broken down. The house was not at all what she had expected. It was as though she had wanted it to be a time machine rather than a relic. A novel rather than an obituary. She wanted to know the people who had lived there" (36). What does Clare desire? The Rosetta Stone or a living book? Perhaps at this point in her development as a ("post")colonial child, she wants both. In desiring the Rosetta Stone, she seeks something she can rely on to remain "true," a sense of reality that is fixed. And yet for so long the code of the Rosetta Stone lay unbroken—the tablet did not speak. Clare combines her wish for the clues on the Rosetta Stone with her desire to enter history as a revising author. Gayatri Spivak reminds us that "[h]istory cannot be reversed or erased out of nostalgia. The remaking of history involves a negotiation with the structures that have produced the individual as agent of history."[34] Clare's wish to remake history is reflected in her desire for the house to be a novel or a time machine. Clare (like Cliff, the writer) seeks to enter the past as author, as active agent capable of learning from it as well as rewriting it, to effect some rationalization for the uncertainties with which she is faced.

Clare's seemingly contradictory longings reflect a difference between memory and history as ways of knowing the past. Pierre Nora's article, "Between Memory and History: *Les Lieux de Mémoire*," suggests a helpful distinction: "Memory is a perpetually actual phenomenon, a bond tying us to the eternal present; history is a representation of the past" (8). Clare's desire for a time machine would make her an actor in the perpetual phenomenon of memory. But Nora's clarifications help explain Clare's desire for the Rosetta Stone, too, since he emphasizes that memory is not abstract, and in fact it "takes root in the concrete, in spaces, gestures, images, and objects." History, on the other hand, "binds itself strictly to temporal continuities, to progressions and to relations between things" (9). It is the linear temporality of history that is constructed by Clare's father and the St. Catherine's School for Girls, and Clare attempts to reject it. But as an adolescent, "She was at that point at which some children find themselves, when to move forward would mean moving away. She was not ready or prepared for this action—perhaps later, if the place in her which might effect this was nurtured carefully, she could bring it off" (76). Clare is dissatisfied with, or confused by, various representations of the past and she looks instead for phenomena and traces that speak of the past, longing for an impossibly unmediated voice. Through its multiple and fractured glimpses of various characters, time frames, and voices, *Abeng* presents these traces and phenomena, instead of (re)representing a monologic Jamaican history.

Natural Bodies/Bodies and Nature

Though both social relationships and historical discourse in *Abeng* are shown to be shifting and lacking "one true thing that doesn't come and go," the novel also resists the temptation to posit the natural world as a fixed, safe, or reliable alternative realm of certainty. Edouard Glissant, referring to the inadequacy of realism as an interpretive paradigm for the New World, sees landscape itself as both a character and a creator of history, adding that landscape "is not saturated with a single History but effervescent with intermingled histories."[35] Cliff's novel names specific flora and fauna of the Jamaican landscape and sets up the countryside as "a landscape which was wild and real" for Clare and her friend Zoe's imaginations to explore (95). The countryside is also the place where, in rare moments of intimacy, Clare's mother Kitty "would take Clare into the bush with her, where they would go barefoot, and hunt for mangoes or avocadoes out of season" (52). Cliff's repeated descriptions of rot, of the landscape's ability to erase and encompass human history, imbue the landscape as a character with immense power. The narrator describes a predawn moment when Clare ventures out from her grandmother's house:

> There was a deep musty smell which traveled through the darkness of the coffee piece. Of leaves and manure and eggshells and fishbones and vegetables her grandmother used to thicken the earth. Above this smell was the thin sharp scent of urine, because Miss Mattie emptied their chamberpots near to the edge of the planting. All these things rotted silently in the moisture and darkness of this part of the property where the earth was most damp.... At the end of the coffee piece ... were two graves of former landowners.... People around said that the graves were as old as slavery times—and the names, of a planter and his wife, had been erased by rains, and the spaces where the names had been, obliterated by a heavy green mold. (111–12)

This power of the landscape to both absorb and erase human history recurs persistently in Cliff's writing.[36] She opens her second novel, No Telephone to Heaven, with a definition of ruinate, and has elsewhere described the power of ruin as akin to the power of chaos: "When a landscape becomes ruinate, carefully designed aisles of cane are envined, strangled, the order of empire is replaced by the chaotic forest.... A landscape in ruination means one in which the imposed nation is overcome by the naturalness of ruin."[37] Here landscape is presented as chaotic in opposition to human projects of order, nation, and meaning, as if to suggest that such projects must ultimately fall when confronted with the greater force of nature's "ruin." This allegorization of landscape can be seen as antimodernist "because it speaks of the inevitable reclamation of the works of man by nature."[38] But the passage can also be interpreted using the romantic image of an ever-regenerative natural world that "heals" the hurts of human history. I want to suggest that Abeng does not romanticize "nature" as infinite plenitude, endlessly capable of regeneration. Rather the novel implies a parallel between the natural world and the political/social world in the ways that these systems absorb horror.

One site for reading nature is the body, and Cliff's novel questions our ability to read human corporeality as truth. Abeng figures the body in multiple ways. On one hand, it is the Rosetta Stone that Clare seeks—the marks of historical events are inscribed with some degree of permanence on the body. Clare's right thigh is marked by "a two-inch scar, long and white, where she had been stung by a jellyfish, a surprise because the animal seemed so incapable of attack" (23). Though the outer appearance of the jellyfish is a false representation that masks its potential for danger ("a pink and transparent being carried by the sea, in and then out again"), its aggressions are marked on the body with the permanence of a scar (23–24). But other bodily markings, though seemingly as "permanent" as the etchings on the Rosetta Stone, show themselves to be as vulnerable to shifting discursive interpretations as the words on that ancient tablet. Cliff locates the body within racial discourse as a site of differently interpreted markers. In one scene, Clare asks her father how she can be "white" if her mother is "colored," and she tries to read answers to these and similar questions in the physical characteristics of her own flesh: "She was waiting for her father's answer, but her mind was also back a ways and she was considering how she could be white with a colored mother, brown legs, and ashy knees" (73). Color as a marker of racial identification becomes more and more indeterminate for Clare, calling attention to the ultimately semantic, and therefore unstable, construction of racial categories. In racial discourse, there is no "one true thing that stays the same," especially in New World societies. Paul Gilroy writes, "[T]he unashamedly hybrid character of these black Atlantic cultures continually confounds any simplistic (essentialist or anti-essentialist) understanding of the relationship between racial identity and racial non-identity."[39] The reliance on the immediately visible falters in Clare's environment, but to let go of vision as a way to know feels dangerous to Clare. The visual marker of skin shade enters Clare's school:

> The shadows of color permeated the relationships of the students, one to one. When the girls found out that Victoria Carter, whom everyone thought was the most beautiful girl in school, was the daughter of a Black man who worked as a gardener and an Englishwoman who had settled in Jamaica, her position in their eyes was transformed, and the girls who had been quite intimidated by her, now spoke about her behind her back. (100)

The visual codes of Victoria Carter's body grant her respect, yet they conceal aspects of her "race" and class history that determine where she is placed in the shifting semantic field of the schoolgirls' racial discourse. Like the jellyfish, she is not what she seems. In "Passing," a section of *Claiming an Identity They Taught Me to Despise*, Cliff writes, "To this day camouflage terrorizes me. The pattern of skin which makes a being invisible against its habitat. And—yes—this camouflage exists for its protection. I am not what

I seem to be" (6). The jellyfish is dangerous specifically because it does not seem so, and yet camouflage offers safety to beings that need to blend into their environment. The notion of camouflage exists within a logic of vision that Cliff's novel, as part of its antirepresentational project, calls into question. Amy Robinson's work on racial and sexual passing reminds us of the centrality of the visual within totalizing paradigms: "Within a Western metaphysical tradition that has naturalized visibility as the locus of ontological truth-claims about the subject, vision masquerades as the agent of unmediated facticity."[40] Cliff's literary representation of Jamaican social worlds is thus as shifting for the reader as it is for the protagonist. Clare cannot depend even on corporeality as something solid or fixed. Cliff's novel continually problematizes the ways that the human physical body both lies and slips from view, the ways it is both the site of optical surety and potentially false representation. At the same time, however, within representational systems that are themselves violent and partial, the body remains a material site that bears the (undeniable, yet denied) marks of horror.

Abeng poses questions about how the social body can absorb scenes of horror, of the physical body's excess of pain. Cliff links such questions to the acts of historical representation, to the definitional stories that people tell about other people as they represent them. For example, her previous discussion of the label human/inhuman, of the dangerous power wielded by one who uses such labels and definitions, draws connections that extend far behind and beyond Clare Savage's schoolgirl hissing on a street corner. The narrator explains that European explorers and "discoverers" of the New World consistently imagined indigenous peoples as inhuman monsters. Cliff likens this imaginative force to science fiction creation and exposes the violence enabled by these and other fantastical projects of representation. She explains that the primary feature of "imagined inhabitants,"

> is their difference from white Christian Europeans. It is *that* heart of darkness which has imagined them less than human. Which has limited their movement. The fantasies of this heart infected the Native tribes of North America with smallpox and with syphilis. Destroyed the language of the Mayans and the Incas. Brought Africans in chains to the New World and worked them to death. Killed nine million people, including six million Jews, in the death camps of Europe. This is one connection. These are but a few of the heart's excesses. (79)

Material bodily violence is the result of representational fictions and fantasies. The novel asks, if discourse about the body is indeterminate, where does our knowledge of horror reside? What forms of bodily horror cannot be absorbed? Cliff critiques the human social machine for its capacity to absorb horror, for its attempts to rationalize it, by focusing on the literal, biological absorption of the body's horror by both the natural world and the human corpus. The bodies themselves, the physical remains of suffering human victims, may slip away through discourse, through rationalization, fantasy classification, historical imaginings. In trying to visualize and imagine the death camps,

> [Clare's] mind cast [the Holocaust's] environment in places that she knew on sight. Her mind tried to picture acre upon acre of shantytowns and acre upon acre of alms houses—and in this expanse of misery she placed inhabitants. Without thinking that these places were already inhabited with people the society had discarded . . . she didn't really think of the people who were actually there. (76)

Clare's epileptic classmate, Doreen Paxton, also slips from the minds of the schoolgirls after her public bodily trauma.

Cliff shows that not only the human mind, but the natural world can absorb human horror. At the place where Clare's great-great-grandfather Justice Savage tortured his slaves to death, "The bones fell to the ground where they melded with the earth, fertilizing the cane with potash" (30). The bones of the hundred slaves he burned "made the land at Runaway Bay rich and green. Tall royal palms lined the avenues leading to the houses of the development. Breadfruit trees, branches fat with their deep green lobed leaves, created shade around the stucco [vacation] bungalows" (40). Rather than read this as the regenerative power of nature to transvert suffering to plenitude, Cliff shows the sickness of the human capacity to absorb horror—it is a corporeal, physical illness she relates in her discussion of the smoke from the Holocaust. Those who would deny, ignore, or erase the horror of the Holocaust from historical narratives are nevertheless marked physically by its actuality, its presence as undeniable fact:

> The smoke from six million bodies burning had passed across the surfaces of continents and the slopes and peaks of mountain ranges and moved over bodies of water. The bones of six million people had been bleached stark white by the same sun that traveled overhead day after day, its circuits telling time. And when the bones started to crumble in their dryness, some of the dust had also been carried across land masses and bodies of water— while the rest seeped under the ground to fertilize the earth. The smoke from the bodies and the dust from the bones made a change in the atmosphere—

in the air that people breathed and the water they drank. Did no one notice
the steady change in their environment? Their lungs—their good Christian
lungs—must have been filling with the smoke from burning Jewish bodies.
Just as the clouds of Hiroshima and Nagasaki entered the bodies of women
and emerged as milk from their breasts. (71)

Cliff's meaning here is clearly not a positive ashes-to-ashes, dust-to-dust
implication of cycle or regeneration. Rather, she is calling attention to Pierre
Nora's distinction between memory and history. History, which exists in
language and is fixated on events, has the capacity to absorb, via rationalization, multiple forms of terror. But overwhelming events of human cruelty,
such as racial slavery and the Holocaust, remain as traces on the body politic
as well as on the human physical self, there to be recalled in the reworkings
of memory. Cliff's challenge as a novelist is how to capture these memories
without fixing them as artifacts. Perhaps we can say that she attempts to
write in the space that Richard Wright confronted at Christianborg Castle
when his "mind refused to function." Out of his confrontation with the
walls of that castle, Wright imagines the tear of a female ancestor. Cliff
attempts to fashion multiple stories out of that woman's tear.

In his critique of Enlightenment modernity, Lyotard writes, "The nineteenth and twentieth centuries have given us as much terror as we can take.
We have paid a high enough price for the nostalgia of the whole and the
one, for the reconciliation of the concept and the sensible, of the transparent and the communicable experience."[41] Michelle Cliff uses her fiction to
ask, "What do people do with their history of horror? What does it mean to
bear witness in the act of watching a retelling? What does it mean to carry
cultural memory in the flesh?"[42] These are also questions about representation, about vision and spectatorship. Hortense Spillers sees the history, as
well as the actuality, of slavery as a founding memory of the New World:
"[T]he sociopolitical order of the New World . . . with its human sequence
written in blood, *represents* for its African and indigenous peoples a scene of
actual mutilation, dismemberment, and exile."[43] Spillers's phrasing makes us
think about the social locations of spectators and those represented in much
the same way that African American visual artist Pat Ward Williams asks,
"Can you be BLACK and look at this?"[44] Donna Haraway reminds us further
that "vision is *always* a question of the power to see—and perhaps of the
violence implicit in our visualizing practices. With whose blood were my
eyes crafted?"[45] Cliff's depictions of the physical connections between the
horrors of the flesh and human life question the extent to which horror is
at once absorbable and that which cannot be denied. That is, while the

rationalizing mind may discursively erase the existence of horror, its persistent presence exerts itself in human lungs, milk glands, stomachs, eyes, and noses.

And yet in tension with this notion of a bodily trace is "the difficulty in defining and delimiting one's own corporeality" as a central problematic for writers of the Caribbean diaspora.[46] The body politic of Jamaican society, through racial discourse, attempts to control and regulate the definitions and limits of corporeal meaning. As in the episode of Victoria Carter, Clare's "white" then "black" schoolmate, optical human mechanisms are insufficient for racial classification: it is linguistic knowledge of Victoria's "black" father that makes her "black" in the eyes of the schoolgirls. And yet within this realm of language, visual clues and marks on the human body are not only scrutinized and classified, but manipulated. Though hair may be either "good" or "kinky," it can be straightened in many ways. Clare's father

> tutored her about the expectations he had with regard to her pursuit of shade.... Boy taught his eldest daughter that she came from his people — white people, he stressed—and he expected Clare to preserve his green eyes and light skin—those things she had been born with. And she had a duty to try to turn the green eyes blue, once and for all—and make the skin, now gold, become pale and subject to visible sunburn. These things she should pursue. (127)

The visible markings of race can be preserved and pursued in an ongoing genealogical effort to fix racial classification "once and for all." Cliff posits that within this society where hybridity is prevalent, during this time in Clare's life (puberty) where the body is in exaggerated flux, nevertheless the social machine draws lines, fixes rules, and enforces codifications in the discursive realm to preserve hierarchical arrangements. Sylvia Wynter sees this process of codification as the second half of an apposite process of homogenization:

> The social machine homogenizes—as in its constitution of the "negro," a process during which it homogenized multiple cultures, multiple genetic strains into one entity.... But once it has homogenized it needs to differentiate, to demarcate, to inscribe, so as to produce the multi-layered levels necessary to the hierarchical structures of production.[47]

As a developing adolescent, Clare struggles with these arrangements, wondering, "Why did everything seem so fixed? So unchangeable.... She felt split into two parts—white and not white, town and country, scholarship and privilege, Boy and Kitty" (118, 119). The adolescent child tests the limits of this fixity, pushing against social boundaries in ways that her elders will condemn and punish. For example, when Clare accidentally shoots her grandmother's bull, none of her adult relatives can see that her motivations in venturing out with a gun were multiple and quite complex. In her parents' eyes, "She had stepped out of line, no matter what, in a society in which the lines were unerringly drawn. She had been caught in rebellion. She was a girl. No one was impressed with her" (149–50). Rebellion is frowned upon in all middle-class children but especially in girl children. Part of Clare's social maturation entails the inculcation of gender roles, a process in no way unconnected to a schooling in proper class behavior. Thus as punishment for shooting the bull, Clare's parents send her to live with a "proper" old (and racist) white lady "from one of the oldest families in Jamaica," Mrs. Phillips (150). In explaining this banishment, Kitty tells Clare,

> You have to learn once and for all just who you are in this world. Mrs. Phillips is a lady, and you are getting to the age when you will need to be a lady as well. . . . When you are grown you can want anything you want. You can be anything you want to be. A doctor. A teacher. But to get there you have to learn the rules. That girls like you don't fire guns. Girls like you have a better chance at life than other girls. I know what I am talking about. . . . Mrs. Phillips can teach you to take advantage of who you are. (150)

Kitty's words here echo those of her husband, who urges Clare to turn the family's green eyes blue "once and for all." Both of Clare's parents construct her as a "lady" and attempt to lodge her (and perhaps through her, the family) in a fixed and stable ("once and for all") racial and class identification of white-lady-ness.

Despite the fixity desired by Clare's mother, however, the novel, true to its antibildungsroman qualities, ends in both irresolution and change. At the moment of its closure, Clare has begun to menstruate and she sits with her diary in her lap; her life as she authors it is located at the physical site of an adult sexuality, enabling her to script a counternarrative of female adulthood that is opposed to the one foisted on her by her parents or Mrs. Phillips. Clare does not come into a full or unified understanding of herself in a non-contradictory way because hybridity is part of her Caribbean identity, which is best seen as processual, rather than linear and finite. *Abeng* rewrites Franklin's and Jefferson's "Enlightenment" discourses against "racial mixing" in its last pages when Clare visits Mrs. Phillips's "crazy" sister, condemned by her family for loving a black man. This woman, Miss Winifred, has internalized miscegenation discourse and tells Clare, "What I did was wrong, you see. I knew better. I knew that God meant that coons and buckra people were not meant to mix their blood. It's not right. Only sadness comes from mixture. You must remember that" (164). Beginning to accept a multiply diasporic location, Clare responds, "But, Miss Winifred, there's all kinds of mixture in Jamaica. Everybody mixes it seems to me. I am mixed too" (164). The novel does not end with Clare's stable location in one particular race, gender role, or social class, but instead points her toward what Teresa de Lauretis has termed an excessive, eccentric, critical position, "a position attained through practices of political and personal displacement across boundaries between sociosexual identities and communities, between bodies and discourses."[48] It is only in Cliff's second novel, *No Telephone to Heaven*, that we see Clare fully accept the often dangerous politics of this coalitional location. Both of Cliff's semiautobiographical novels demonstrate her engagement with the multiple positionings that make up her own cultural inheritance(s).[49]

For Cliff, Caribbean identity is always/already dispersed, as she indicates in the quote that begins this chapter. This dispersal makes the writing of Jamaican history complicated and multiple; she must appropriate multiple vocabularies in her revisionary work. Cliff writes fiction as a politics of resistance, like Trinidadian writer Merle Hodge, who claims, "Creative writing becomes, for me, a guerrilla activity. We are occupied by foreign fiction. Fiction which affirms and validates our world is therefore an important weapon of resistance"[50] For Cliff, the space of creative writing becomes the place where she can validate a world and a history that she wants to claim as hers and that she also wants to revise and critique. Richard Wright's essays in *White Man, Listen!* become for him a way to critique the exclusions implied in a U.S. national identity that defines "the Negro" as a second-class citizen. In response to these exclusions, Wright searches in his writings for a "home in the heart." Cliff's work, on the other hand, can be seen as part of a constellation of feminist narrative practices that remain skeptical about the redemptive possibilities of "home." Both Wright and Cliff negotiate the multiple meanings of diasporic kinship as a concept unavoidably linked to the histories of slavery. Like Wright, Cliff writes from the space of expatriation, using her novel *Abeng* to claim an identity that is both national and diasporic: Jamaica is the nation with which she chooses to identify, yet she rejects the exclusions that stratify Jamaican social locations.

Part II

From Discrimination and Insult to Homes in Diaspora

3

Harlem on My Mind:
Exile and Community in
Chester Himes's Detective Fiction

REPORTER: What does the King verdict say to you as a black man living
    in America?
INTERVIEWEE: What it says to me is I'm living on the wrong continent.

—*TV newscast following the acquittal on April 29, 1992,
of all four police officers who beat Rodney King*

Chester Himes, an American author who never found a "place" in the American literary scene in his lifetime, wrote his detective novels during his French expatriation, setting them in the nostalgic milieu of a Harlem he half created in his own imagination. In the second volume of his autobiography, *My Life of Absurdity: The Later Years*, Himes states emphatically, "*The Harlem of my books was never meant to be real; I never called it real; I just wanted to take it away from the white man if only in my books*" (126). Himes's detective novels evoke a geographic and social landscape at once surreal and recognizable. Nightmarishly vivid scenes of almost hilarious violence and mayhem occur on named streets, in landmark churches and nightclubs. The consistency of the descriptive tone throughout the novels elicits a vision for the reader of "Himes's Harlem," allowing us to see the way that the author uses his writing to reclaim the space of "home," to "take it away from the white man," and to invest this reauthored space with a radical politics of black freedom and community.

Himes's work in the detective fiction genre was extremely successful in France and made him a celebrity of sorts. His first detective novel, *For Love of Imabelle*, won France's coveted literary prize, the *Grand prix de roman policière*, in 1958 for the year's best detective novel.[1] The popularity of Himes's detective fiction in France and the celebration of Himes by the French as a "great black American writer" are facts that exist in tension with Himes's lifelong ambivalence about America as a possible home for black people in general and for a black writer in particular. In his autobiography, Himes reflects triumphantly on this time when he was finishing *For Love of Imabelle* and receiving his first advance check from his publisher: "Now I was a French writer and the United States of America could kiss my ass" (113). It is slightly ironic that Himes describes himself as a French writer since he never learned to speak French, though he remained in Europe for the rest of his life. Later in his autobiography, Himes describes a time around 1968 when, he says, "I still felt as much of a stranger in Paris as I did in every white country I had ever been in; I only felt at home in my detective stories" (381). Himes's work in the distinctly American popular genre of the hard-boiled detective novel provides an excellent opportunity to study the ways that writing can become a space of home for an expatriate diasporic author. Issues of racial and national identity are prominent in Himes's sense of exclusion from the American body politic: France and America represent "white countries" for him, and his detective writing provides him with a space of home that is not racially exclusive, a traveling home in blackness.

How does the author insert himself into the space of fiction, having been rejected by, or perceiving himself to be outside of, an American literary tradition? Himes describes this writerly process as a journey: "I entered the world which I created. I believed in it. It moved me and troubled me. But I could control it, which I have never been able to do to the world in which I really live."[2] In his detective novels Himes was able to exercise a control over U.S. racial politics that he (like most people) could never exercise in life. In a 1970 interview, Himes explains the nostalgic pleasure of his literary journey to fellow black American writer, John A. Williams:

> I went back—as a matter of fact, it's like a sort of pure homesickness. . . .
> I began creating all the black scenes of my memory and my actual knowledge. I was very happy writing these detective stories, especially the first one, when I began it. I wrote those stories with more pleasure than I wrote any of the other stories. And then when I got to the end and started my detective shooting at some white people, I was the happiest.[3]

What are the ways that writing becomes, for Himes, "a sort of pure home-sickness," containing the experiences of both pain and pleasure? Himes speaks of the pain he felt in being denied the identity of a "famous writer" by the American publishing industry and reading public, saying, "Nothing in all my life hurt me as much as the American rejection of my thoughts."[4] Himes refers here to the poor critical reception of his two protest novels, *If He Hollers Let Him Go* (1945) and *Lonely Crusade* (1947). He links his pain directly to the place, America, from which he desires to be free, and his sense of hurt causes Himes to turn in 1953 to France as a place where he sees a larger space for the articulation of his thoughts. French scholar Michel Fabre quotes Himes as saying,

> For me France was the opportunity to write without the barriers imposed by race, politics, my state of health, finances, or my appearance. . . . The U.S. offered me no future. . . . Richard Wright was then having his turn. But France had attributed fame and fortune to Alexandre Dumas and his son and many other blacks.[5]

Himes, however, does not leave "home" behind when he crosses the Atlantic. Rather, his writing itself becomes a pleasurable visitation of home. This chapter will examine what generates this pleasure, and the ways that, for Himes and his readers, the pleasure is not simply nostalgic, but also political.

Himes's immensely popular detective series becomes a way for him to control an urban African American experience and to briefly imagine refashioning U.S. law enforcement practices. Himes served time in the Ohio State Penitentiary for armed robbery, from December 1928 to April 1936, and it was in prison that he began writing. He first published stories under his prison number in *Abbott's Monthly and Illustrated News*, *Bronzeman*, *The Pittsburgh Courier*, and *Atlanta Daily World*, leading finally to several stories being published in *Esquire* magazine in 1934.[6] Though originally sentenced to serve twenty to twenty-five years, Himes was released for good behavior (perhaps also because of his status as a published writer) after seven and a half years. Thus Himes's identity as a writer was initially connected in both symbolic and material ways to his experience of imprisonment and his access to freedom. The relationship of U.S. law enforcement institutions to African American people becomes a dominant theme throughout Himes's writing.[7] In a 1952 letter to Richard Wright, Himes describes his prison novel, which was published that year under the title *Cast the First Stone*: "The book is a simple story about life in prison; maybe the boys can stand

the truth about life in a state prison better than they can stand the truth
about life in the prison of being a Negro in America."[8] The idea that America is a prison for black people has a long history, beginning, of course, in
the "prison-house of bondage" that was racial slavery. Malcolm X told his
audience in 1963, "Don't be shocked when I say that I was in prison. You're
still in prison. That's what America means: prison."[9] In "American Prisons
and the African-American Experience: A History of Social Control and
Racial Oppression," Robert Johnson explains that "[t]he pervasiveness of
prison and prison-like environments in the African-American experience
has led some thoughtful observers to contend that America itself is a prison
for blacks, offering men and women in the 'free world' a life that is little
more than a replica of existence in confinement" (28). Himes resists this
confinement, using his writing practices to continually revise the spaces of
incarceration that make life a prison for "black" people in "white" countries.
In writing, Himes, like Richard Wright and Michelle Cliff, revises the
exclusionary politics and policies that attempt to delimit and confine black
identities.

Freedom and Safety: "He may run, but he can't hide..."

Himes's experience of being "black" in America makes issues of citizenship,
safety, and policing central to his analysis of democracy. So much of Himes's
writing was centered around a revision of law enforcement practices because
of what Robert Johnson calls the "criminogenic conditions" of black urban
life in America. Johnson explains that "[n]o other group in American history
has faced such conditions of continuing deprivation and injustice, often
under the authority of law (including laws that explicitly allowed slavery
and, later, racial segregation)."[10] These conditions produce a high rate of
street crime and a high rate of incarceration, leading to more social isolation, more crime, and more incarceration, in a vicious cycle that leaves those
people who are caught up in it profoundly alienated and, I would add, "un-
homed." Johnson cites multiple studies dating from 1928, 1935, 1970, and
1995 to show that black Americans throughout history have experienced
"lawlessness and injustice at the hands of formal authorities."[11]

In 1944, if not earlier, it was clear to Himes that U.S. police procedures
did not offer protection to African Americans. Throughout his career Himes
wrote about African Americans' need for physical safety as the most basic
requirement for fulfilling the promise of democratic freedom for all citizens.
In 1921 the prominent African American historian, Carter Woodson, stated

in no uncertain terms, "The citizenship of the Negro in this country is a fiction."[12] Woodson's statement comes from his essay, "Fifty Years of Negro Citizenship as Qualified by the U.S. Supreme Court." This experience of the failure of democratic freedom, the sensation and knowledge that one's citizenship is a fiction, is precisely the form of racial exclusion that so many black writers resist and revise in their multiple discursive modes. Perhaps we could say, then, that Himes uses his detective fiction to revise the fictional nature of black citizenship. He also uses a journalistic mode to address issues of citizenship and participation in democracy. In a 1942 article in *Opportunity* entitled "Now Is the Time! Here Is the Place!" Himes explains the willingness of Negro Americans to fight in World War II:

> Does not, also, the nation of the United States of America, in a comparable degree, belong to the Negro American by right of creation, by right of development, by right of occupation? Are not these the inalienable rights by which peoples claim nations? What question can there possibly be of the Negro Americans' loyalty? This is our native land, our country; our participation in the war effort is a fight for what is ours. Our fight at home is simply for the possession of it. (273)

Elsewhere in the article Himes demands racial freedom at home, alongside the building war rhetoric of freedom worldwide. It is important to note here that in 1942 Himes articulates the "Negro" struggle in the terms of fighting for the *possession of a home*. Himes's own history of incarceration is important to his thinking since he experienced life in the exile of prison, not home but locked in the "big house," with his citizenship revoked.[13] The possession of a home in the national body politic implies freedom and safety as the necessary benefits of citizenship. When the state sanctions violence against a group of people in the form of police brutality or accepts a lack of police protection from racist brutality, that group is effectively excluded from the benefits and rights of citizenship. These are the reasons that Himes, Wright, Baldwin, and so many other black Americans cross the Atlantic. And yet, Himes uses his writing, indeed his fiction, to simultaneously inhabit the U.S. political space that excluded him and to question the fictional nature of the citizenship of "the Negro in America."

In 1948, Himes was asked to address a creative writing class at the University of Chicago. In this speech, later published as "Dilemma of the Negro Novelist in the U.S.," Himes sheds light on why he consistently wrote about the national identity that had excluded him. He tells his audience that the black American writer cannot "return to African culture" as an escape from the "race consciousness" that pervades American culture:

He cannot accomplish this departure because he is an American. He will
realize in the end that he possesses this heritage of slavery; he is a product of
this American culture; his thoughts and emotions and reactions have been
fashioned by his American environment. He will discover that he cannot
free himself of race consciousness because he cannot free himself of race;
that is his motive in attempting to run away. But, to paraphrase a statement
of Joe Louis's, "He may run, but he can't hide." (53)

This statement is laced throughout with the desire to flee, depart, and run,
yet it is linked to the great Joe Louis, who so effectively stayed and fought;
as such, it provides a critical way to read Himes and other black expatriate
writers who use words as their weapons in the fight. Himes, however, did
not see words as the only necessary weapons, explaining in 1970 to his
friend John A. Williams that "[a]nything can be initiated, enforced, contained or destroyed on the American scene through violence. That's the
only thing that's ever made any change, because they have an inheritance
of violence; it comes right straight from the days of slavery."[14] Himes's language echoes that of Du Bois's explication of a race concept in *Dusk of Dawn*,
as we see how the social "heritage of slavery," continued in "discrimination
and insult," both provoke Himes's exile and incite his literary response. In
writing, via the medium of ink, he gains the measure of control that enables
him to feel at home in his detective novels. Himes rejects the exclusionary
politics of the "white country" for a (written) home in detective fiction, a
popular American genre featuring the elements of violence, crime, and
policing so central to Himes's ideologies. Through his work in this genre,
Himes moves from the articulation of a black identity that is not "convict"
or "number 59623" (Himes's prison number and the only signature for some
of his stories published from prison), to a roomier cultural space where he
can say, "I am a famous French writer."

For Himes, the first requirement of citizenship is the assurance of safety and
protection from violence. Himes describes African Americans' lack of physical safety in "Negro Martyrs Are Needed," published in 1944 in *The Crisis*:

> Riots between white and black occur for only one reason: *Negro Americans*
> *are firmly convinced that they have no access to any physical protection which they*
> *do not provide for themselves.* It is a well-known and established fact that
> this conviction is rooted in history: *Negroes in fact do not have any protection*
> *from physical injury inflicted by whites other than that which they provide for*
> *themselves.* (174)

Writing from a space of expatriation, Himes performs a literary intervention
in this state of affairs by creating his two famous detectives, Coffin Ed John-

son and Grave Digger Jones, as "the cops who should have been," the cops who could offer protection to the African American urban community. By analyzing two of Himes's detective novels, *The Real Cool Killers* (1959) and *Blind Man with a Pistol* (1969), we can chart the progress of these proposed heroes. In *The Real Cool Killers*, Himes constructs Coffin Ed and Grave Digger as viable folk heroes for the urban community.[15] But by *Blind Man with a Pistol*, the characters' effectiveness as heroes is undercut by the changing landscape of racial politics in the United States. Thus the home space that Himes writes back to does not exist in an idealized unchanging apolitical realm; instead, his expatriate vision responds to changes "at home." There is, in fact, a dialogue between the image of home and the text that represents this image.

The Real Cool Killers: Coffin Ed and Grave Digger as Heroes Who Will "Serve and Protect"

Himes's second detective novel, *The Real Cool Killers*, opens with the blues lines, "I'm gwine down to de river, / Set down on de ground. / If de blues overtake me, / I'll jump overboard and drown" (5). This epigram signals a reading of Himes's novel grounded in the vernacular. Like the blues themselves, the novel can be read as the response of the disenfranchised to white power. But the words of the blues lines imply a different and more pessimistic response to life in a racist society than the response suggested by the novel. The characters in *The Real Cool Killers* employ specifically community-based, folk-heroic strategies of self-defense and solidarity in the face of an intrusive, dominating power structure embodied by white cops. They employ these strategies as a way to make their "home" a habitable space, despite their exclusion from the larger city. In all of his detective novels, Himes sets up Harlem as particularly unreadable and mystifying, especially to white "visitors" and cops. In contrast, the local residents of the neighborhood are able to both read Harlem and manipulate its unreadability, and these skills afford them a certain amount of self-protection.

Most governmental systems of ordering and labeling urban spaces are not applicable to Himes's Harlem. When Grave Digger questions a suspect to find out an address, the evasive response he gets is, "You don't never think 'bout where a gal lives in Harlem, 'les you goin' home with her. What do anybody's address mean up here?" (115). The unreliability of official labels functions in several ways in the novel. First, it completely baffles the white cops (especially chiefs and lieutenants) and frustrates their efforts to

apprehend criminals. On another level, it allows Himes to project Coffin Ed
and Grave Digger as empowered inside readers of an otherwise baffling
milieu. It also enables the residents of Harlem to manipulate the particular
codes that confound white cops, thereby providing them with a measure of
safety and self-protection. In *The Real Cool Killers*, the white cops continually express their frustration at being unable to find a systematic way to de-
cipher their surroundings. Their inability to understand their environment
is directly tied to their preconceived racist stereotypes, as seen in the exas-
perated statement of one white cop to another: "What's a name to these
coons? They're always changing about" (121). It is language that enables the
local residents, in effect, to "take Harlem away from the white man," making this neighborhood "their own." Thus their strategies are in many ways a
mirror for the literary performances of Himes himself, as he uses the languages of his fiction to repossess "home."

The context that makes street-level strategies of manipulation both necessary and successful is the historical presence of white law enforcement in
black urban communities and the way this white presence has been seen by
those community residents. Chester Himes had stated in 1944, "It is a rather
deadly joke among Negroes (especially since the Detroit riots) that the first
thing to do in case of a race riot is not to call the police but to shoot them. . . .
'Man, what you mean call the police; them the people gonna kill you.'"[16]
John W. Roberts explains that "the tremendous amount of power vested in
white law enforcement officers in the late nineteenth century caused many
African Americans to view them as the embodiment of the 'law' and, by
extension, white power."[17] Because these law officers were not community
insiders and only entered these neighborhoods for work, their knowledge
of the territory was limited, and African Americans soon developed self-
protecting strategies for exploiting this ignorance and manipulating codes.
Himes gives us Lieutenant Anderson and Captain Brice as the mid-twentieth-
century embodiments of the "law." But Himes creates an intermediary: the
black police officer, in the form of his two heroes, Coffin Ed and Grave Digger.[18] Robert Johnson's analysis of race and incarceration shows that "garden-
variety street crime . . . is a common adaptation to blocked opportunities for
assimilation into American society and achievement of the American
dream of material success."[19] Though Coffin Ed and Grave Digger do not
condone such "petty" crimes as theft and prostitution, they are more concerned with a different form of crime in the ghetto.

The Real Cool Killers opens with the murder of a white man, a "visitor" to
Harlem. This fact brings the white cops to Harlem in full force, armed with

both weapons and racist projections: "'Rope off this whole goddamned area,' the sergeant said. 'Don't let anybody out. We want a Harlem-dressed Zulu. Killed a white man.... Pick up all suspicious persons'" (22). When white power (in the form of armed white police officers) invades the neighborhood, every black person becomes a potential suspect, a potential scapegoat. And because the crime is the murder of a white man, every black person becomes a potential victim of lynching by the white mob. Himes specifically suggests this potential when he describes the cops' intrusive presence swarming over the neighborhood:

> [The white chief of police] turned and pointed toward a tenement building across the street. It looked indescribably ugly in the glare of a dozen powerful spotlights. Uniformed police stood on the roof, others were coming and going through the entrance; still others stuck their heads out of front windows to shout to other cops in the street. The other front windows were jammed with colored faces, looking like clusters of strange purple fruit in the stark white light. (41)

Himes's imagery of "colored faces" should be read in the context of both its musical and literary antecedents, specifically Billie Holiday and Jean Toomer.[20] In this imagery, the specter of slavery enters the text and is refigured in the modern context of police brutality. The last two stanzas of Toomer's "Song of the Son," from *Cane*, read:

> O Negro slaves, dark purple ripened plums
> Squeezed, and bursting in the pine-wood air,
> Passing, before they stripped the old tree bare
> One plum was saved for me, one seed becomes
> An everlasting song, a singing tree,
> Caroling softly souls of slavery,
> What they were, and what they are to me,
> Caroling softly souls of slavery. (14)

The words of Toomer's poem, "squeezed and bursting," suggest the violence of slavery and the pressure of exploitation, and these images resonate with the conditions of social inequality in contemporary urban environments. Himes draws on this African American literary antecedent to signify in language the social heritage of slavery and the modern extensions of state-sanctioned racialized violence.[21]

Billie Holiday's famous blues song, "Strange Fruit," articulates the image of lynching even more overtly in a way that is crucial to Himes's own description of the relationship between white law enforcement and black communities. Her musical version of a poem by Abel Meeropol (aka Lewis

Allan), recorded April 20, 1939, has potent resonance not only for an American audience, but for an international one as well.[22] Holiday's song represents lynching in its reference to "black bodies swinging" on southern trees;
she sings of the "strange fruit" that these southern trees bear, their leaves
and roots marked with blood. The song's lyrics powerfully combine the pas-
toral "scent of magnolia" with the "smell of burning flesh." Singing to an
urban New York audience at Café Society in Greenwich Village in 1939,
Billie Holiday contextualizes Southern racism and oppression for the Northern audience, making it relevant to them. Himes uses these same metaphors
for lynching; for the pine-scented squeezed-plum imagery of "Song of the
Son" and the antipastoral vision of "Strange Fruit," he substitutes the modern, signally urban decaying tenement flooded with police spotlights, surrounded by uniformed white cops, perhaps urban equivalents of hooded
Southern embodiments of white power. This resonance between the voices
of Himes, Holiday, and Toomer sets in motion a critique of Southern racism
by bringing it to a Northern urban context and showing the way that lynch
mob "law enforcement" is replicated in the modern city when a white is
presumed murdered by a black. It is this linking of lynching and the law
that underscores the social isolation felt by African Americans when they
have no recourse to legal protection in their homes.

Holiday's recording of "Strange Fruit," and her various performances of it
throughout the 1940s, especially, became iconic. The song was recognized
as the first overt antilynching statement in popular music.[23] It is significant
that both Holiday and Himes here insert the horror of slavery into the *popular* genres of the blues and detective fiction. For both black artists, this reference has been misread, perhaps because of its placement in a popular
form. In a long article, "Les Paroissiens de Chester Himes," published in
1965, French critic René Micha reads Himes's detective novels within the
discourses of exoticized travelogue. Micha echoes Himes's descriptive passages without quotes, stating,

> It's the vision itself which transports us . . . which offers a comic beauty. *Ut
> pictura poesis*. . . . We push open a door: on the white-washed walls, some
> graffiti forms a long fresco, always the same: enormous genitals on tiny
> bodies, like an orchard of strange fruits.[24]

The "we" here, the French reader, is actually transported, via Himes's visual
imagery, into the distant scene, which is marked symbolically by a sexualized
trope: larger-than-life genitalia. Given the popularity of blues and jazz in
France, it is probable that Micha knew Billie Holiday's song "Strange Fruit."

The contrast, then, between Holiday's horrific antipastoral vision of lynching and Micha's almost ecstatic "transport" here is quite striking. In *Lady Sings the Blues*, Billie Holiday tells a story of another rhapsodic, and sexualized, misreading of this imagery:

> Over the years I've had a lot of weird experiences as a result of that song. It has a way of separating the straight people from the squares and cripples. One night in Los Angeles a bitch stood right up in the club where I was singing and said, "Billie, why don't you sing that sexy song you're so famous for? You know, the one about the naked bodies swinging in the trees." Needless to say, I didn't. (84)

As castration was commonly a part of lynching, Micha's description perhaps unselfconsciously recalls Southern racism. Micha's (and the "bitch's") reading of Himes and Holiday replicates a fetishistic logic of the sexualization of blackness, a form of "eroticised othering" made doubly disturbing in its misappropriation of lynched bodies, not live ones.[25]

In *The Real Cool Killers*, true to the lynch-mob mentality, the white cops descend on the neighborhood, looking for any "Harlem-dressed Zulu" who can "hang" for the crime. But no criminal appears apprehendable, and the police chief is in danger of losing face before the white press. The master has been duped; he's caught unable to read the signs, solve the mystery, and appease the mob with a lynching. So he must get his hands on a black body quickly. A teenage gang called the Real Cool Moslems is suspected of being involved, and gang member Sonny Pickens becomes the scapegoat for the chief, who says, "We haven't got anybody to work on but him and it's just his black ass" (43). In the cops' mentality, Pickens's black ass is much less valuable than the white ass of Galen, the murdered man. This inequality cannot be balanced. Himes's expatriate analysis is that one dead black ass does not equal one dead white ass in the U.S. racial economy of 1959. This unequal economy of bodies becomes the central issue of much of Himes's detective fiction as he attempts to imagine how black people can be at home in America.

Coffin Ed's and Grave Digger's roles are made complex when white people come to Harlem seeking the exploitative vice available there, literally hoping to buy its citizens' bodies. When visiting customers in a Harlem bar question Grave Digger's "tough" police language, he responds, "I'm just a cop, if you white people insist on coming up to Harlem where you force colored people to live in vice-and-crime ridden slums, it's my job to see that you are safe" (65). Digger's comment here is important because it names the invidious complicity of white socioeconomic oppression and white participation

in exploitative vice. But his comment also invites a reading of his job as
protecting *white people*. This surface reading has caused some critics to condemn Ed's and Digger's seeming allegiance to white law at the expense of
brutality toward blacks. I would argue that Digger and Ed are skillful readers
of the particular politics of violence and law enforcement in the urban community, and that their ultimate aim is the protection of *black people*, and
especially black neighborhood security.[26]

This goal, of course, is one that is not recognized by the police force. Ed's
and Digger's reading of this police force's ideology demonstrates that the
best way to ensure the security of black bodies is to keep the lynch mobs at
bay. This goal can be accomplished by means that may seem circuitous but
are actually crucial: protecting the singular white body in Harlem. As we
have seen, only one white death in Harlem brings the cops en masse to the
area, with unquenchable lynching fervor, and importantly, one white stiff
ends up equaling four black corpses and one maimed black body. If Coffin
Ed and Grave Digger use violence in their questioning procedures, their
goal is to solve crimes so that white cops stay out. The complexity of Coffin
Ed and Grave Digger as heroes rests in this double-edged quality of their
behavior: their violence is both directed at members of their community
and used as a force to prevent the more uncontrollable violence of lynch
mobs. John Cawelti, writing on "hard boiled" detective fiction, explains
that "the action of legitimized violence . . . resolves tensions between the
anarchy of individualistic impulses and the communal ideas of law and order
by making the individual's violent action an ultimate defense of the community against the threat of anarchy."[27] Lynch-mob police brutality represents the anarchic violence that threatens the neighborhood's safety, that
endangers the home-space. In their protection of the community against
the anarchic forces of white law enforcement, Coffin Ed and Grave Digger
are complex black heroic figures. Possessing some of the traits of the trickster, badman, and slave driver, they stand apart from all these.

In *The Real Cool Killers*, Coffin Ed and Grave Digger are respected within
the tough-guy codes of the neighborhood. For example, their guns are
extremely formidable symbolic images and very real instruments of destruction known by all the community. At least one scene in each of Himes's
detective novels introduces these guns. In *The Real Cool Killers*, for example,
Himes writes: "Coffin Ed drew his pistol from its shoulder sling and spun the
cylinder. Passing street light glinted from the long nickel-plated barrel of
the special .38 revolver, and the five brass-jacketed bullets looked deadly in
the six chambers" (13). Here the gun literally reflects the street, the life of

the neighborhood, and the gun's image repeats its power in the community's imagination when Choo-Choo, one of the Real Cool Moslems, fantasizes, "What I'd rather have me is one of those hard-shooting long-barreled thirty-eights like Grave Digger and Coffin Ed have got. Them heaters can kill a rock" (49). Choo-Choo's hyperbolic description of the guns' power is tied to similarly legend-infused tales of Coffin Ed's and Grave Digger's own power, based on their quickness to use these infamous weapons. But Coffin Ed and Grave Digger play a very complex and multilayered role in their negotiation of the city's white power structure and their relationship to the black community, and there is less ambivalence in their behavior than there is conscious manipulation and folk heroic maneuvering in a very tight space of operation.

Coffin Ed's and Grave Digger's brutality is also part of the general cartoon-like excessive violence of Himes's detective fiction as a whole. For Coffin Ed and Grave Digger, violence or its threat (which is effective due to community knowledge of their capacity to do actual violence) is what enables them to get informants to talk. As cops, Coffin Ed and Grave Digger have official sanction from the white police department to be excessively brutal. This caveat removes the traditional prohibition against police brutality, which in many cases is only nominal anyway. But this particular nod from their white superiors functions differently for the white cops than it does for Coffin Ed and Grave Digger. As the chief says to Grave Digger, "You know Harlem, you know where you have to go, who to see.... I don't give a goddamn how many heads you crack; I'll back you up" (44). Thus their license to commit brutality is based on the police department's utter reliance on them as skilled readers of Harlem's behavioral and linguistic codes. This reliance recalls the role of black slave drivers during slavery. Roberts tells us that "in the black slave driver, the masters, from their point of view, had an individual who could be held responsible when enslaved Africans violated the rules of the system and whose loyalty could be counted on."[28] While this is what the plantation owner, and the white police force, *think* they are getting in the black slave driver, the actual allegiance of the driver may indeed be elsewhere. Hence during slavery a body of folklore emerged celebrating the driver as a trickster hero, portraying "John as a talented and skillful exploiter of his exploitation by Old Master, his dupe or foil in most of the tales."[29] To understand the ways that Coffin Ed and Grave Digger are able to function as *protectors* within their community, we must be aware of this difference between white perceptions of black behavior and black loyalty and the realities of that behavior and loyalty.

In 1970, Michel Fabre of *Le Monde* asked Himes whether his black detectives were traitors to their race. In response, Himes raised an important issue that has special bearing on *The Real Cool Killers:*

> Coffin Ed and Grave Digger would be traitors to their race if they were realistic characters. This is not the case: they represent the type of cop who *should* exist, who lives in the community, knows it well, and enforces respect for the law in a humane way. I believe in them. I created them: two people who would be enemies of Blacks in reality, but whom I intended to be sympathetic.[30]

Himes's statement is confusing in the ways that it champions, yet denies realism. When Fabre asks whether Coffin Ed and Grave Digger are traitors, he is speaking of their characters, not "real" black cops in general. Yet Himes does not respond directly to this request to discuss his *portrayal* of the cops, but instead hypothesizes that "real" black cops would be traitors. I take Himes to mean that Coffin Ed and Grave Digger are ideal types, that "real" cops who are black are necessarily traitors to their race, but that these two are sympathetic and their allegiance is above all to their community. Perhaps the writer in exile is perfectly placed to create such an ideal—a type that paradoxically could not exist.

Himes creates Coffin Ed and Grave Digger as a way to prevent the abusive presence of law enforcement from invading black neighborhoods. Ed and Digger can be read as artful strategizers of police procedure, whose perhaps imperfect methodology of protecting one white body (their overt, white-perceived purpose) has as its goal the effective prevention of a general lynching of black bodies. While such a goal was possible for Himes to articulate in the U.S. racial environment of 1959, even Himes knew it was not possible to realize; in the end Coffin Ed and Grave Digger cannot fully prevent the lynching, and innocent black citizens are killed. Ten years later, with the publication of *Blind Man with a Pistol*, Coffin Ed's and Grave Digger's strategic methodology is much less plausible even to articulate and is shown to be absurd.[31]

Blind Man with a Pistol: Riots and Revolutions

In the ten-year span between the publication of *The Real Cool Killers* and *Blind Man with a Pistol*, U.S. racial politics gained international exposure, and civil rights mobilization was met by both overt and covert forms of state repression. The assassinations of Martin Luther King Jr. and Malcolm X had violently demonstrated U.S. institutional response to powerful black heroes. In a discussion of 1960s social movements and African American literature, W. Lawrence Hogue explains that the increasing economic disparity between blacks and whites had led to riots and rebellions across the nation and to civil rights and black power struggles that "continued to undermine and bring into question the authority and legitimacy of the dominant ideological apparatus."[32] Himes's own political philosophizing moves from an assertion of defensive violence to an aggressive violence but within the construct of making the United States ultimately a *safer* place for blacks, a place where black people could feel at home. For Himes, white law enforcement continues to represent the greatest threat to personal safety for African American urban dwellers. In an environment pervaded by racial oppression, the first requirement of freedom is protection from lynch mobs and the feeling that one's home is not besieged and one's body is not endangered. But Himes's long career of writing about the United States reflects the fact that he saw this safety and security as no more attainable in the 1960s and 1970s than it had been in the 1940s, when he asked, "Is the Constitution jim-crowed? Is freedom for white only?"[33]

Late in Himes's detective series, Coffin Ed and Grave Digger, by virtue (or fault) of their connection to the institutional power structure of the police force, meet with challenges to their previously unquestioned authority. The nationalist impulse energizing urban black communities in the 1960s sees white power as centralized and therefore fightable. As emblems of the state, all police are seen as opponents, and no exception is made for skin shade: there is no intermediary role, then, that Coffin Ed and Grave Digger can play. If they are cops, they are the enemy, not the heroic protectors of the community. During his expatriation in Europe, Himes kept attuned to internal and international U.S. politics and ideology. He explains the genesis of *Blind Man* this way in his preface to the novel:

> A friend of mine, Phil Lomax, told me this story about a blind man with a pistol shooting at a man who had slapped him on a subway train and killing an innocent bystander peacefully reading his newspaper across the aisle and I thought, damn right, sounds just like today's news, riots in the ghettos, war in Vietnam, masochistic doings in the Middle East. And then I thought of some of our loudmouthed leaders urging our vulnerable soul brothers on to getting themselves killed, and thought further that all unorganized violence is like a blind man with a pistol.

Given the social circumstances outlined by Hogue, the creation and function of Coffin Ed and Grave Digger as ideal heroes and community protectors becomes entirely implausible for Himes. In effect, the street writes back to Himes's creation of these well-known characters, and he must respond to their shifting environment if they are to be kept alive. In the absence of Ed's and Digger's protective function in *Blind Man*, widespread random violence ensues in Harlem, and in this, Himes's last completed detective novel, we return to his long-held critique of unorganized violence, as initially set forth in *The Crisis* in 1944.

While *Blind Man* is less a traditional detective story than any of Himes's previous detective fiction, there is the premise of a mystery within the novel. Like *The Real Cool Killers*, it involves a white man who lives outside Harlem journeying to the neighborhood to buy a black body for sex and ending up dead on the street. As *Blind Man* progresses, it becomes obvious that if Ed and Digger's former heroic strategies were ever viable ones, they can no longer succeed, for in 1969 the mood on the street is very different from that of 1959. In addition, the corruption of the police force, previously alluded to, now works to circumscribe Ed and Digger's behavior. Predictably, the dead white man on the street brings on the white cops in full force, and Grave Digger and Coffin Ed try futilely to protect the citizens from the ensuing lynch mob. At the scene of the crime, Grave Digger says to Coffin Ed,

> "I just wish these mother-rapers wouldn't come up here and get themselves killed, for whatever reason."...
> ...Coffin Ed turned on [the crowd of black onlookers] and shouted suddenly, "You people better get the hell away from here before the white cops come in, or they'll run all your asses in."
> There was a sound of nervous movement, like frightened cattle in the dark, then a voice said belligerently, "Run whose ass in? I lives here!"
> "All right," Coffin Ed said resignedly. "Don't say I didn't warn you." (35)

While Coffin Ed and Grave Digger are still following their earlier strategy of protecting Harlem citizens from the anarchic wrath of white law enforcement, the scene has changed. The unidentified belligerent voice, who contests Coffin Ed's demands and asserts his rights as a resident speaking from and for his home, is the voice of a new generation that respects neither Ed and Digger's authority, nor the intimidating practices of the white cops. Ed's answer back to the voice is "resigned," a new way to describe Ed and Digger's behavior in a crowd. The new, more militant generation of Harlem citizens has less respect for "the law" in any form. Confronting some young kids threatening another kid with violence because he is too chicken to stone the white cops, Coffin Ed and Grave Digger are neither automatically recognized, nor feared. One kid boldly challenges the once terrifying Coffin Ed:

"You scared of whitey. You ain't nothing but shit."

"When I was your age I'da got slapped in the mouth for telling a grown man that."

"You slap us, we waste you."...

"We're the law," Coffin Ed said to forestall any more argument. Six pairs of round white-rimmed eyes stared at them accusingly.

"Then you on whitey's side."...

"Go on home," Grave Digger said, pushing them away, ignoring flashing knife blades. "Go home and grow up. You'll find out there ain't any other side." (140)

Here Coffin Ed and Grave Digger express their recognition of the pervasiveness of white power. "Whitey's side" is the ruling paradigm, and they do not see the nationalist moment as viable, the opponent as fightable. The younger generation of Harlem citizens, however, represents a popularized version of nationalism, which Himes's novel will ultimately critique. Himes's novel depicts "the people" on the street as possessing the impulse of anger toward white power, the refusal to tolerate further oppression; but they lack the organization of purpose that Himes sees as essential to revolutionary efficacy.

Not only the people on the street, but the narrator characterizes the formerly heroic Ed and Digger as laughable. Throughout the novel they are frequently described using clownlike imagery: "They looked like two idiots standing in the glare of the blazing car, one in his coat, shirt and tie, and purple shorts above gartered sox and big feet, and the other in shirtsleeves and empty shoulder holster with his pistol stuck in his belt" (141–42). Their former possible heroic stance, Himes's ideal creation of the cops who "*devrait exister*," is no longer even a viable part of his own imagination. Their role has been fully obviated. Ed's and Digger's authority is also sharply curtailed by the white cops who run the force. In one scene the white cops who have basically taken charge of the investigation of the white man's murder are accompanied by Ed and Digger, following the blood trail to a tenement's basement room:

The blood trail ended at the green door.

"Come out of there," the sergeant said.

No one answered.

He turned the knob and pushed the door and it opened inward so silently and easily he almost fell into the opening before he could train his light.

Inside was a black dark void.

Grave Digger and Coffin Ed flattened themselves against the walls on

each side of the alley and their big long-barreled .38 revolvers came glinting
into their hands.

"What the hell!" the sergeant exclaimed, startled.

His assistants ducked.

"This is Harlem," Coffin Ed grated and Grave Digger elaborated:

"We don't trust doors that open." (60)

We recognize this Ed and Digger, acting in tandem, keenly reading the visual
clues of the environment they know by heart. But despite their obviously
superior knowledge, they are not allowed to act alone, they are not allowed
to do their job, which is to investigate. In *Blind Man*, Coffin Ed and Grave
Digger's investigative skills lead them too close to uncovering embarrassing
connections to Harlem's vice industry on the part of the white power structure and the deeper levels of corruption and complicity within the police
force. Therefore Captain Brice and Lieutenant Anderson curtail their activity. As Brice tells them to leave the investigation to the D.A.'s homicide
bureau, he asks,

> "What do you think you two precinct detectives can uncover that they
> can't?"
>
> "That very reason. It's our precinct. We might learn something that
> wouldn't mean a damn thing to them." (95)

Ed and Digger here have no social position to occupy: the people on the
street see them as cops and enemies, and the cops reduce them to the equiv-
alent of people on the street: "precinct detectives." Ed and Digger know
that their professional identities had existed between these poles: it is their
relationship to their "precinct," their ability to be at home on these streets,
that had enabled them to manipulate the racist procedures of the police
department. However, over a twelve-year development as characters, Ed
and Digger have lost any earlier optimistic idealism:

> The two black detectives looked at one another. Their short-cropped hair
> was salted with gray and they were thicker around their middles. Their faces
> bore the lumps and scars they had collected in the enforcement of law in
> Harlem. Now after twelve years as first-grade precinct detectives they hadn't
> been promoted. Their raises in salaries hadn't kept up with the rise of the
> cost of living. They hadn't finished paying for their houses. Their private
> cars had been bought on credit. And yet they hadn't taken a dime in bribes.
> Their entire careers as cops had been one long period of turmoil. When
> they weren't taking lumps from the thugs, they were taking lumps from the
> commissioners. Now they were curtailed in their own duties. And they
> didn't expect it to change. (97)

Thus, while Coffin Ed and Grave Digger may have begun the series with the heroic potential of ideal figures, the further institutionalization of racial discrimination throughout U.S. society has rendered them ineffectual. Caught in the middle, taking lumps from both thugs and commissioners, Coffin Ed and Grave Digger are no longer "at home" in their professional lives, and they do not fully own their homes in their personal lives. Their sense of social exclusion is palpable.

Not only has white power cemented its position, but it acts to prevent any public discovery of its complicitous actions. Coffin Ed and Grave Digger's previously folk-heroic strategies for maintaining community security have become absurd. Even as they attempt to pursue their original investigation of the white man's death, they are now aware of this absurdity, and they identify its racial basis. Astute readers of police force ideology, Ed and Digger clearly see, and state, the racial politics behind the restraint placed on them. When Anderson denies them access to someone they know is a key suspect, Grave Digger responds,

> "Listen, Lieutenant. This mother-raping white man gets himself killed on our beat chasing black sissies and you want us to whitewash the investigation."
> Anderson's face got pink.
> "No, I don't want you to whitewash the investigation," he denied. "I just don't want you raking up manure for the stink."
> "We got you; white men don't stink." (111)

Coffin Ed and Grave Digger's initial strategies fail as their political consciousness rises. The more they know about the inner workings of the white-run police force, the more they realize that the premise of their role as detectives or investigators is flawed and ineffectual at its base. They may be ultimately unable to make Harlem a safe home for its residents.

But as increasingly savvy readers of the racial politics of policing, Coffin Ed and Grave Digger are quite able to name the culprit. What they cannot do is apprehend "him." During the course of Blind Man, Harlem has been the scene of several riots, and the white cops have given Grave Digger and Coffin Ed the task of finding out who is the cause of these seemingly inexplicable riots. Confronting Lieutenant Anderson toward the end of Blind Man, Ed and Digger point the blame on the unapprehendable criminal they have been chasing their whole careers. In this key scene Himes writes his dialogue to emphasize the way his two detectives are closely attuned to one another. They speak in a close call-and-response pattern that frustrates Anderson, who exclaims,

"All right, all right! I take it you know who started the riot."

"Some folks call him by one name, some another," Coffin Ed said.

"Some call him lack of respect for law and order, some lack of opportunity, some the teachings of the Bible, some the sins of their fathers," Grave Digger expounded. "Some call him ignorance, some poverty, some rebellion. Me and Ed look at him with compassion. We're victims."

"Victims of what?" Anderson asked foolishly.

"Victims of your skin," Coffin Ed shouted brutally, his own patchwork of grafted black skin twitching with passion.

Anderson's skin turned blood red. (153–54)

Ed and Digger are quite clear here on the balance of law and order on their beat: while the rioters may be black citizens, the instigator, the criminal responsible, is in fact the white racism that causes poverty, ignorance, the hypocrisy of religion, and the "criminogenic conditions" of life in the ghetto. In naming Anderson's white skin as the source of their victimization, they identify what George Lipsitz has termed "the possessive investment in whiteness," the ideology responsible for centuries of policies that have "widened the gap between the resources available to whites and those available to aggrieved racial communities."[34] Coffin Ed and Grave Digger's own allegiance remains on the side of the victims. Himes's writing here is at its resonant best as he focuses on the twitching patchwork of Ed's grafted skin. As any reader of the detective novels knows, Ed's face was scarred early in the series by an acid-throwing criminal. Ed's face is a narrative reflection of the violence borne by these two would-be protectors and defenders against white lynch-mob law enforcement, as are the other scars and marks that attest to Ed's and Digger's life work. But the pastiche of skin on Ed's face can also be read as a mirror reflecting the arbitrariness and absurdity of race as a determining category, of the truth of blackness as a social construct. By calling attention to the "grafted-on" nature of Ed's black skin and juxtaposing it to Anderson's white, then red face, Himes implicitly questions the fictions of race, especially as they are manipulated by the (white) police force.

In the same year that *Blind Man* was published, Himes gave an interview to John A. Williams. In the interview, Himes adds some history to his discussion of the "cause" of U.S. "race riots":

Well, this whole problem in America, as I see it, developed from the fact that the slaves were freed and that there was no legislation of any sort to make it possible for them to live. . . . What is it that they have in heaven — milk and honey? That some poor nigger could go and live on nothing. Just to proclaim emancipation was not enough. You can't eat it; it doesn't keep the cold weather out.[35]

Himes makes a similar statement in an italicized "Interlude" in *Blind Man*, where Grave Digger and Coffin Ed name Lincoln as the instigator of the riots: "He hadn't ought to have freed us if he didn't want to make provisions to feed us" (135). Though Ed and Digger can supply the name of the singular culprit so doggedly desired by Anderson and the police force, of course he cannot be apprehended, and further, if he were, he couldn't be convicted— because he's white. Says Coffin Ed, "Never was a white man convicted as long as he plead good intentions" (135).

Blind Man ends with less resolution than any of Himes's previous detective novels, a point noted by many critics as Himes's ultimate stretching of the detective fiction generic limits. A. Robert Lee writes, "*Blind Man with a Pistol*, especially, approaches antic nightmare, a pageant of violence and unresolved plot-ends which, true to the illogic of a dream, careens into a last chapter of senseless riot."[36] Coffin Ed and Grave Digger are reduced to the inanity of shooting at rats fleeing a burning tenement. In *Blind Man*, then, Himes returns to his own long-standing political philosophies about both "senseless riot" and the absurdity of racism. In Himes's 1944 *Crisis* article he states, "The first step backward is riots. Riots are not revolutions. . . . Riots are tumultuous disturbances of the public peace by unlawful assemblies of three or more persons in the execution of private objects—such as race hatreds."[37] Himes uses his detective fiction to revisit this analysis in his ending to *Blind Man*, critiquing what he sees as the ineffective methodology of chaotic violence. In his 1970 *Le Monde* interview with Michel Fabre, Himes explains the genesis of *Blind Man*:

> Several years ago, numerous riots erupted in America followed by spontaneous riots after the assassination of Martin Luther King and battles between the Black Panthers and the police. I thought that all this unorganized violence that the Blacks unleashed in America was nothing other than shots fired blindly, and I titled my novel *Blind Man with a Pistol*. Such was my commentary on the inefficacy of this type of violence.[38]

It is important to note that Himes does not condemn the use of all violence as a political tool, only unorganized violence. In fact, throughout his life he wrote in favor of planned revolution as a political strategy. Edward Margolies, in his article, "Experiences of the Black Expatriate Writer: Chester Himes," quotes from an English transcript of Himes's 1970 *Le Monde* interview with Fabre:

> I realized that subconciously that was the point I had been trying to make in *[Blind Man]*. . . . I think there should be violence . . . because I do not believe that anything else is ever going to improve the situation of the black man in

America except violence. I don't think it would have to be great shattering
and shocking violence. If the blacks were organized and if they could resist
and fight injustice in an organized fashion in America, I think that might be
enough. Yes, I believe this sincerely. (427)

While Himes sees unorganized riotous violence as ineffective, it is important to trace out his "call" for successful planned revolution. What does it
mean to "call" for revolution from an expatriate stance of nonparticipation?
In Himes's discussions of what "the black man in America" should do, he
stands outside the implied group of actors, whom he refers to as "they." When
Himes does not see himself as a "black man in America" anymore, he is
keen to prescribe action quite similar to what he had previously described as
"some of our loudmouthed leaders urging our vulnerable soul brothers on to
getting themselves killed" (preface to *Blind Man*). Himes's various writings
then, in multiple genres, shed light on the shifting ways in which he sees
himself in relation to the concept of race as it is deployed in America. Writing from a position of expatriation, outside the "home country," he articulates a revolutionary politics that sacrifices immediate personal safety for
the goal of future social change.

In order to trace the movements in Himes's political thinking about
safety, revolution, and violence, we should recall the title of Himes's 1944
Crisis article, "Negro Martyrs Are Needed." This article describes the role of
a single martyr in the revolutionary cause. Himes did not discard this idea
after the 1940s, and we encounter this martyr again in his short story, "Prediction" (1969). "Prediction" is an important story in Himes's oeuvre because it also contains the prefigurings of his final detective novel set in the
United States, *Plan B*, which was not published in America until after the
author's death. Himes's philosophies about the need for organized violence,
as articulated in "Prediction" and "Negro Martyrs," can be seen as an in-
verted economy of bodies, bearing in mind his earlier idealized construction
of Coffin Ed and Grave Digger as protectors of one white body in order to
ultimately protect many black bodies. What happens in the economy of
"Prediction" and "Negro Martyrs Are Needed" is an ideologically revolutionary inversion: one black body is martyred in the interest of creating
more white corpses. In "Negro Martyrs," Himes states, "The first and funda-
mental convictions of the political tactician fighting for the human rights
of the people are: (1) Progress can be brought about only by revolution;
(2) Revolutions can be started only by incidents; (3) Incidents can be created only by Martyrs" (159). Himes specifically counterpoises this idea of a
planned incident by a martyr to what he sees as more random, spontaneous

rioting, which he condemns as ineffectual and based in self-interest as opposed to race betterment and the achievement of democratic equality. Elab-
orating in 1970 on his ideas about the role of the martyr, he tells John A.
Williams,

> Even individually, if you give one black one high-powered repeating rifle
> and he wanted to shoot it into a mob of twenty thousand or more white
> people, there are a number of people he could destroy. Now, in my book [the
> uncompleted *Plan B*], all of these blacks who shoot are destroyed. They not
> only are destroyed, they're blown apart; even the buildings they're shooting
> from are destroyed, and quite often the white community suffers fifty or
> more deaths itself by destroying one black man.[39]

In tracing out Himes's varied positionings, the ways that the black international writer speaks to (and for) particular communities at various moments, we should note the contrast between Himes's comments to John A.
Williams, a fellow black American writer, and those he makes to Michel
Fabre, a white French literary critic. Though both interviews took place
around the same time, Himes's divergent expressions of revolutionary ideology reveal both ambiguities in his own thought and alterations for his perceived audiences. To Fabre he states (assures?) that "great shattering and
shocking violence" is not necessary. Blacks should just use violence "to
resist and fight injustice in an organized fashion."[40] His words here seem
like platitudes as he implies a specific and localized enemy who could be
systematically resisted. The author of *Blind Man*, however, knows there is
no easily vanquished enemy. On the other hand, the act of shooting a repeat-
ing rifle into a crowd of twenty thousand, as Himes describes to Williams, is
fairly "shattering and shocking violence." And Himes's literary portrayal of
this act in "Prediction" emphasizes the graphic nature of the violence. While
the philosophy of limited black deaths in order to produce larger numbers
of white deaths seems to be a reversal of the economy of bodies in the discourse of *protection* articulated in the detective novels, the ideology behind
these acts understands white behavioral motivation in the same way. The
white reaction to black violence against whites is one that crushes anything
in its path. "Prediction" presents us with a more advanced stage of the lynch-
mob police response that we see throughout the detective novels. In "Prediction," this crushing white reaction is disembodied in the form of a tank
with a brain.

The story, which later becomes chapter 21 of *Plan B*, opens with an all-
white police parade "headed north up the main street of the big city."[41]
Instead of the precisely located Harlem geography of the detective novels,

the incidents of "Prediction" and *Plan B* could theoretically occur in any U.S. city. In a harshly satiric tone, the narrator tells us that this police parade "had been billed as a parade of unity to demonstrate the capacity of law enforcement and reassure the 'communities' during this time of suspicion and animosity between the races. No black policemen were parading for the simple reason that none had been asked to parade and none had requested the right to parade" (281). Grave Digger and Coffin Ed would be out of place in this symbolic display of the social exclusions that make "the main street of the big city" home to white people, but not black people. Himes mocks the idea that U.S. law enforcement can create unity between different races or "communities," and he describes at length an all-white scene: white cops, white crowds, white workers, are all visible on the street. Himes has shifted his scripting of home, and instead of presenting a neighborhood in which African American people are the majority, he here draws a very different portrait: "In fact the crowd of all-white faces seemed to deny that a black race existed" (281). Where is the black neighborhood in this story about Main Street, Big City, U.S.A.? The narrator explains that "there was only one black man along the entire length of the street at the time, and he wasn't in sight" (281). This unnamed man, hidden in a church with an automatic rifle, is Himes's martyr for the cause of black liberation: "Subjectively, he had waited four hundred years for this moment and he was not in a hurry" (282). Just as Lincoln can be fingered as the criminal responsible for the riots in *Blind Man*, the legacy of racial oppression since slavery is the instigator of the revolution that will follow this triggering incident. The martyr knows, however, the nature of white reaction to his planned crime—he is aware of the lynch-like response to follow: "He knew his black people would suffer severely for this moment of his triumph. He was not an ignorant man" (282). The man is "consoled only by the hope that it would make life safer for the blacks in the future. He would have to believe that the children of the blacks who would suffer now would benefit later" (282–83). Note here the demand for safety and protection running throughout Himes's depictions of "life in the prison of being a Negro in America." This language exists in dialogic relationship with the language of equality, with greater emphasis on safety as at least the first most important condition of freedom for African Americans. Law enforcement, as an institutional agency, has not fulfilled its role of providing safety for African Americans, of ensuring that the "main streets" of the country can be a safe home to black communities.

In "Prediction," Himes enacts his revenge. When the police parade reaches a key position on the street, the black gunman opens fire and begins mowing down rows of officers. Himes's depiction of this carnage shows his writing at its maximally grotesque:

> [The commissioner] wore no hat to catch his brains and fragments of skull, and they exploded through the sunny atmosphere and splattered the spectators with goo, tufts of gray hair and splinters of bone. One skull fragment, larger than the others, struck a tall, well-dressed man on the cheek, cutting the skin and splashing brains against his face like a custard pie in a Mack Sennett comedy. (284)

The unseen martyr decimates row upon row of parading white police officers. After their commissioner has been splattered, "the brave policemen with their service revolvers in their hands were running helter-skelter with nothing to shoot at while being mown down by the black killer" (285). Combined with the more obvious political reasons, this level of graphic description of white deaths caused by blacks is something Himes knew U.S. publishers, and by extension, the reading public, would reject. Discussing *Plan B* with John A. Williams, he says, "I don't know what the American publishers will do about this book. But one thing I do know, Johnny, they will hesitate, and it will cause them a great amount of revulsion."[42] The gunman's slaughter causes general pandemonium in the crowd, with police officers firing at each other, at civilians, and so forth, in their frustrated confusion and inability to find the sniper. Now the police force's anarchic response makes the main street of the big city signally dangerous, not just for African Americans, but for anyone who happens to be on it, as innocent bystanders and white cops are all killed randomly. The police (and civilian) response is still, however, racialized, and the lynch-mob ethos is still present:

> All were decided, police and spectators alike, that the sniper was a black man for no one else would slaughter whites so wantonly. . . . And in view of the history of all the assassinations and mass murders in the U.S., it was extraordinarily enlightening that all the thousands of whites caught in a deadly gunfire from an unseen assassin, white police and white civilians alike, would automatically agree that he must be black. (285)

In an apocalyptic climax, the lynch mob itself takes the form of the technologically developed war machine, a riot tank endowed with a brain and an eye searching, at first futilely, for the hidden sniper:

> Its telescoped eye at the muzzle of the 20-mm. cannon stared right and left, looking over the heads and among the white spectators, over the living white policemen hopping about the dead, up and down the rich main street with its impressive stores, and in its frustration at not seeing a black face

> to shoot at it rained explosive 20-mm. shells on the black plaster of
> paris mannequins displaying a line of beachwear in a department store
> window. (286)

Police procedure has here reached an anarchic level of absurdity in shooting at plaster images of black bodies when it cannot find a human black
body. This destruction, in turn, triggers further mass hysteria and the killing
of vast numbers of innocent bystanders until finally the tank demolishes the
church with the sniper inside. Even this last act, however, is not conclusive
for the white mob, since it does not produce the desired black body: "It did
not take long for the cannon to reduce the stone face of the cathedral to a
pile of rubbish. But it took all of the following day to unearth the twisted
rifle and a few scraps of bloody black flesh to prove the black killer had
existed" (287). When whites are killed, only a black body will appease the
lynching mob, and the capturing—dead or alive, whole or in pieces—of this
body becomes the all-important aim. *Plan B* portrays the apocalyptic climax
of a racist society, in which blackness itself is made to function as redun-
dancy in white power's hegemony. After four hundred years of oppression,
white power is still, redundantly, emptying its bullets into an already beaten
black "opponent."

In the mind of the martyr, because of the number of whites he has killed,
the exchange of his body for their deaths seems fair: "He was ready to die.
By then he had killed seventy-three whites, forty-seven policemen and
twenty-six men, women and children civilians, and had wounded an additional seventy-five, and although he was never to know this figure, he was
satisfied. He felt like a gambler who had broken the bank" (286). In 1944,
Himes envisions this kind of a murderous gamble as the key move to trigger
more widespread planned violence by blacks, "which will mobilize the forces
of justice and carry us forward from the pivot of change to a way of existence where everyone is free."[43] The martyr's gamble succeeds financially as
well, since "[i]n the wake of this bloody massacre the stock market crashed.
The dollar fell on the world market. The very structure of capitalism began
to crumble" (287). In *Plan B*, the lack of safety available to African Americans finally becomes a condition experienced by the entire U.S. population, as black men all over the country begin arming themselves and killing
white people at random. After the incident of the martyr, "the reaction of
whites to the massacre in front of the cathedral was of such murderous in-
tensity that the very structure of their civilization was threatened" (183).
Perhaps "Prediction" and *Plan B* can be read as Himes's satiric warnings,
indeed predictions, about the long-term effects of the social exclusion and

personal danger experienced by African Americans in the United States. And yet in *Plan B*, the martyr's actions do not lead to the freedom Himes was able to envision in 1944. It is telling that he also predicts at least one form of white response to black revolutionary activity: "Eventually whites demanded that many large modern prisons be erected all over the United States, and that all blacks be locked up in them, except for the few needed to look after their food and sanitation" (146). Indeed incarceration now represents perhaps the greatest risk and danger faced by black American youth, and in 1996 "almost one of every 10 young black male adults in America were behind bars."[44] Himes saw the ways that the United States uses the prison system as a form of internal exile for those who are relegated to the margins of society.

In resistance to the confinement of black identities enacted by social exclusions of all kinds, Himes uses his detective fiction to reenter the home space and revise the institutions of law enforcement in the United States. He ends his revision with a satiric look at his own heroes, perhaps laughing at his imaginative creations, as he embroils them in the final confrontation between the so-called forces of law and order and a radical black revolutionary politics.[45] In his autobiography, Himes states, "I began writing a book called *Plan B*, about a real black revolution in which my two black detectives split up and eventually Grave Digger kills Coffin Ed to save the cause."[46] In *Plan B*, Grave Digger is then killed by another satiric character, Tomsson Black.[47] *Plan B* was published in France in 1983, one year before Himes's death, but the detectives live on in the international imaginations of Himes's global reading publics. Taking account of Himes as a black international writer allows us to attend to the ways in which he felt displaced from multiple "white countries," excluded from various national publics, and to see how he crafted an international home in writing, a diasporic identity in authorship.

4

"A Landmark in a Foreign Land": Simon Njami's Parisian Scenes

> Having been prepared by colonial education, I knew England from the inside. But I'm not and never will be "English." I know both places [England and Jamaica] intimately, but I am not wholly of either place. And that's exactly the diasporic experience, far away enough to experience the sense of exile and loss, close enough to understand the enigma of an always-postponed "arrival."
>
> —*Stuart Hall*

Stuart Hall describes an inside-out relationship to Europe that is also recalled in the writings of other African diasporic authors, such as James Baldwin in "Stranger in the Village" and Caryl Phillips in *The European Tribe*. Simon Njami echoes this multiplicity of identification when he says, "I don't feel any belonging. And I think it's partly due to my strange life. Because whenever I say I'm an African I feel like I'm saying a lie. But when I say I'm a European, I feel the same way. Because I've never lived in Africa, but I'm an African. I've lived all my life in Europe, and I'm a European; but in another way I'm not a European."[1] These authors convey their experience of the limitations of national identity at the same time that they reject the idea of an identity based on "race." In the previous chapters, I have argued that black international authors use writing as a way to resist the social exclusions of nation-states as they craft social identities that can be called diasporic. In this chapter, I will trace some of the ways that diaspora identity is articulated in literature over and against other terms of group membership, specifically nation, community, and family. In the writings of Simon Njami, a black author of Cameroonian descent living in Paris, we see that it is often the condition of expatriation that generates the very concept of diaspora as a link that connects people designated as "black." Far from their many home-lands, it is often in an adopted land that various peoples choose to designate themselves as united by a diasporic framing of identity.

Writing is a key site where black international authors pose questions about identity in multiple ways, and these diverse framings of identity are neither static nor monologic. The literary works of black international writers generate intertextual conversations about the global politics of black-ness. The popularity of Chester Himes's detective fiction in France creates networks of influence between Himes's Harlem and the literary landscapes of other black international writers. This chapter will examine the dias-poric conversation about global black identities that Himes's texts invite. One of the most fascinating recent manifestations of international interest in Himes can be seen in a detective novel by Simon Njami. Born in Switzer-land in 1962, Njami is the author of four novels, a collection of essays, and a biography of James Baldwin. He is also editor-in-chief of *Revue Noire*, the leading African diasporic art journal in France. In its engagement with African American authors, Njami's work sheds light on the social construc-tion(s) of black identities in multiple global locations. Thinking back to the detective novels of Himes, we recall the ways that Himes uses his fiction to write and revise "home." In the process, his literary work becomes "a landmark in a foreign land," providing a space for a new generation, and specifically Simon Njami, to continue a conversation about global black identities and writing.

The novels of Himes and Njami, when read together, raise questions about the freedoms of discursive spaces and the confinements of urban spaces— about a writer's ability to create a home on the page, and to write a world. Njami's detective novel, *Coffin & Co.*,[2] also poses questions about family and community and what these terms mean in relation to the idea of a homeland and to the condition of exile that sustains that idea. Like Himes's work, Njami's fiction enables us to see the ways that expatriate black writers enact a relationship to home in their fiction.

Coffin & Co. is situated in the middle of a conversation about diaspora identity and literature because the plot of the novel looks from Europe to both Africa and America. The novel's style is informed by both the Harlem-

based detective fiction of Himes and a literary subgenre of postcolonial literature called "Parisianism" by its practitioners. In her study of contemporary
African writers in Paris, Bennetta Jules-Rosette explains that Parisianism is
a literary movement different from earlier French-language movements
centered around either Négritude or the *Présence Africaine* writers. Jules-
Rosette explains that the term *Parisianism* is used by contemporary African
authors living in Paris to "describe their own works and to assert their cultural claim of belonging to French society."[3] For these writers, "belonging to
French society" is not the same thing as defining oneself as nationally
French. Yodi Karone explains: "On the whole, to be Parisian does not mean
to be French. I am Cameroonian, but I am also Parisian."[4] This is part of
what Stuart Hall means when he describes knowing England from the inside
but also being not-English. Karone's rejection of a French national identity
echoes recent resistant social practices around immigration and citizenship
in which "some young North and sub-Saharan African immigrants elect
not to assume French nationality, even when offered the legal possibility to
do so. This perplexing situation has baffled French authorities, who, despite
posing obstacles to French nationality, always suspected that all immigrants
would ultimately want it."[5] As a literary movement, Parisianism focuses on
the cosmopolitan life of Paris as experienced by the city's African diasporic
residents, and their writings show how France's "official ideology of opportunity coupled with responsibility does not coincide with immigrants' lived
experiences of social blockage, discrimination, and disillusionment."[6] This
disjuncture between the state's language of equality and black peoples' experiences of social exclusion runs as a current through the work of African
diasporic authors. We also see these tensions in the work of Simon Njami.

Njami's postcolonial novels problematize notions of community as homogeneous as defined by terms like *nation* or *race*. The protagonist of *Coffin &
Co.* is Amos Yebga, a Cameroonian journalist living in Paris and writing for
a newspaper called the *World*. Like other Parisianism novels, *Coffin & Co.*
describes the expatriate community of black people living in Paris, hailing
from various African and Caribbean countries, and questions the very connections that might cause us to call this diverse group a community. The
novel interrogates the meaning of diaspora identity as it is defined both
in terms of shifting communities of social relationships and as against an
idealized or nostalgically desired "home" land. The novel, then, has a triple
focus: though its plot centers around the city of Paris, the sites of Harlem and
Cameroon are also invoked. Njami's work also continues Himes's engage-

ment with the impact of police procedures on black people in urban locations and expresses his protagonist's longing for an antiurban nostalgized
past in Cameroon.

(Re)Calling Chester Himes

Coffin & Co. concerns not only the migrations of Africans to Paris, but
also a journey of African Americans, as the novel engages in a postmodern
literary play with the work of Chester Himes. Njami brings the supposed
prototypes of Himes's classic two detectives, Coffin Ed Johnson and Grave
Digger Jones, out of Harlem and into Paris. When Njami's characters, two
Harlem cops named W. Jones Dubois and Ed Smith, learn that Himes (an
actual character in the novel) has just published a new novel in French in
which Coffin Ed and Grave Digger are killed, they travel to Europe to track
down Himes and persuade him not to translate the book into English. (*Plan
B* is this novel, which had not yet been translated into English when Njami
published *Coffin & Co*).[7] Dubois and Smith, it seems, have been playing a
role in which they have claimed that Himes modeled his characters on
them, that they are the "actual" Grave Digger and Coffin Ed. If Himes kills
them off, their real-life drama ends. Hence they venture across the Atlantic
for the first time in their lives

> to meet the author who for so many years had served as both their memory
> and model. . . . Without Himes their lives would have been the same long
> descent into hell that bedeviled other unfortunate guys appointed to
> maintain order where whites had imprisoned blacks: in corruption and
> chaos. (41)

Here we see that Njami continues Himes's focus on policing and the various
confinements experienced by people of color in the urban spaces of "white
countries." Njami's engagement with Himes is the result of a transatlantic
diasporic literary influence, the perhaps ironic fact that Himes really was a
"famous French writer."[8] This influence is paralleled in the novel's plot as
Jones and Dubois are first informed about the existence of Himes's new
novel by their friend, Little Cassius, a student at Columbia University, in
Harlem. Cassius breaks the news to the two detectives: "'One of my buddies
at Columbia is African,' he said. 'His parents live in France. They always
send him piles of books. This month he received the latest Chester Himes'"
(6). This triangular cross-cultural exchange between Harlem, Africa, and
France plays a major role in Njami's work as editor of *Revue Noire*, a journal

covering artistic expression throughout the black Atlantic world, and also
in his own writerly topics. He has authored a biography of James Baldwin
and a biography of Leopold Senghor. The brief early chapters of *Coffin &
Co.* are set in Harlem, and they offer an opportunity to see how Himes's
Harlem is (mis?)translated, as Njami's Harlem is clearly not the same urban
space as Himes's Harlem. Njami alludes to the intellectual life of Columbia
University, and the music Little Cassius plays on his boom box is Bruce
Springsteen (2). When Smith shouts to Little Cassius to turn down "the
racket," the young man replies, "You're just not with it. Bruce Springsteen's
great." Smith retorts, "Any spade'd make that kind of music has got to be
crazy. That kind of racket's not our style, boy." When Cassius informs them
that "Springsteen's not black," they snap back, "That's even worse" (2).

When Dubois and Smith realize that what Cassius says is true, that the
next Himes novel means the deaths of their "characters," they know they
must cross the ocean and confront Himes:

> For forty years these two ordinary cops from a rotten neighborhood had
> linked their lives to two imaginary characters, whose existence they had
> substituted for their own.... According to them, Chester Himes had become
> a sort of bard or *griot* canonizing their livelier adventures. But with this
> latest book reality was taking its revenge, coming to claim its due. The
> usurped titles, the borrowed risks, the myth of two extraordinary lives, had
> to be restored to the fiction from which they had departed. (9)

Here the text highlights the ways that Himes's literary act produces the
(fictional) identity of Dubois and Smith. The self-reflexive nature of Njami's
fiction alludes to the performative nature of identity and the way that fiction
can be the site of multiple identity stagings. When they arrive in France,
the two detectives stop first at Himes's Paris publishing firm, Gallimard, but
they "didn't have time to wonder how a guy like Chester Himes, writing the
books he wrote, could survive in an ambience of whispers, kiss-ass smiles
and boudoir shadows, a thousand leagues from the lures of the 'Big Apple'"
(26). Traveling on to Alicante, Spain, they meet Himes's British wife, Lesley, and tell her part of their mission: "We've come to bring him some news
from back home. To let him know how blacks are doing back there.... We
came to remind him. He's a great man, but back there, if you're black,
you're still only considered half a man" (42). Smith and Dubois, whose own
lives have been bolstered by the literary life of Himes's writerly creations,
seek a way to maintain the fiction they have enacted, a way to inhabit a
heroic space of black identity in America. Their concern with identity con-

struction in America resonates with (the actual) Himes's own statements about the possibilities of American identity for black people. As Himes states in an article about Harlem that was published in the French journal, *Présence Africaine*, in 1963,

> You can eat like an American, dress like an American, speak like an American, [think] like an American. But if you are Black, you are less American than a foreigner.[9]

As we have seen in chapter 3, Himes vacillated throughout his life about the extent to which he saw himself as a part of America and identified with American blacks. Part of this shifting was tied to his role as a writer and the American public's neglect of his writing and his professional self-definition. National identity is a fickle label, and for Himes what was more important was to be allowed discursive space, to be granted the literary reception that allows for the expression of his professional identity as a writer. The space of literary or artistic expression can serve to locate the writing subject, in perhaps a geographic as well as a psychic sense. The location of a writer's identity is commonly evoked when we speak (also in geographic terms) of a literary landscape or field. Mae Henderson implies an even broader spatialized understanding of culture itself when she writes, "Criticism [of *Lonely Crusade*] from all classes and political persuasions signified that the novel failed to locate Himes within American culture."[10] What this failure points to, then, is the finiteness of the discursive space available, specifically to a black writer, a perception we know that Himes felt keenly. American culture has historically provided a limited space for black artistic expression, at times even prescribing how that expression must be shaped. In the case of Himes's *Lonely Crusade* (1947), the American audience was unwilling to accept a black novel on the terms in which Himes wrote it. Gilbert Muller links the reception of *Lonely Crusade* directly to Himes's move to France:

> Great in scope and ambition—one of the most radical novels about the structures of American domination and about California life as a symptom of the corrupt power of both capitalism and communism—*Lonely Crusade* was reviled by critics of both the left and the right. . . . And the hostile reception of *Lonely Crusade* convinced [Himes] to leave the United States forever.[11]

The popularity of Himes's detective novels in France grants him a professional identity as a famous (French) writer. The detective stories become for Himes a psychic home, locating him within French culture, paradoxically *as* a great black American writer. Alas, however, it is too late for the author to assist Njami's characters, Smith and Dubois, in their ongoing quest to play heroic roles in Harlem.

When Smith and Dubois finally meet the great author, Himes is on his deathbed. Their meeting with him is almost comically anticlimactic, as the dying writer appropriately falls asleep while they are pleading their case about the importance of heroes in black America and the worsening U.S. racial divide:

> It seemed grotesque and obscene to them that reality could avenge itself to such an extent. Himes, the combatant, the everyday companion, the one who knew all the tangles, all the bad ranks of the neighborhood, Himes who had robbed a bank and done time, whose presence ran throughout Harlem . . . had become this old man with emaciated features. (44)

Njami's story begins, then, with the death of the influencing author, perhaps a classic literary patricide. Himes's novelistic death, however, marks a new chapter in the lives of Smith and Dubois, who decide to stay in Paris a while. Before they know it, the two Harlem cops are involved in a mystery as we watch them try to translate their detective skills to this new milieu, an urban neighborhood both similar and quite different from the streets they know so well back home.

Though the two detectives play a central role in *Coffin & Co.*, the main protagonist is Amos Yebga, a Cameroonian journalist living in Paris and writing for the *World*.[12] We first meet Yebga replaying the messages on his answering machine. Njami depicts these random quotes from often unnamed callers as floating on the page, cut off from full explanation; they represent multiple and varied points of communication and social connection, as Yebga "paraded all these callers through his mind, thinking they made up a strange group. They reminded him of his own vagabond life" (19). The novel gives us this "strange group" as a microcosm of Yebga's expatriate life. Indeed, it is a criminal investigation that makes it necessary for Yebga to sort out his relationships to the individuals within this group, as well as to the notion of the group itself.

Yebga's presence in Paris is the direct result of French colonial rule in West Africa and the historical processes of decolonization and nationalism. He is part of a wave of immigration described by Jules-Rosette: "From 1960 to 1992, the number of sub-Saharan Africans residing in Paris virtually exploded. The rising African migration rates do not include the considerable Antillian population from Martinique and Guadeloupe," who are French citizens and counted in different census categories.[13] Njami's narrator tells us that Yebga "had chosen to exile himself to France, because Cameroon was not ready to confront its own corruption" (18). Yebga critiques the politics of the neocolonial bourgeoisie in power in Cameroon more than he does the politics of French colonialism. However, throughout the novel Yebga's critique of present-day Cameroon drops out, replaced by a nostalgic desire for something he and other male Africans label "traditional arrangements." Family becomes the term around which this social space is defined, but it is a very patriarchal definition of family that the novel enacts. Like Michelle Cliff, then, Njami is a postcolonial writer whose work juxtaposes a precolonial past with contemporary politics in the "homeland"; the gender dynamics of their engagements, however, are quite different.

Early in the novel, Yebga defines himself as only tenuously connected to the black international community in Paris; he rejects the idea that he is a part of a group. Perhaps against his will, Yebga is pulled into this group and into involvement by one of the random voices on his answering machine, a Maktar Diop who wants to give Yebga, the reporter, some important information. When Diop later misses their meeting because he's been killed, Yebga begins the investigative work of tracing connections. As in Himes's novels, it is the racialized policies of law enforcement and their impact on the black "community" (however that may be defined) that begins the detective plot of the novel. Though the French police immediately label Diop's death an "accident" (he was hit by a car), Yebga suspects it may have been murder, and exclaims to his editor: "These stupid cops who conclude right away it's an accident. You know if Diop had been white..." (46). Yebga pursues the case because of his suspicions about this injustice:

> In light of the fact that this "accident" had taken place so fast, and in so
> "natural" a manner, Diop's telephone messages took on new meaning.
> Diop had feared for his life. Yebga had hesitated to believe in Diop's anx-
> ious threats and disclosures. Now it was his professional duty to get to the
> bottom of this affair. If he had really been murdered, perhaps he had known
> something. (46)

Yebga's investigative efforts bring him into contact with various members of the expatriate African community in Paris. When an African waitress, Myriam, tells Yebga, "If you really are a reporter, I hope you won't forget us," he stumbles over this group identification:

> Who was "we" anyway? She, him, blacks?... The "community," that hypo-
> thetical and abstract family of which they wanted to make him a slave, had

to be put and would be put in the background. He was from Cameroon; he lived and worked in France, with whites. (49)[14]

In *Keywords*, Raymond Williams traces historical definitions of the term "community." He remarks, "What is most important, perhaps, is that unlike all other terms of social organization (*state, nation, society*, etc.) it seems never to be used unfavorably, and never to be given any positive opposing or distinguishing term" (66). And yet it is this term that leaves a bad taste in Yebga's mouth early in the novel. Yebga perceives this form of "abstract *family*" as extremely oppressive, to the point of being enslaving. The narrator's bracketing of the word *community* becomes central to Yebga's searching, throughout the book, for a way to see himself in relation to his Parisian environment. Paradoxically, this search leads him to another form of (conservative) "family" structure. Despite his discomfort in claiming membership in an expatriate African community (or being claimed by it), each move that Yebga makes in his attempt to answer some of the questions raised by Diop's death pulls him deeper and deeper into this community, which he would have preferred to ignore. Perhaps we can say that it is the common experience of discrimination and insult that generates the linkages between the various black people in Paris. Until Yebga experiences the discrimination, he does not accept the linkage.

Also determining Yebga's propulsion into the mystery is his desire to break from his intellectual routine and become a "man of action," perhaps the same desire that led Dubois and Smith to emulate Himes's Harlem cops. At the beginning of the story, Yebga suffers from what seems like a classic existential malaise. In contemplating his options, Yebga thinks,

> Or he could write a novel full of the odor of exhaust fumes, something without social pretensions, the opposite of a story for the *World*. A novel which would serve no purpose but to contain his sorrow, to mark out the boundaries of his imagination, so that for once he might have a place all his own in this foreign city. (33)

This quote establishes an important connection between Himes and Njami as black international authors whose writing constructs identity in geographic terms, but terms based on literary discourse: discursive space is seen as having the potential to domesticate a geographic and social space that is in other ways inhabitable. Writing becomes a way to revise the spaces of exclusion and social alienation often experienced by black people living in European countries and in America. Recall Himes's way of placing himself from the second volume of his autobiography: "I still felt as much of a stranger in

Paris as I did in every white country I had ever been in; I only felt at home in my detective stories."[15] Here Himes's and Njami's narrative comments about writing evoke the same imagery of geography and the ability of words and artistic creation to contain and define a space of identity for the "black" subject in a "white country."

Yebga's social life is composed of "Paris white and Paris black," and early in the novel this combination represents in his eyes "success for a black man" (19). Resisting an idea of group membership based on "race," Yebga prefers to define social success as the forming of relationships that transcend racial boundaries. His girlfriend, Faye, is described as physically very white: "She was really blond with blue eyes and veins running along her transparent skin" (38).[16] And her white identity is made additionally significant because the narrator represents Yebga's union with Faye as indicative of his isolation from part of his own cultural history: "The day he'd decided to share his life with Faye, he'd broken off from the world of traditions in which he'd been raised" (39). Yebga specifically hides any knowledge of their relationship from his parents "back home" in Cameroon. Thus, in his alignment with "Paris white," Yebga decides to cut himself off from "Africa black."

Faye herself would deny not only history, but present social reality in seeking an isolated union with Yebga. Toward the end of the book, after the mysteries have deepened and Yebga has drifted away from their relationship to spend more time at bars like The Sunny Kingston with his new friends, Smith and Dubois, she asks him, "Why have you changed? We were getting along so well. The two of us, just you and me. Why are you letting the world come between us?" (139). As a white woman, Faye has the privilege of believing in a mythical place outside "the world" where their relationship could flourish. But of course such a location does not exist. Yebga's relationship with Faye represents another implicit link to the work of Chester Himes, specifically his short novel A Case of Rape, which Mae Henderson reads as "both measure and emblem of the failure of expatriation for the black American artist."[17] A connection can be drawn between Faye and Elizabeth Hancock, the white woman in A Case of Rape who is involved with Scott Hamilton, a black American. Elizabeth Hancock had left the financial security of her (unhappy) marriage, exiling herself from "her home and her children and her kind to come to him and lose herself in the soft dark night of his love."[18] The narrator's description of Elizabeth's form of escape focuses on color, just as the above quoted passage from Coffin & Co. focuses on Faye's whiteness: "To her [Elizabeth] he [Scott] was not only escape, but a dark void of peace beyond escape, free from all the anxieties and hurts and demands of her race and culture. A dark void without thought, that had no past or future, no pretensions or necessities."[19] Desiring an apolitical, romanticized union with blackness, "Elizabeth's description of Scott reveals that the freedom she seeks is that of historical oblivion."[20] Yebga bursts this bubble for Faye. As Diop's murder investigation draws Yebga further into relationships with other blacks in Paris, he begins to reject Faye and her desire to live outside history. He says to her,

> It would be ideal for you if we were stranded on a desert island, right?. . . There are no more desert islands. . . . I thought there were, too. I thought we could live apart from the world, leading our own lives, safe, protected. But we're affected by other people, our illusions are destroyed. Suddenly everything seems to be out of control because we weren't prepared for the shock. . . . At first I knew what it was that I wanted. I understood my slightest gestures, my slightest words. Now, it's as if I'm no longer living inside of myself. . . . We were living a lie. It couldn't last. (159)

Henderson, in her discussion of A Case of Rape, states that the failure of expatriation is linked to the failure of Scott's relationship with Elizabeth: "Inscribed within the relationship are both the possibilities as well as the limits of expatriation."[21] If Yebga previously saw success in expatriation as measured by his living and working with whites as well as blacks, perhaps Coffin & Co. traces the same limits as A Case of Rape. As Yebga drifts away from Faye, he has brief liaisons with black women, often in violent and exploitative ways.

The Diaspora on the Seine

After the character Himes's death, early in Coffin & Co., Dubois and Smith are also inadvertently drawn into the mystery of Diop's death when they stumble on Yebga being attacked by thugs in a black Mercedes limousine. They fend off his attackers and save his life, saying, "We've got to look after this one, he's a brother. I bet he wouldn't be too happy to wake up at the police station after an incident like this" (83). Though Yebga is clearly the victim in this violent incident, Dubois and Smith know that waking up in the police station would not be a guarantee of Yebga's safety or presumed innocence. Knowledgeable about the racialized politics of law enforcement, the two Harlem cops protect Yebga as a "brother." Dubois and Smith's subsequent pursuit of criminals on French soil extends beyond this brotherly

sentiment and soon becomes tied to their desire to create themselves outside of Himes's fiction:

> They hoped their mission would permit them to cast off, once and for all,
> their phony alter egos, without embarrassment or loss of face. To succeed
> would make them heroes in their own right. Himes could roll over in his
> grave for all they cared. Alone, on foreign soil, on their own, without
> Captain Brice's fictional support, or Lieutenant Anderson's literary cover,
> they planned to make these rich men pay in blood for using petty hench-
> men to kill blacks. (184)[22]

Yet Smith and Dubois's crime-solving skills are hampered by their unfamil-
iarity with the Parisian landscape and their inability to speak French.

Himes's characters, Grave Digger and Coffin Ed, succeed in Harlem
specifically because of their special insider status, their knowledge of intri-
cate Harlem social connections, and a specialized language that repeatedly
baffles their white superiors. The cognitive and spatial map of the neighborhood is all-important. But here in Paris, Dubois warns his partner, "It's
not our beat, man" (93). Recall that though Himes claimed himself to be a
"French writer," France was never really his "beat" either. In all his time
spent in France he never learned to speak French, he wrote all of his detective novels in English, and Marcel Duhamel had them translated into French
for publication. The language difference seems most baffling for Dubois and
Smith, and this resonates with Himes's Harlem novels, where linguistic play
is possible and powerful in the closed community milieu. Smith and Dubois
search for the signs that might enable them to translate Paris to New York,
to map the city in terms that would be familiar to them. In a rundown area,
they ask Yebga, "Is this the black neighborhood?" as they seek "clear explanations which were cleanly cut like keys to the vast works of the world. It
was easy to conclude, from having seen this gray building with its stinking
elevator, that blacks were cooped up here" (120). Though their conclusion
here proves to be wrong, certain similarities in the urbanness of the New
York and Paris landscapes do provide moments of familiarity for the two
cops. The violence that pulls them into the investigation appears as a familiar marker: "Paris was beginning to look like New York City; blood, wounded
people sprawled out in the street, it was a real Harlem sidewalk!" (82). They
can read the signs of urban violence and are able to function successfully as
investigators, at least for a while.

Dubois and Smith soon become friends with Yebga, who takes them to
all the local hangouts frequented by exiled Africans and Antilleans. Despite

his early claims that he is not tied to an African "community," Yebga clearly has many connections with expatriate Africans by virtue of his role as a newspaper reporter. Yebga's social life shows us the transnational nature of diaspora identities, the ways in which "diasporic identities are at once local and global. They are networks of transnational identifications encompassing 'imagined' and 'encountered' communities."[23] In a particularly telling example of the confluence of the local and the global in Yebga's Parisian world, the narrator explains:

> The one good thing about exile was that it strengthened bonds which might not have existed back in Africa. The simple fact of being black and African created affinities which gave an illusion of strength to these poor devils abandoned in the turbulence of Paris. You were not alone. You recreated family structures modeled on those you had left behind. Paradoxically, it was only away from home that Africans formed a real nation. In Paris, Congolese, Ivorians, Cameroonians, and Senegalese considered themselves brothers from the same country. African unity could only exist outside the frontier, in reaction to the surrounding hostilities. (72–73)

This quote is important in many ways, and reveals some of the complicated ways in which diaspora identity is expressed. The quote describes affinities formed by the social experience of "being black and African" but explains that these affinities would not exist in Africa. It is only in a state of abandonment, in the "turbulence of Paris," that the affinities create bonds. The embattled social space shared by these various individuals generates a connection based on, and in response to, "the surrounding hostilities." I am particularly interested here in the way that the response formed is articulated in terms of patriarchal and traditional family structures. The "family structures" in the adopted land are modeled on a vision of those left behind, and throughout the novel older African men instruct Yebga in the importance of the homeland, as the adopted land reveals its exclusions and its experiences of discrimination and insult.

In the conservative discourse of these men, we see the ways that "exile is the nursery of nationality," even as nation stands for continent.[24] Nation here is not defined by geopolitical boundaries but is reconstructed in completely new terms, far from the soil of the politically defined "nations" of each African's original birthplace. In the foreward to *Black Paris*, Njami explains, "Africa does not exist. Africas exist. Only on a neutral territory, and while facing a common adversary, can a lyrical brotherhood develop which will bring together the children of Mali and Cameroon, of the Côte

d'Ivoire, and the West Indies" (xii). It is outside the homeland that supra-
national bonds are formed, based on the social experience of being a "raced"
subject, rather than on an essentialist assumption of racial "unity." When
the word "community" is figured in this way, in terms of the evidence of
experience rather than the imprint of genetics, it can be a site of resistance
to those specific social exclusions, and it can also potentially allow for a
multiplicity of identities. A potentially liberatory understanding of community is retained when we consider that "the bonding of different experiences
through their spatialization displaces the common implications of exclusion
that the geographies of *communities* can imply."[25] Repeatedly we see the
ways that black international writers articulate the formation of bonds in
response to a common adversary. Their writings depict multiple strategies of
resistance, at the same time that the writings themselves become the sites
of future bonds.

Recalling the literary bond between Njami and Himes, we can note the
way that Himes discusses his own Parisian milieu in the second volume of
his autobiography:

> I must point out that all the soul people in Europe made up a club and when-
> ever soul people from other cities came to town we celebrated. It made no
> difference whether we knew one another or not.... In this respect we were
> the tightest club on earth. All that was required to be a member was proof
> we had paid our dues. The dues were estimated according to the degree we
> had suffered in the U.S.A. because of race.[26]

Himes's words do not construct an imagined community with "a single and
internally consistent set of rules, values, or beliefs," but rather describe "club"
membership among all the "soul people" in Europe as based on a shared,
lived personal experience of "race" and racism.[27] Similarly, the community
that Yebga may find with other black people in Paris is generated by a commonality of *experience*, based in postcolonial expatriation within the former
colonial center. Bell hooks's essay, "Postmodern Blackness," helps us see
that there is a difference between naming a socially formed community and
reverting to essentialized notions of unity. She emphasizes the importance
of lived experience as formative of social identity as she stresses the need

> to critique essentialism while emphasizing the significance of "the authority
> of experience." There is a radical difference between a repudiation of the
> idea that there is a black "essence" and recognition of the way black identity
> has been specifically constituted in the experience of exile and struggle. (29)

A shared diasporic consciousness that connects Africans in Yebga's Parisian world need not be the same thing as "a black 'essence,'" though in fact this is a distinction that is not apparent to Yebga at various moments in the text.

Africa Travels; or, Continental Shifts and Gender Roles

In its portrayal of intersections among the lives of individual Africans living in the French capital, *Coffin & Co.* reveals the ways that "African" in Africa is different from "African" in Paris. How does the black European writer, self-described as a "citizen of the world," address the symbol of Africa itself? Speaking of what the label *African* means to him as a writer, Simon Njami rejects a continental designation, stating, "An artist should not be governed by a geographical map. I have always been bothered by the labels 'African writer,' or this type of writer, or that type of writer, as if everyone has a domain reserved for him out of which he cannot move. But today, the new generation of which we speak—and I am part of that generation—has no frontier."[28] In the discursive world of the novel, as in the social world of Black Paris, there are multiple Africas. Seeing the multiplicities of Africas can help us to see the multiplicity of forms of diasporic identifications. The novel describes the varying relationships that various characters have to the symbol of Africa. Smith and Dubois's own relationship to Africa, as African Americans, shifts throughout the book. At one point the narrator tells us,

> Every time they spoke about Africa, they said "the motherland," the way Christians in Jesus' temple believe that paradise was established in the sky, behind the clouds. They didn't want to give up this ultimate dream. (140)

This seeming nostalgia for a phantasmal Africa, however, is balanced by a coldly realistic assertion of their identity as defined by place of birth in national terms. When Dubois and Smith meet Rastafarian Dread Pol, he tries to convince them of their universal brotherhood, saying, "There are no black Americans. We blacks have only one land, one nationality. We are Africans" (107). While Dread Pol speaks for a diasporic self-identification based on "race," Smith grounds his angry reply in a different historical/experiential reality:

> We are Americans, pal. Whether you like it or not, and there's a good chance that our fathers' fathers were sold into slavery centuries ago by your fathers' fathers. Since then we've fought every God-given day to achieve the rank of human being.... Africa let us down, brother. Don't ever forget that. Ever. (107–8)

Dubois and Smith echo Richard Wright's pause at the limit of diaspora identification in the case of slavery and the selling of slaves. Africa here functions as both nostalgic homeland and the site of originary enslavement for
the two Harlem cops. Living under conditions of racial and economic oppression in Harlem, American blacks like Smith and Dubois experience social
exclusion in America. But perhaps they also see that Africa is not a solution
and cannot be an alternative homeland. Indeed, like Wright, they go so far
as to indict Africa as the metonymic (and guilty) origin of their oppression.

In his autobiographies, periodical writings, and detective novel *Cotton
Comes to Harlem*, Chester Himes expresses similar ambivalence about Africa
as a "homeland" for black Americans.[29] Himes tells John A. Williams, "[T]he
American black doesn't have any other community [besides a predomi-
nantly white American community]. America, which wants to be a white
community, is their community, and there is not the fact that they can go
home to their own community and be the chief and sons of chiefs or what
not."[30] In Himes's words we see the strength of a longing for community,
due to the exclusions within "American community." Where does the black
American insert his/her identity when the "American community," however
falsely, defines or desires itself to be "white"? Himes's own life in Europe was
marked by vacillating nostalgia for, or identification with, America and
black American communities, as well as the realization that America wasn't
"his" country. Similarly, given the history of French colonialism and French
racism, where does the postcolonial person of African descent locate his
or her identity within "French community"? Yodi Karone's statement that
"Parisian" is not the same thing as "French" suggests that black writers in
Paris articulate Parisianism specifically as a resistant way to locate themselves
in an alternative space both within and without "French community."

The subject in diaspora vacillates between desire and awareness: desiring
an idealized "home"-land as antidote to the exclusions of the adopted land,
but also aware of the contradictions implicit in the "home"-land itself. Bennetta Jules-Rosette describes this tension in Parisianism literature as characterized by narratives of longing and belonging:

> The narrative of longing idealizes holding on to the past while the subject
> takes a leap into the future. Africa is envisaged as a nurturing mother for
> whom one longs, and as an authoritarian father whose constraining paternal
> traditions must be destroyed by an act of patricide.... The narrative of
> longing clashes with the counternarrative of belonging to a new culture
> and society—a modern world, which, although tainted, possesses its own
> symbolic and magical attractions.[31]

Diasporic writers express multiple and shifting visions of what the site and the name of "home" might mean, and this is part of the inherent multiplicity of the project(s) of writing diaspora. Njami's novel depicts both Yebga's desire for an idealized return and its ultimate impossibility.

Expatriate Africans in Njami's novel mark their attachment to the Continent with traces of a symbolically authentic African past: tourist art. For example, N'Dyaye, who is one of the "petty henchmen" that Yebga, Smith, and Dubois encounter during their investigation, has "a lighter inlaid with diamonds that marked the positions of the major metropolises on the African continent" (61). His apartment is described as

> a veritable jungle. There were plants; African musical instruments, amulets and masks were hanging on the walls. . . . N'Dyaye had been bent on reconstituting in his world the Africa he carried within himself. It was a chaotic Africa, full of contradictions and lies. Two fake crystal chandeliers hung above the tables, mythic stamps of occidental grandeur. (122)

N'Dyaye's interior decorating, with its "chaos, contradictions, lies, fake crystal," and "mythic stamps of occidental grandeur," mirrors the corruption Yebga will soon uncover among the powerful members of the African community in Paris. Africa becomes a symbol laden with different meanings for various members of the expatriate community of Njami's novel. The narrator tells us that one of the reasons Yebga has left Cameroon is that it is internally corrupt. In tracing the interconnectedness and complicity of the African expatriate community in the seemingly unexplainable crime he sees around him, he begins to generate nostalgia for an Africa marked by traditional, patriarchal social arrangements. This desire for a safe "home" is juxtaposed to Yebga's disillusionment with Paris as the site of his expatriation. It is also a desire for a home in the impossibly temporal past, an impossible return.

Yebga's nostalgia for a social simplicity is tied in his mind directly to his childhood in Africa and is established very early in the book in his first encounter with Dubois and Smith: "The graying hair on their heads and cheeks evoked for him a confused image of his own grandfather from Yaoundé. He had died when Yebga was ten" (22). Yebga's nostalgic reminiscences about Africa are all narrated through sensual imageries of childhood:

> He started singing softly to himself, until the ground beneath his feet felt not like concrete but baked mud, like the floors of the big house in Douala. He remembered a large table, where at night the whole clan gathered to palaver. . . . He remembered his happiness as a child, too, playing blind man, fists clenched against his lids, the clucking of startled chickens, the feel of mud walls, and his mother's gentle scolding. (181)

Njami's text depicts this form of longing for home as ultimately insatiable and critiques Yebga for seeking an equally impossible return to unquestioned patrilineal social structures. Samba, an African club owner in Paris, becomes a voice for a patriarchal, temporally distant social order after a senseless murder occurs outside his club. He warns Yebga that his investigation of these Parisian incidents is dangerous because it may implicate fellow Africans as criminals. As in Himes's *Blind Man with a Pistol,* Samba implies that the real criminal is elsewhere, is larger, is unapprehendable.

Samba's warning to Yebga emphasizes "traditional" social orders, located somewhere in the past, as he tells the younger man, "We're living in times of great confusion. . . . I'm worn out. The keys my grandfather entrusted to me don't open any doors now. I'm going back to Ziguinchor. I'm selling out and leaving" (177). Samba expresses a dream of sense and morality established in previous generations through male "keys." Many of the older African men whom Yebga encounters in his investigation echo this patriarchal ordering of social relationships. When Yebga gets too close to implicating a "fellow" African as a criminal, the older men warn him, appealing to a concept of continental (African) solidarity based on family as they articulate a kind of conspiratorial brotherhood. When Yebga questions N'Dyaye to gain information regarding Diop's death, the older man answers,

> A few years ago, this insult would have been settled between your father and me. I would have called him and said to him, "Your son is young. He doesn't know anything about life yet. He came to my place and insulted me." Your father would have apologized for you and we would have decided on your punishment. Unfortunately those days are over! We live in times of trouble and disorder. The West has ruined your minds. (74)

With its lack of familial respect and structures of address to determine appropriate behavior, the contemporary West represents disorder and chaos, while a "traditional" African past is viewed nostalgically as ordered, respectful, and comprehensible. This idealized past may be located in a nationalist politics promoted by the decolonizing moment. Partha Chatterjee's discussion of nationalist ideology in India provides an explanation for the persistence of social conservatism in these otherwise "liberatory" movements. He says, "The new politics of nationalism 'glorified India's past and tended to defend everything traditional'; all attempts to change customs and lifestyles began to be seen as the aping of Western manners and thereby regarded with suspicion. Consequently, nationalism fostered a distinctly conservative attitude towards social beliefs and practices."[32] In such a framework, the West is seen as the corrupting influence, against which a traditional national culture must assert itself. Chatterjee's article, like Njami's novel, shows how this conservative move promotes the home and family as the site for the preservation of tradition. The "lyrical brotherhood" described by Njami and depicted in *Coffin & Co.*, however, may be discordant for expatriate black women, who are excluded from or subordinated to the patriarchal bonds enacted by men.[33] As readers, we need to consider, what are the gender politics set in motion by the privileging of the home and family as site of the maintenance of traditional culture and traditional gender roles?

The definition of familial order and meaning in Samba's and Yebga's nostalgia is specifically patrilineal. Samba sees contemporary "Western" family arrangements as too limited:

> The word "family" means nothing to young Africans in France. You want to forget where you came from. You want to lock yourselves up between four walls with a woman and some children. That's where your family stops.
> You don't have any brothers or fathers or grandfathers or uncles or aunts or cousins. How do you manage to live alone like this? (178)

Samba here does not criticize "French" people per se, but rather the "young Africans in France," that is, this generation of expatriates, the next generation, whom he sees becoming even more removed from the traditional values of the home space. Women in particular are marginalized in Samba's ideal social world. Only one of the categories of missing relatives in Samba's definition of family is clearly marked as female (aunt), and it is a collateral relationship, rather than one of direct lineage. More important, in the course of his investigation, Yebga crosses a formerly forbidden behavioral boundary when he brutally attacks an African woman, Sarah M'Bamina, whom he considers a "lying slut": "This was the first time in his life that he had ever hit a woman and he felt a genuine thrill" (148). He continues to beat her in what becomes a highly charged public scene in a hotel lobby. When a barman responds to Sarah's cries for help, Yebga warns him with a raised fist, "I don't advise you to come closer you little prick. Mind your business. You can fuck our women, but you can't stop us from disciplining them!" (148). Yebga as disempowered black male uses his abuse of a black female to wield an illusory power over white men, whom he here verbally desexualizes also: "you little prick."[34] The postcolonial female here occupies the most dangerous position—the target of both the potential misogyny of conspiratorial male bonding and the patriarchal structuring of community relationships. Unlike Faye, Sarah has neither the privilege nor the option of living in an ahistorical oblivion, on a deserted (a)social island (and such a position is also a fiction for Faye).[35] Sarah occupies a social position in which her perceived "race," her country of origin, and her gender make it possible for Yebga to define her as one of "our women," and so to be disciplined by men like him.

As a racially designated "black" immigrant in Paris, however, Yebga occupies some of the same social positions as Sarah. His public display lands him in the police station, listening to racist comments from the French police officers. To Yebga, his arrival at the police station seemed inevitable: "Yebga tightened his jaw. His fists were clenched. It had taken fifteen years for him to come to this experience, and finally here it was, and at first hand. At the paper, he'd specialized in ironic comments on the 'paranoia' of blacks. Now he was getting his just desserts" (151). In effect, the social experience of police racism scripts Yebga as black in Paris. The first scripting is soon repeated as he descends to the Halles metro station and "three cops accosted him and asked to see his identity papers. It was the first time he'd been harassed like this in the fifteen years since he had come to France" (175).

Yebga's discovery of the complicity of the African community in the crimes around him causes him to reassess his relationship to Africa. In one scene he tells Dubois and Smith stories of an African past, but "These memories made Yebga aware that Africa had become his prey, his pasture, his theme, in short, his livelihood, but that it had not been his vital element for years" (140). While this quote seems to indicate that Yebga has a growing awareness that a divergence may exist between the Africa in his mind and "the real Africa," his continued idealizations suggest that he has not transformed this nascent awareness into a developed political consciousness that would acknowledge historical process. The quote also readily recalls Himes's own relationship to Harlem, about which he has said,

> I didn't really know what it was like to be a citizen of Harlem. I had never
> worked there, raised children there, been hungry, sick or poor there. I
> had been as much of a tourist as a white man from downtown changing
> his luck. . . . *The Harlem of my books was never meant to be real.*[36]

Perhaps the fantastical nature of Himes's Harlem is part of why he is able to feel at home there. Against an actual, historically contingent Africa (or Harlem) may be posed a fantasy, or desired, ahistorical Africa (or Harlem). Writing is a place where these projections are worked out. And yet Himes was much more than a literary tourist in Harlem, since he did not create facile or regressive nostalgia, instead using his writing to revise the spaces of incarceration that can make life a prison for black people in America.

In *Coffin & Co.*, Njami presents Yebga as an antihero caught in the fantasy of family articulated by the older men and driven by these patriarchal definitions of community to abuse women. Onto the temporal past of Cameroon he projects a dream of being home. Yet as Biddy Martin and Chandra Talpade Mohanty explain,

> "Being home" refers to the place where one lives within familiar, safe, protected boundaries; "not being home" is a matter of realizing that home was an illusion of coherence and safety based on the exclusion of specific histories of oppression and resistance, the repression of difference even in oneself.[37]

Where would Sarah M'Bamina fit into Yebga's illusory African "home"? Her specific history of oppression and resistance is excluded by the male expatriate African community's attempts to reinscribe a nationalist patriarchal social order and sense of community.[38] While the male African and Caribbean characters in *Coffin & Co.* occupy such professions as writers, newspaper editors, club and restaurant owners, and businessmen, the only roles that black women occupy in Yebga's Parisian world are prostitutes, fashion models, and waitresses. Avtar Brah reminds us that "all diasporas are differentiated, heterogeneous, contested spaces, even as they are implicated in the construction of a common 'we.'"[39] Indeed, these constructions are never seamless or fixed. Recall that it is Myriam, whom the narrator describes as "a mulatto waitress" at the Sunny Kingston (35), who first suggests to Yebga his connection to a "we." Ironically, it is also Myriam whom Yebga phones from the police station where he is held after his attack on Sarah. Myriam willingly comes to his rescue, suggesting that her idea of "we" might not necessarily encompass other women. In each particular articulation of community, the novel suggests, we must ask, "Who is empowered in a specific construction of the 'we'?"

Caught between narratives of longing and belonging, *Coffin & Co.* replays a particular formation of diaspora identity even as it critiques that formation. William Safran's definition of diaspora consciousness explains why the myth of a homeland retains such a powerful pull, functioning as a psychologically healing balance to the experience of oppression:

> Both diaspora consciousness and the exploitation of the homeland myth itself are reflected not so much in instrumental as in expressive behavior. It is a defense mechanism against slights committed by the host country against the minority, but it does not—and is not intended to—lead its members to prepare for the actual departure for the homeland. The "return" of most diasporas (much like the Second Coming or the next world) can

thus be seen as a largely eschatological concept: it is used to make life more tolerable by holding out a utopia—or *eutopia*—that stands in contrast to the perceived *dystopia* in which actual life is lived.[40]

Of course, an actual return has historically been a part of certain diasporic ideologies, and many of the members of the African community in Njami's novel do plan to return. The point is that, at least for Yebga and perhaps for others as well, the Africa to which they may return will probably be quite different from the Africa they imagine. In his discussion of Africa as "homeland" for diasporic communities, Paul Gilroy identifies the notion of Africa as a *political* sympathy, rather than as a place to which one could return.[41] Yebga, not yet articulating this developed political consciousness, instead seeks a "mystical unity" that is "outside the process of history," located in the irretrievable past of his childhood.[42]

Feeling disoriented and out of place, fantasizing about the homeland of his childhood, Yebga, a black international writer himself, stumbles through Paris toward the novel's end. He is nearly blind to his French landscape, so enwrapped is he in a daydreaming nostalgia for the sensual features of his African childhood, and he almost stumbles into

> a building made of glass and steel in the rue du Commandant-Mouchotte. He glanced up at the address. His efforts had not been wasted, after all. Chester Himes had lived here in May of sixty-eight. So, he *wasn't* all alone! His intuition had not abandoned him. Neither had his energy. He had found a landmark in a foreign land. (181)

It is significant that the architecture of this building is not marked as French. It is not a typical nineteenth-century Parisian building, but rather an emblematic part of a contemporary urban cosmopolitan landscape. Thus in this most provocative juxtaposition of the dueling forces of tradition (nostalgic memories of Africa) and a postmodern novelistic play, at a symbolic juncture where the mud walls of Douala meet the glass and steel of Paris, Yebga finds an anchor for his questions about identity and community. The expatriate writer Amos Yebga, African journalist for the *World*, finds his most solid place in a literary field: a "landmark" that withstands time and events. Himes, a fellow exiled black writer, becomes his geographical identity marker, a landmark implying Yebga's own membership: he was not alone. Thus, rather than a questionable bond with patriarchal members of the expatriate community (the "we" he had questioned in Myriam's words), he ends up defining community as a union with another black writer. This is an affinity based on the diasporic connections of a literary identity that is also linked to the experiences of being "black" in major metropolitan areas of "white countries." Yebga and Himes share the experiences and themes of being a black writer in a profession dominated by white publishers, writing about the racialized politics of law enforcement in contemporary urban locations.

Mirroring Yebga's own connection to Himes, we can also say that Njami, diasporic writer of a postmodern detective novel in French, enters an important dialogue with the work of African American author Himes, whose voice and characters and actual personage inhabit his novel. While the character Yebga "can't go home again" to an uncomplicated Africa of his childhood, in aligning himself with Chester Himes as a literary forefather, he replicates a similarly paternal social bond or "family." Frustrated by the false alignments among the expatriate community, Yebga finds solace and relief in another, more abstract literary community (which he may be idealizing in the same way). Himes is dead and Yebga (and Njami) can make of him what he wants. Of course, while such a father/son literary relationship creates certain bonds, it can also invite conflict and patricidal desires. This situation can be seen to echo Himes's own Parisian milieu, which centered around a group of black male writers and artists at the Café Tournon; and contemporary African American literary history itself has until recently been largely theorized in terms of a patrilineal order, with Richard Wright generally seen as a forefather of sorts.[43]

The final pages of *Coffin & Co.* find the two detectives, Smith and Dubois, in an unfamiliar environment. Previously, the traits that Paris shares with Harlem, the signs of urban life (violence, congested built environments, and so forth) enable Smith and Dubois to investigate fairly well in this similar territory, despite the linguistic and cultural differences between Paris and New York City. Smith and Dubois's investigation breaks down most dramatically when the two detectives must operate in Neuilly, an affluent suburb of Paris. The detectives have followed the investigation to the suburban mansion of an unnamed African "minister." In the neighborhood of Neuilly (an environment composed of long gravel driveways, high security gates, expansive green lawns rimmed by box hedges, and opulent old mansions), Dubois and Smith meet their death on the novel's last page. Njami's description heightens the economic and geographical differences between an affluent suburb and a poor urban neighborhood:

> Ed Smith and Jones Dubois pulled their hats down low over their foreheads. The minister's neighbors were nowhere in sight, probably too busy, thought Dubois, tasting the soup, or amusing themselves with the maid, to pay

attention to the sidewalk. Even if one of these trust funders took his dog out for a pee, he would probably take Smith and Jones [sic] for thieves, rousing the indigenous population to safeguard his wife's pension, his son's security, his daughter's dowry, Aunt Clarissa's silverware. (194)[44]

This suburban space is a new and unfamiliar terrain for the two detectives, who are shot by the private security guards of the mansion after a black Mercedes limousine enters the gates. The suburban scene does not offer up recognizable or solvable configurations of culpability or criminality. Their dying calls to each other are the names of their literary predecessors: "Ed!" "Gravedigger!" (195). At the novel's close, then, Dubois and Smith, in the personages of Coffin Ed and Gravedigger, are also represented in union with Chester Himes. Njami writes, "He'd better watch out up there, that old spade Himes. From here on in, Coffin Ed and Gravedigger Jones would have all of eternity to dictate their adventures to their Maker" (195). For Yebga, as for the two detectives, it is finally the literary tie that binds.

Writing to Homelands/Writing to Diasporas

In Amos Yebga, *Coffin & Co.* depicts a character caught by a vision of home that may never be recouped. Njami's novel shows us the dangers, in fact, of desiring this idealized vision of home. The yearnings of Amos Yebga and other male characters replay a patriarchal vision of the homeland that is ultimately injurious to postcolonial women. In this sense, Njami's literary relationship to the idea of a homeland is quite different from that which we see in Michelle Cliff's novels, especially *No Telephone to Heaven,* which rewrites a feminist nostalgia for the homeland. In Cliff's vision of Jamaica, postcolonial women are the agents of social change, rather than the stabilizing factor expected to maintain nationalist "family values." In *No Telephone to Heaven,* Clare Savage inhabits a revolutionary political position only in her return to the island, not in the metropolitan space of immigration in London.[45] Njami's novels focus instead on the politics of immigration, not the politics of return. In doing so, they open up the metropolitan space to the voices of the diaspora as they point the way out of binary models of immigration and assimilation. The webbed histories of colonialism mean that many African cultural workers in various international metropoles "never had the luxury of being completely inside or completely outside of African, European, or American culture, but instead experienced them together at all times."[46] The quotes by Stuart Hall and Simon Njami that began this chapter speak to the lived experience of histories of migration, which demand more capacious understandings of identity than those enabled by nationalism. Haitian writer Yanick Lahens states, "It seems possible and urgent on the eve of the twenty-first century to rethink the question of identity, of nationality, and of origin in order to get out of the inside/outside alternative."[47] Hall and Njami describe being English but not English, African but not African. I argue that diaspora literatures are key sites for the rethinking of these questions of identity, nationality, and origin.

Diaspora literatures deconstruct the falsely monolithic categories of national identity. French itself is deterritorialized by the presence of African writers in Paris, enriching the French language, as Calixthe Beyala has noted. So, too, does the French language become the very site enabling the diasporic literary conversation between African American author Chester Himes and black European author Simon Njami, neither of whom was born in France.[48] Homi Bhabha reminds us that "the Western metropole must confront its postcolonial history, told by its influx of postwar migrants and refugees, as an indigenous or native narrative *internal to its national identity.*"[49] As Russell King, John Connell, and Paul White, the editors of *Writing across Worlds* explain, "For those who come from elsewhere, and cannot go back, perhaps writing becomes a place to live" (xv). I take this to mean that writing becomes a way to revise the political space in which one lives, to generate a cultural politics that would make this space more habitable. Writing becomes a strategy by which black authors resist the discourses of the state that would script their identities in negating ways. Through their writing, black international authors provide alternate narratives, alternate ways of defining habitable global black identities.

5

History's Dispersals:
Caryl Phillips's Chorus of the
Common Memory

For people of color, doing time is only one among many forms of
imprisonment legitimized by the concept of race.

—*John Edgar Wideman*

Survival and Freedom

The varied oeuvre of black British writer Caryl Phillips traces the multiple
and complex meanings of the term *diaspora*. Throughout several novels and
travelogues, his writing retains a deep skepticism about the meanings of
terms like "family" and "membership." Rather than grant such terms an
unquestioned status as key tropes underlying the concept of diaspora,
Phillips's writing excavates the myriad ways that a term like "family" is
played out at the level of individual identities. Hence, first-person fictional
narratives compose a large part of his novelistic work as he tells specifically
local stories about a global phenomenon. Many of Phillips's novels enact a
restless traveling back and forth across the Atlantic and across centuries as he
places before us local stories that complicate a global understanding of diaspora. Phillips presents characters that are paradoxically in exile at home, and
his texts can be read as literary examples of what Avtar Brah means when
she describes "diaspora space" as a concept that "foregrounds the entanglements and genealogies of dispersion with those of 'staying put.'"[1] For Phillips,

the concept of diaspora refuses to rest on a false binary between home and exile, and his work repeatedly mines the complicated archives of both black and white histories of slavery, exposing their endlessly interrelated natures.

One of the recurring questions raised in Phillips's work is the meaning of survival. Phillips has stated that he "come[s] from a place which is characterized by survivor guilt."[2] This place is not solely geographical, but is also mapped in social identities, and it becomes a part of the literary explorations of diaspora identity that Phillips's work undertakes. Phillips's writing can be read as a provocative conclusion to many of the issues raised in the work of Richard Wright, Chester Himes, Simon Njami, and Michelle Cliff. All of Phillips's novels concern the intertwined histories of diaspora, histories of people from multiple social (and racial) positions as they are, or have been, shaped by the fact of slavery or by its heritage in contemporary discrimination. Phillips's third novel, *Higher Ground*, traces a tension between survival and freedom, engaging multiple diasporic perspectives and interacting with texts by Richard Wright, Chester Himes, George Jackson, and Michelle Cliff.

Higher Ground is a novel told in three disparate parts, encompassing the voices of an African middleman residing at a slave fort on the west coast of Africa probably in the mid-eighteenth century; a black American prisoner writing letters to his family from Max Row in the late 1960s; and a mentally unstable Polish-Jewish refugee woman living in England just after World War II. What are the linkages between these temporally and geographically very different narratives? Part of the answer lies in Phillips's understanding of diaspora as constituted not by the binary of home and away, but by complicated connections and histories that do not at first glance seem to be linked. The novel opens with an epigraph quoting a spiritual: "Lord plant my feet on higher ground," a sentiment suggesting homecoming, heaven as home, and the slave's hope for freedom in this world or another. Indeed each story is about someone displaced, either geographically or institutionally, from his or her place of birth and from a social location of original identity. Two of these displacements, however, become in themselves at least temporary means of survival. Phillips's text asks, in the context of slavery and the Jewish Holocaust particularly, whether survival is a crime or an act of heroism or perhaps something in between. His novel explores the conditions under which one may be forced to survive, and he plumbs the moral predicament of an individual survival that in some ways depends on the endangerment of others. True to Phillips's complicated and beautiful writ-

ing, he presents characters that are both guilty and innocent, imperfect victims of difficult histories.

The first two stories in *Higher Ground* focus on language as the means by
which we can know something about identity; it is the method by which we
come to our knowledge of the slave trade and the prisoner's thoughts. In the
first section, entitled "Heartland," Phillips presents an unnamed character
who is a linguist, a man in the middle responsible for translating between
two sides that do not remain quite so binarily opposed. Though the narrator's literacy affords him a position of relative safety within the slave fort,
translation is never purely innocent, and it can ensnare one in many ways.
Similarly, in the second section, "The Cargo Rap," the letters of Rudi, the
prisoner, (usually) reach the outside world, but they are censored by the
prison guards and may even provoke disciplinary tactics and punishments
against Rudi by these other "readers." Phillips thus raises questions about
the space of writing, about freedom of speech, and about the ability of language to reconceive social identity. In the third section, "Higher Ground,"
the protagonist, Irina/Irene, has "spent a small life writing unanswered
letters" to the beloved sister, mother, and father she was forced to abandon
in Warsaw when her father boarded her onto the Kindertransport that
undoubtedly saved her life, but separated her from her family forever. Phillips
uses these three characters to write a map of the central displacements that
imperil the notion of freedom: slavery, incarceration, and genocide.

"Heartland": Searching for Wright's Guilty Seller

The title of *Higher Ground's* first section, "Heartland," refers to a realm of
affect, since its setting is not the geographical heartland of the continent,
but the coast, the shoreland, the edge of Africa. Perhaps this coast is also an
emotional heartland, a place connected to the hearts (emotions) of diasporic peoples.[3] The unnamed African narrator, a translator working at a slave
fort on the African coast, is caught in the middle of the first phase of the
institution of slavery, translating at the edge of the continent, before the
harrowing departure to the middle passage. Phillips's narrative shows that
the man-in-the-middle is in many ways an untenable position in this power-
laden situation. The narrator is alienated from both the whites he serves
and the people of his own culture, to the point that he is unrecognizable to
them and does not automatically recall certain social mores when he is
among them.

Phillips's text can be linked to Richard Wright's *Black Power*, and Wright is an author whom Phillips identifies as a key influence. As a young student at Oxford in the late 1970s, Phillips met a black American fellow student who introduced him to African American political thought and literature. Phillips then traveled to the United States in search of this political milieu and has described picking up a copy of *Native Son* in a bookstore in Southern California. He took the book to the beach early one morning and remained rooted to his beach chair until dark, the waves of the Pacific lapping at his feet, transformed by Wright's prose.[4] *Black Boy* had a similar effect on him, and Phillips quotes from *Pagan Spain* in his own travel narrative, *The European Tribe*.[5] As an intellectual, a writer, and a black man in Europe, Wright may represent a landmark for Phillips in the way that Chester Himes did for Simon Njami. (Phillips was also a friend of the late James Baldwin, spending time with Baldwin at his home in St. Paul de Vence.)[6] *Higher Ground* specifically takes up a question raised by Wright in *Black Power* and explored in chapter 1 of this work: How can we come to understand the multiple complicities that enabled the slave trade? Whereas Wright, the African American author, somewhat tortuously answers this question by retreating into a binary opposition of "you fellows who sold us" versus "we descendants of slaves," Phillips, the black British (Caribbean-born) author, seems to revisit Wright and use fiction to flesh out the character of Wright's betraying ancestor. Wright's travel narrative never took this fictional turn, and it is in the fictional fleshing out that a complex understanding of this person emerges. Whereas Wright's record of his travel in West Africa leaves him bitter about this ancestor and without any further understanding of what motivated his actions, Phillips invents a character to create a way to understand. He leaves us with a more humanly complicated sense of a person's decisions and life course, as opposed to Wright's hurt brushing aside. It is as if Phillips, facing his precursor's frustration, has taken up the challenge to ask a further question, to continue the conversation that Wright cut short.[7]

The bulk of the "Heartland" section takes place at the slave fort on the coast. Phillips enters these architectures of trauma repeatedly in his work. In *The Atlantic Sound*, he reads the 1766–1811 letters of Philip Quaque, an African who lived at Cape Coast Castle for fifty years, working as a chaplain.[8] The contemporary novelist describes Quaque: "This African man lived with the British slavers as their chaplain, and literally resided above the dungeons in which were held thousands of his fellow Africans awaiting transportation to the Americas" (176). Phillips explains in this text that it is through reading this man's letters that he first discovered the name of

Cape Coast Castle (175). Phillips's literary practice involves spending a great deal of time researching historical material in addition to writing novels, since the history of the diaspora is a major theme of all his work.[9] We can see the fictional trace of this archival reading in *Higher Ground*. Answering the questions formed at Wright's fingertips as he moved through the passageways of the slave dungeons on his 1954 visit to Ghana, Phillips attempts to give life to the particular human relationships that might have characterized existence at this edge of the ocean. Phillips considers the role of literature to be its ability to give flesh to these archival documents. He identifies this as a subversive role: "You subvert peoples' view of history by engaging them with character. I don't think you subvert it by arguing schematically about ideas."[10]

The slave fort is a liminal place, a world between worlds where each person who arrives is displaced from one social category to another. African villagers are captured, branded, and become slaves (and potential future rebels). The narrator has been displaced from his original village, his family relationship with his wife and son erased forever. Due to his linguistic abilities, the narrator is then displaced from being a member of the group of African captives to being a translator between the captives and the captors. But before the section ends, he is again displaced from his position of relative privilege, remanded back to the status of slave as we leave him in the Americas, waiting to be sold at auction. The European men who live and work in the castle are also displaced from "their people," as Phillips's writing demonstrates the ways that the slave trade displaces all who play a role in it. As the section begins, a new governor arrives at the fort and engages in conversation with the narrator, telling him of his life back in Europe; he describes it as a "good life," which the narrator imagines as "a life spent with ledgers and files, with clerks and arithmetical equations in sunless rooms, a life of profit and loss. Presumably his people acknowledge such a life as 'good.' I do not know for I am familiar with only the rump of his countrymen" (12). As the narrator was cut off from his village and family, the new governor is now cut off from this "good life." In the false world of the fort, then, perhaps it is tempting for the narrator (and the reader) to see the inhabitants as "all trapped by similar circumstances" (20). Indeed the new governor soon dies of a tropical illness after returning from his first slave-gathering expedition into the heartland. But the section makes clear that the power imbalance between black and white people that defines the slave enterprise in all of its various moments and manifestations does not, in fact, create "similar circumstances." The narrator thinks that "[w]ithin the confines of the Fort my position is secure, if low and often unbearable. I now find it difficult to conceive of a life either before or after this place. I need to feel safe" (19). And yet within the confines of the fort his position is actually highly insecure, ultimately affording him little safety, and he finally ends up in the dungeon, shackled along with the other recent captives, bound for the Americas to be sold as an old man.

It is in the physical movement away from the liminal world of the fort that the narrator must confront his untenable position as a man in the middle. Caught in a power struggle between the new governor and Price (the European man in charge of the soldiers at the fort when the new governor arrives), the narrator is ordered by Price to take him on horseback to the nearest village. This journey from the world of the fort to the world of the village reveals the narrator's superficially secure social position to be highly unstable. Much to the narrator's shock, Price orders the narrator to ask the Head Man of the village for a girl that he can take back to the fort and then return "unharmed." Confronting the village Head Man, the narrator thinks, "It is moments such as these that I loathe. Marooned between them, knowing that neither fully trusts me, that neither wants to be close to me, neither recognizes my smell or my posture, it is only in such situations that the magnitude of my fall strikes me" (22). The narrator's ability to sustain this painful middle position has also required the psychically violent act of "murdering the memory." Not only is he disremembered by his "own people" and disrespected by the new people he is among, but to live in this space he must also disremember his own identity as father, husband, and villager. This position is not achieved without pain, and requires the implicitly violent "art of forgetting—of murdering the memory" (24). At the village, familiar sounds and the smells of local food cause him to "recall [his] youth and feel an overwhelming sense of loss" (25), as memory itself becomes a "territory too painful to inhabit" (24). Phillips's exploration of memory is complicated here, as the narrator implies that he needs to violently murder memory to survive.[11] *Higher Ground*'s other two protagonists, Rudi, the prisoner, and Irina, the Holocaust survivor, also describe numbing certain parts of their emotional identities to survive. Through these characters, Phillips traces a Fanonian inquiry into the damages done to the psyche, to identity, in surviving violence, discrimination, exclusion, and incarceration. Though forgetting may enable survival, what are the various psychic and social costs of this amnesiac survival? Perhaps paradoxically, memory is a territory that the *writer* will endure the pain of inhabiting.

The narrator characterizes his position of social displacement as a fall, indeed a fall from recognition. In the world of the fort, he is not recognized as an equal because difference is stigmatized through the lens of race. Back at the village he is not recognized because he serves the white man. Yet the narrator's guilt or innocence, his responsibility for his own fall, is complicated. At the village, as they wait for the girl, the village elder spits on the narrator, who then wonders:

> Why do they seem intent upon blaming me? Have I, unlike their Head Man, ever made profit for myself? I merely survive, and if survival is a crime then I am guilty. I have no material goods, no fine hut in which to dwell, nobody to wait on me. I set the circumstances of my existence against those of these Elders and I laugh. They are able to justify their way of life by pointing to people like myself whom they consider guilty of a greater betrayal. But observe the price of their treachery. Their sons and daughters are gone from them for ever. Yet I, who stayed behind, am expected to be something other than I am; which is an ordinary man doing an extraordinary job in difficult times. They blame me because I am easily identifiable as one who dwells with the enemy. But I merely oil the wheels of their own collaborationist activities. (24)

Phillips's text asks, through each of its stories, whether survival is a crime and under what conditions it can be seen to be one. Later in this section, when the trading party returns to the fort with new captives, the narrator, as translator, is ordered to separate the captives "to help arrange the shackling of one man to another man of a different tribe and language or dialect, in order that difficulties of communication might further induce isolation and prevent the planning of communal rebellion" (57). "I nod and begin, knowing that I am despised by my own for my treachery. This is surely the worst tragedy that can befall a man; but I am a survivor" (57). How do we interpret this last sentence? Wouldn't the worst tragedy have been being separated from his wife and child? Having survived that trauma, he is now faced with the tragedy of being despised and treacherous. Will he survive that? We do see him survive the middle passage and land on the American shore, and the section is not written to show its trace as historical; this is not the record of his life, not letters or diaries that would let us know that indeed he also survived the final tragedies.

The narrator's role as interpreter causes him to fall, losing his status as a fellow countryman. What is it that causes him to fall (again), losing the status he thought he enjoyed, the relative safety and security he thought he had inside the fort? This fall occurs when he steps outside the role allotted to

him by the power structure of the slave fort's bizarre world, when he assumes that the white men will recognize him as an equal. The Europeans'
own power depends, however, on their refusal to recognize the African as a
human. The narrator can perform the role of translator and assist them in
their enterprise, but he is not allowed to display human traits beyond the
fulfillment of this role. The African girl becomes the catalyzing force in the
narrator's third transformation. After torturing her and raping her for several days and nights, with her screams echoing throughout the fort, the evil
Price orders the narrator to return the girl to her village, where she, too, is
now unrecognized by "her people," chief among them her own father, who
is now revealed to be the Head Man of the village. The narrator eventually
is moved enough by a sense of concern for her that he risks his life to return
to the village and take her away again, this time for protection rather than
degradation. The narrator hides the girl at the fort, and they soon form a
bond characterized by mutual physical and emotional affection, an emotion
that effectively cannot exist in the world of the slave fort. When their situation is discovered, they are both led in chains to the dungeon, separated
forever. A love relationship between them is not a part of this social world,
and cannot be recognized since it demonstrates their humanity; the narrator is remanded to the position of slave.

Though the narrator is once again transformed from a translator with a
relatively privileged position into a captive about to endure the middle passage, he is still a linguist and he is still a survivor. It is important to note,
however, that he alters his relationship to language. In his role as translator
for the whites, he has been replaced by another African man: "Price stands
with the new linguist, a young man who barks orders at us in our language
and then turns and converses with them in theirs. I pity him" (60). Here
the narrator has a chance to see his former self from the perspective of the
captives to whom he had once barked orders. Instead of barking orders or
translating, he now finds himself communicating with the captives in a new
way. The description of this communication becomes one of the most powerful parts of this novel, and also resonates with several of Phillips's other
books on the topic of diaspora:

> Under my breath I begin to mutter. Other lips move independently, and
> without organization we swell into a choir. I realize that this is the same
> choral chant that I would listen to when I was the man next to Price, the
> same hitherto baffling rebellious music that now makes a common sense for
> we are all saying the same thing; we are all promising to one day return,
> irrespective of what might happen to us in whatever land or lands we

eventually travel to; we are promising ourselves that we will return to our
people and reclaim the lives that are being snatched away from us. And the
promise comes from deep inside of our souls, it comes from a region where
it is impossible to pretend, it comes from the heart. (60)

Here we see that the final transformation this character will undergo is indeed
a linguistic one: where once the sound was baffling, it now signifies not
only rebellion but return. We see that this is not even the final transformation, that there will be yet another. Phillips uses the geographic metaphor
signaling that the heartland of the title is in fact the region of the heart, sig-
nifying perhaps not only love of homeland, but more important, the love
that formed between the narrator and the girl, the love that caused him to
risk his own survival to help her. Despite being separated into many diverse
languages, the captives sing in a chorus, united in their *meaning* of rebellion
against the dehumanizing goal of the enslavers and toward the promise of
an eventual return to one's identity, to one's life. The linguist narrator no
longer translates the white man's dominative power; rather, he participates
in the common promised song of "his people." This promised song connects
a scattered diaspora "in whatever land or lands we eventually travel to."

The notion of a chorus resonates elsewhere in Phillips's work. "Choral"
could serve as a description for the writing style that he uses in many texts
as he creates multiple songs of diaspora. Though each singer speaks a different language, a harmony results, rather than fracture and fragmentation.
This harmony signifies not only survival, but love—indeed that it must be
love that enables survival against such odds. Phillips's most resonant evocation of this idea occurs as the final section of his 1993 novel, *Crossing the
River*, where he describes this singing as "the many-tongued chorus of the
common memory" (235). This is not a joyful song, nor does it entirely pal-
liate the many horrible conditions that Phillips describes:

In Brooklyn a helplessly addicted mother waits for the mist to clear from
her eyes. They have stopped her benefit.... A barefoot boy in São Paulo is
rooted to his piece of earth, which he knows will never swell up, pregnant,
and become a vantage point from which he will be able to see beyond his
dying *favela*.... For two hundred and fifty years I have listened. To voices in
the streets of Charleston. (The slave who mounted this block is now dying
from copping a fix on some rusty needle in an Oakland project.)...I have
listened. To reggae rhythms of rebellion and revolution dipping through the
hills and valleys of the Caribbean. (235–36)

The corpus of Phillips's work charts a movement away from fracture and
toward the expression of this chorus. In *Higher Ground* (1989), Phillips's

narrator joins this chorus on the African side of the Atlantic, but it is fractured by the time he reaches the Americas: standing on the auction block
the narrator thinks, "I am an old man. The yoking together is over. My
present has finally fractured; the past has fled over the horizon and out of
sight" (60). By the time he publishes *Crossing the River* in 1993, however,
Phillips revises this figuration; though he paints no rosy picture, he emphasizes that those like the narrator in *Higher Ground* who made it to the
Americas, living through the middle passage, must be seen as heroes, "Sur-
vivors all." The African drumbeat of centuries past, which begins *Crossing
the River*'s final section, merges into a combination of historical and contemporary diasporic musical, literary, and revolutionary sounds:

> For two hundred and fifty years I have listened. To the haunting voices.
> Singing: Mercy, Mercy Me (The Ecology). Insisting: Man, I ain't got no
> quarrel with them Vietcong. Declaring: Brothers and Friends. I am Toussaint
> L'Ouverture, my name is perhaps known to you. Listened to: Papa Doc. Baby
> Doc. Listened to voices hoping for: Freedom. Democracy. Singing: Baby,
> baby. Where did our love go? Samba. Calypso. Jazz. Jazz. Sketches of Spain
> in Harlem. In a Parisian bookstore a voice murmurs the words. Nobody
> Knows My Name. (236–37)[12]

In a 1994 interview, Phillips explains his ideas about this final section of
Crossing the River: "I perceive an annealing force that comes out of fracture.
I wouldn't say I've always wanted to be an explorer of the fissures and
crevices of migration. I have seen some connectedness and 'celebrated' the
qualities of survival that people in all sorts of predicaments are able to keep
hold of with clenched fists."[13] Phillips's reference in *Higher Ground* to this
promised return made by the captives is a promise made from the heart-
(land) of each person. Against a literal return, he here posits a return as a
"symbolic imaginary" as described by Stuart Hall.[14] In later works such as
The Atlantic Sound, Phillips casts a critical eye on contemporary diasporic
"returns" as enacted in what he sees as commodified touristic experiences.
In *Higher Ground*, I would argue, he alludes to a reclamation of self through
political acts like revolution and/or escape: a return to a political self, not
necessarily a geographic space.

The Cargo Rap: Live From Death Row

Higher Ground's second section borrows heavily from *Soledad Brother: The
Prison Letters of George Jackson*, as many of Phillips's books borrow from
previously published or archival letters, diaries, and documents composing

the histories of the African diaspora.[15] Phillips's writings make clear that these documents do not belong solely to the history of the diaspora, but rather compose the history of the modern world since slavery. Through his fictive sampling in these archives, he writes "new" chapters on the history of British colonialism (Cambridge), the history of American institutions of incarceration (Higher Ground), and the histories of the Jewish Holocaust (Higher Ground). "The Cargo Rap," the second section of Higher Ground, shifts our focus from the middle of the eighteenth century and the developing slave trade to a new form of slavery in the twentieth century.[16] Higher Ground was published in 1989; the next decade in the United States would see the prison population explode, with the numbers for African American men far outstripping those of other races.[17] In a 1991 interview, Phillips describes being in Alabama and visiting several jails, recounting "[t]he actual physical horror, for the first time in my life, of being in a couple of prisons which had huge black populations and were primarily staffed by bigoted, Southern rednecks—I had to write something about all of this."[18]

In including the life of the prisoner in his transcontinental novel of three parts, Phillips also brings the site of the prison into a discussion of diaspora. The contemporary scholar/activist collaborative, Critical Resistance, makes this link clear when Gina Dent, in conversation with Angela Davis, explains that

> the prison is itself a border. This analysis has come from prisoners, who name the distinction between the "free world" and the space behind the walls of the prison. This is an important interpretation that undoes the illusions of the powerful nation-states on the one hand and the seeming disorganization and chaos of capital's travels on the other. There is a very specific political economy of the prison that brings the intersections of gender and race, colonialism and capitalism, into view.[19]

Indeed the work that Davis, Dent, and other members of the Critical Resistance project undertake in analyzing what Davis has called the "prison industrial complex" has become increasingly global in its scope. The potent analysis of the prison as a border can connect the prisoner's experience to other forms of extranational identity, such as exile or displacement. The prison is both home and not-home. In a carceral society such as the United States, the prison as "big *house*" replaces the possibility of *home* for those locked up, or likely to be locked up.[20] What Soledad Brother, Malcolm X's Autobiography, and "The Cargo Rap" all claim, however, is that America itself can be seen as a prison. When Rudi, Phillips's fictional prisoner, writes to his mother, he echoes Malcolm X's words in "Message to the Grass Roots":

"Do not assume that you all are free. You are not. Most of you cannot see your chains. This is a serious error that some of us both inside and outside are fighting to correct."[21] Chester Himes's representation of American urban police practices as modes of containment has been discussed in chapter 1. Phillips's *Higher Ground* revisits American law enforcement by examining the life and letters of one fictional prisoner, and also by mirroring the text of a more iconic actual prisoner, George Jackson. Jackson's *Soledad Brother* stands as a seminal example of the radicalization of one prisoner, which echoed throughout a generation.

Phillips's Rudi writes to his family members and lawyers, telling his narrative of modern enslavement and captivity. In a letter to his father, dated January 1967, he describes his conditions this way: "I am a captive in a primitive capitalist state. I live on Max Row in a high-security barracoon. Forty-five percent of my fellow captives are of the same colour as the captors. Fifty-five percent of us—the wretched of the earth—are Africans. We live on the bottom level of this social swill bucket" (66). Rudi rejects American identity as simply a form of mental captivity and refers to himself as an African. Like Chester Himes, Richard Wright, James Baldwin, and so many other black international writers, Rudi has given up on the possibility of equality in America. Rudi chooses Africa, not Europe, as the future location for a free black self. In another 1967 letter to his father, he asks,

> Is this America, the civilized country of satellites and color television? Of Hot-Dogs, Coca-Cola, and Mickey Mouse? What dark part of this bright nation have we been condemned to, Joe, you and I? We must fell and burn bridges behind us as we leave. We are Africans. If we want our children to visit a Disneyland then let it be our own African Disneyland. The dice are loaded, the terms are unacceptable, the American odds are too long. (107)

Rudi mocks the consumeristic terms of freedom espoused by capitalist culture as he envisions his "African Disneyland." George Jackson's letters, too, often speak of Africa as home, for perhaps more overtly political reasons than those espoused by the fictional Rudi. In a 1968 letter to his father, Jackson says, "Africa is a most wonderful continent. They have everything in the way of human and natural resources. Oil in Egypt, Libya, Tunisia, Algeria, and Nigeria. Copper, diamonds, cobalt, and gold in Zambia. There are large deposits of iron ore in Liberia, a whole mountain of it in fact. You name it, and it is found in some part of Africa.... Speaking just for me I would like Tanzania on the East coast if I had to choose a spot to settle. Julius Nyerere is an enlightened and intelligent leader who identifies with the Eastern world" (165). In their brief analysis of *Higher Ground*, Charles

Sarvan and Hasan Marhama suggest that the collapse of democratic regimes in multiple African nations between the late 1960s and the late 1980s "subverts and mocks" Rudi's vision of a more just society in Africa.[22] Caryl Phillips also seems to share this contemporary skepticism about a utopian African home, as we see in his recent work, *The Atlantic Sound* (which I will discuss at the end of this chapter). However, for both Rudi and George Jackson, America is clearly not home.

Like Malcolm X and George Jackson, Rudi fosters his ability to articulate a revolutionary politics about America as antihome for black people through a self-imposed program of reform and reeducation undertaken within the prison cell. None of these prisoners sees this reeducation as a solo process: all three use words as weapons (cf. Richard Wright) and as a way of educating people both within their immediate family and without, via the medium of publishing a literature of rebellion. Rudi describes this self-education to his mother:

> I am entering a very important phase of my development as I try now to marry my political reading with the African-American experience. I feel like a chemist holding two semi-full test tubes, I have to decide which to pour into which. Either way there will be a reaction of some kind, perhaps a loud fizzing, perhaps an explosion, as a new substance is born. You will receive bulletins from my laboratory. (79)

The idea of political literature producing a chemical reaction echoes throughout the work of Jackson and Malcolm X. Asking his father for publication information about the writings of Mao Tse-Tung and W. E. B. Du Bois, George Jackson explains the need for African Americans to unlearn their miseducation in the American school system: "It is difficult, very difficult to get any facts concerning our history and our way of life. The lies, half-truths, and propaganda have won total sway over the facts. We have no knowledge of our heritage.... The ruling culture refuses to let us know how much we did to advance civilization in our lands long ago."[23] Malcolm X describes his prison self-education this way: "I have often reflected upon the new vistas that reading opened to me. I knew right there in prison that reading had changed forever the course of my life. As I see it today, the ability to read awoke inside me some long dormant craving to be mentally alive."[24] Each prisoner speaks of the need for a new literacy, a diasporic literacy that would encompass African heritages, at the same time that they themselves are authoring a literature of rebellion as part of that very archive.

But this newly acquired literacy comes at a cost and is won despite all efforts to limit its potential. The writings of Malcolm X and George Jackson detail the deterioration of their eyesight in prison, the result of reading with poor light.[25] Yet they continue to write and to educate those outside the prisons' borders. Recall that Chester Himes published his first crime fiction from his jail cell in the Ohio State Penitentiary. The earliest African diaspora literatures come from the narratives of ex-slaves, narratives that catalyzed the abolitionist movement. George Jackson's nephew, Jonathan Jackson Jr., suggests that it was the publication of *Soledad Brother* in 1969 that "brought a young revolutionary to the forefront of a tempest, a tempest characterized by the Black Power, free speech, and antiwar movements, accompanied by a dissatisfaction with the status quo throughout the United States."[26] Both Jackson and the fictional Rudi, then, know that their letters represent perhaps one of the last forms of power they can exert in their (mostly solitary) confinement. Says Rudi, "Words are power; they capture things" (68). Jackson writes to his brother Jonathan in August 1969, "I add five words to my vocabulary each day, five new ones, right after breakfast each morning when I have forty-five minutes to kill. It's not enough time for anything else and since I don't want to waste any time, I work on words. It is by words that we convey our thoughts, and bend people to our will."[27] The literature of the prison speaks loudly of the social ills that remain repressed in the national discourse at large.

Speaking such truths in a repressive society, of course, comes with a price. We know that Frederick Douglass had to flee to England after his 1845 narrative was published because its very publication made his free status tenuous. Jonathan Jackson Jr. writes that "George Jackson's imprisonment and further isolation within the prison system were clearly a function of the state's response to his outspoken opposition to the capitalist structure. Political incarceration is a tangible form of state control."[28] We have seen the ways that state repression of the political writings of black people had a material effect on the health of Richard Wright and James Baldwin.[29] Censorship takes many forms, from surveillance by the FBI and CIA on the lives and movements of writers like Baldwin, Himes, and Wright, to the overt censorship that the prison warden imposed on George Jackson's letters. The fictional Rudi warns his father: "I will not be able to explain everything. Should I try this letter will be seized and either returned to me or destroyed. Such is the nature of prison censorship. You must learn from now on to read between the lines of my work, to re-interpret my phraseology and pauses for in everything there is meaning" (83). In between those lines are references to the racist brutality of the prison guards (whom Rudi calls "slave-catcher pigs"), responsible for various physical injuries to which Rudi alludes.[30]

Through Rudi's letters we understand that he is punished for his refusal to succumb to the slave mentality required by the guards and by the prison system in general. He rejects the recognition of self as slave to the guard's attempted mastery. Writing to his father, he analyzes this relationship in Hegelian terms:[31]

> The pigs have gone mad. They openly taunt me. Names have never bothered me—as weapons they are neither sharp nor blunt. I have a mastery of their language far in excess of anything they might achieve. But these days they enter my ten by four cell at will and scatter my papers, destroy my books, and then withdraw laughing and claiming that they did not find what it was they were looking for. Clearly it is a recognizable me that they are looking for. But because I refuse to genuflect before them, because I refuse to wear the garb of humility and stretch out rug-like so they might wipe their feet on me, it appears that I am doomed to suffer their constant visitations. (106)

In *Soledad Brother*, George Jackson describes the relationship between guards and prisoners in similar terms, as the guards seek recognition of their attempted mastery:

> A force of a dozen or more pigs can be expected to invade the row at any time searching and destroying personal effects. The attitude of the staff toward the convicts is both defensive and hostile. Until the convict gives in completely it will continue to be so. By giving in, I mean prostrating oneself at their feet. Only then does their attitude alter itself to one of paternalistic condescension. Most convicts don't dig this kind of relationship . . . with a group of individuals demonstrably inferior to the rest of the society in regard to education, culture, and sensitivity.[32]

The middle section of *Higher Ground*, then, returns to a question raised in the first section's analysis of relationships at the slave fort on the coast of Africa. What is the price of survival? The narrator of "Heartland" enacts a form of survival in which he sees himself as safe, protected within the social world of the fort (which is really a prison). It can be argued, however, that the governor and Price do not recognize the narrator as an equal, and in fact Price's ability to command him to do things that he finds morally reprehensible (asking the chief for a girl) demonstrate that those wielding social power at the fort only view the narrator as a slave. As soon as the narrator rejects this relationship, instead recognizing a commonality in his position across horizontal alliances by siding with the girl, he is punished and forcefully remanded back to the now quite literal status of slave.

For Rudi and George Jackson, there is no middle ground, no space fit to occupy within the social terms set by the prison, except that of revolution-ary. Unlike the narrator of "Heartland," Jackson and Rudi reject a form of survival that entails recognizing themselves as slaves. Rudi, in fact, berates his own family for what he sees as the moral compromises they have made to survive in America. In a 1967 letter to his sister he warns,

> [T]o survive is not the highest morality. To survive with the will to begin again and go on, this is the highest morality. I have lived and died six or seven times in America, but how can they take from me my heritage unless I offer it to them like those fool "Tom" diplomats who accept "foreign" postings among their own people and talk over cocktails about last year's cocoa crop. (97)

Similarly, in a 1965 letter to his father, George Jackson states, "I don't think of life in the same sense that you or most black men of your generation think of it, it is not important to me how long I live, I think only of how I live, how well, how nobly."[33]

Both Jackson and Rudi choose to rebel rather than give in to the logic of submission required for prison survival. The price they pay is further lock-downs, additional solitary confinements, extended sentences, and physical punishment. Both letter writers link their rebelliousness to revolutionary political practices, identifying their inspiration as Malcolm X. In his famous 1964 speech, later published as "The Ballot or the Bullet," Malcolm X rejects Martin Luther King Jr.'s attempt to appeal to the moral conscience of Amer-ica. Malcolm X states: "Don't change the white man's mind—you can't change his mind, and that whole thing about appealing to the moral con-science of America—America's conscience is bankrupt. She lost all con-science a long time ago. Uncle Sam has no conscience. They don't know what morals are."[34] George Jackson's critique of King's politics evolves throughout his letters, beginning with his 1967 accusation that "King and his kind have betrayed our bosom interests with their demagogic delirium. The poor fool knows nothing of the antagonist's true nature and has not the perception to read and learn by history and past events."[35] Jackson's evaluation of King shifts, however, and he writes to his father after King's assassination,

> I was beginning to warm somewhat to him because of his new ideas con-cerning U.S. foreign wars against colored peoples. . . . I never really dis-liked him as a man. As a man I accorded him the respect that his sincerity deserved. It is just as a leader of black thought that I disagreed with him. The concept of nonviolence is a false ideal. It presupposes the existence of compassion and a sense of justice on the part of one's adversary.[36]

Throughout the political development we witness in Jackson's letters, we see the author, like Richard Wright and Chester Himes, further articulate the ways in which (racialized) violent repression is the tool the state uses to maintain its order. And the concomitant move made by Wright, Jackson, Du Bois, King, Himes, and Malcolm X is to internationalize their critique. Jackson comes to realize that this state violence is not simply a function of American politics, but is rather at the service of a global capitalism. Jackson references multiple international sites of violent repression (Leopold II's Congo, South Africa, Sharpsville) and sees violence and economics as linked: "Any claims that nonviolent, purely nonviolent political agitation has served to force back the legions of capitalist expansion are false."[37] Here Jackson knows that he is explicating a politics that is more and more dangerous to his own survival. He states in a June 1970 letter to Angela Davis,

> Do you know (of course you do) the secret police (CIA, etc.) go to great lengths to murder and consequently silence every effective black person the moment he attempts to explain to the ghetto that our problems are historically and strategically tied to the problems of all colonial people. . . . It's no coincidence that Malcolm X and M. L. King died when they did. Malcolm X had just put it together. . . . you remember what was on his lips when he died. Vietnam and economics, political economy.[38]

It is worth noting that thirty years later, Angela Davis has not, in fact, been silenced by the covert repression Jackson warned her about, and her current work on incarceration has become increasingly global in scope. In a 2001 interview she described her international prison-abolition activism: "Our own visits to prisons in Europe, South America, Australia, and the United States have allowed us to begin to think about the appeal of the prison across time and space as the most influential paradigm for punishment over the past two centuries."[39]

Malcolm X is also the inspiration for Phillips's letter writer. Rudi pens a letter to his father after King's death, praising King as a fine orator and writer, but critiquing the efficacy of nonviolence as a political strategy: "King claimed his pacifism was intended to provoke the conscience of the American white man. Why, I wonder, does he imagine that the American white man has a conscience?" (150). Like Malcolm X and George Jackson, Rudi refuses to adopt the strategy of passive resistance within the violent contexts of a prison-like environment. In choosing to reject the status of slave and resist the submission demanded by the guards and police, they forfeit any sense of personal safety (no matter how superficial), and indeed their own survival. Throughout *Higher Ground*, Phillips raises questions about

what such a survival might mean for one's identity. Phillips asks such questions via an international perspective that spans centuries and geographic
locations—from the slave fort on the coast of west Africa to the U.S. prison,
and finally to the last section, which shares the novel's title, "Higher
Ground." Here Phillips locates his examination of survival in Europe, his
survivor now a Jewish refugee who is spared the horror of the Warsaw
ghetto, spared the concentration camp, by a Kindertransport to England.
Each section of Phillips's novel, then, examines places of incarceration and
the costs and possibilities of both surviving in them and avoiding them.
The link to the Holocaust is made in both *Higher Ground* and *Soledad Brother*:
Rudi Williams refers to his cell as a "camp," (92), and George Jackson repeatedly refers to prison as a concentration camp, signing a June 1970 letter,
"From Dachau with love."[40]

Higher Ground: Among the European Tribe

The epigraph to Phillips's novel, a line from a spiritual, "Lord plant my feet
on higher ground," suggests a spiritual (or physical) homecoming, the desire
for a better life than the one currently lived. The third section of the novel
lands us in the middle of a Europe sinking in Nazism.[41] Irina is a Polish Jewish child whose parents find a way to place her, but no one else in her family, on higher ground, that she might survive the rising fascist tide. Irina
indeed makes it across, landing safely in England, but she is sundered forever
from her beloved sister and parents and permanently scarred by the pain of
this separation. By presenting us with the pain of Irina's mental anguish,
Phillips asks what the costs of her survival are. What does the land look like
for those who survive? Working at a library, Irina thinks of saying to her boss,
"'Mr. Lawrence, I'm shipwrecked but alive.... Look at me, Mr. Lawrence,
I'm thirty-seven and I can swim. I'm swimming.' ... She wondered if it might
be possible to stop the wave, to cup it in her hand before it broke, to preserve its curled beauty; to stop swimming for a moment, to sink quietly with
grace and dignity" (182). "Higher Ground" replays the ur-narrative of the
African diaspora, the separation of family members, and thereby links the
Jewish and African holocausts, querying the multiple ways that people survive such traumatic separations. For Irina, survival demands a painful exile,
as she arrives in England, "where she knew nobody, with a suitcase and a
photograph album (and a feeling that she was being punished), and a mind
tormented by the fear that she might never again touch or hold her sister"
(202).

Phillips plumbs the psychological conditions of unease that accompany such displaced survival, describing the children selected for the Kindertransport as they depart from their hometown: "So out and over the cab of the truck they stared, concentrating on going forward, escaping, but even as they did so they realized that a deep guilt was being fused in their souls, a guilt that would be exposed were they now to falter and turn and look back" (209). The need to constantly look forward, to stop the mind's desire for memory, is part of what enables Irina to survive. The cost, however, is her mental health (she spends ten years in a hospital after suffering a miscarriage and a bad marriage and attempting to throw herself under a train). For Irina the hospital, and the ongoing threat of returning to it, represents a space of imprisonment parallel to the slave fort on the coast and Rudi's cell in Max Row. Juxtaposed to this penned survival is the deadly incarceration undoubtedly experienced by her parents and sister, whom we assume become victims of the concentration camps. In *Higher Ground* Phillips meditates on the continuum of imprisonment ever present as a dialectic against the notions of freedom characterizing the discourses of modernity.

Like the narrator of "Heartland," Irina attempts to murder her memory, looking ever forward as she did on the truck, resisting the desire to submerge herself or drown in the past. But these memories threaten to burst forth at any time: "She could not spend another winter in England staunching memories like blood from a punched nose. She could not afford a memory-haemorrhage, but to not remember hurt" (180). The link between memory and blood is a resonant image in discussions of diaspora identity. Phillips's simile recalls the violence (a punch) at the root of a common identification. W. E. B. Du Bois emphasized this commonality, stating that what links members of the diaspora is "a common history," and "one long memory," describing a kinship based not on biology but on the "social heritage of slavery, the discrimination and insult."[42] Memory is not, therefore, identical to the blood and tears that accompany the social heritage of slavery, and yet the specific link *between* memory and the violence that blood reveals may generate certain diasporic affiliations. In "Higher Ground," Irina finally meets Louis, a West Indian immigrant to England who stays only ten days, deciding he would rather leave than deal daily with the type of racism he faces in a pub one night in Britain. "[B]etter to return as the defeated traveler," he believes, "than be praised as the absent hero and live a life of spiritual poverty" (197).

Many of the characters in Phillips's novels are writers: authors of diaries, letters, or other documents. Phillips's work echoes the claim I have been making about writing as a place where diaspora identities are constructed and performed. Rudi's letters from prison are one example of the way that he uses his writing to construct himself as African, not American, despite his physical placement "in the bosom of this country," where he is "a man who is being stretched and tortured for forty dollars. Enough is enough" (163). Phillips's fiction visits these written and unwritten archives to connect the histories of diaspora in the local particularities of their elements. His writing both addresses a trauma and enacts a resistance to it.

Listening for *The Atlantic Sound*

Phillips's recent book, *The Atlantic Sound*, is at once a travel narrative and a historical meditation on the concept of diaspora; it is also a journey across centuries into the lives of individual people affected by the histories of slavery. Phillips shows us how the histories of slavery are always/already multiracial and dispersed. In this book, Phillips presents a first-person narrative of travel from Guadeloupe to Britain, describing a historical tour of Liverpool, his journey to Ghana, and travel circling back to South Carolina. These narratives are interspersed with historical research as he digs in both written and oral archives for the histories of slavery that link Elmina to America, and Liverpool to Charleston. Consistent with Phillips's views on representing history through character, he attempts to excavate these pasts, using the stories and letters of individuals.

In this text and in his recent collection of essays, *A New World Order*, we see Phillips attempting to give place to an idea of *home* that he also wants to leave unplaced. That is, Phillips rejects the notion that any of the journeys he undertakes and describes in *A New World Order* and in *The Atlantic Sound* could represent homecomings. At the same time, in *A New World Order* he addresses what he calls "The 'High Anxiety' of Belonging" that he always felt growing up in Leeds. It is important to note that this anxiety comes specifically from the questions that authority figures and representatives of the British "state" pose to him:

> I grew up in Leeds in the sixties and seventies, in a world in which everybody, from teachers to policemen, felt it appropriate to ask me—some more forcefully than others—for an explanation of where I was from. The answer "Leeds," or "Yorkshire," was never going to satisfy them. Of course as a result, it was never going to satisfy me either. I soon recognised that no sooner had the words "Leeds" or "Yorkshire" fallen from my lips then a corollary question would be asked. My interrogator would paste a smile of benign patronage to his face. "No lad, where are you *really* from?" (303)

This quote highlights the fact that a feeling of belonging, of being at home, is undermined by this process of interrogation. Phillips's own sense of dissatisfaction with the answer "Leeds," indeed his sense of not being at home in Leeds, arises precisely as a result of the early questioning by police, teachers, and others. That questioning, Phillips says, "inevitably affected my ability to embrace Britain as 'home.'" (304)

In a section of *The Atlantic Sound* paradoxically titled "Homeward Bound," however, Phillips recounts another experience of this question(ing) of home, one that comes from a different direction. This time he is on a plane flying from London to Accra, and he is seated next to a Ghanaian businessman. "Whisky, my brother?" the man asks him, followed by "Where are you from?" For Phillips, this is again "*The* question. The problem question for those of us who have grown up in societies which define themselves by excluding others. Usually us. A coded question. Are you one of us? Are you one of ours? Where are you from? Where are you *really* from? . . . Does he mean, who am I? Does he mean, do I belong?" (124). For Phillips, what many might perceive as a friendly attempt to make conversation is instead a trigger for the anxiety of belonging that he has experienced in Britain, making him reluctant to accept the "brotherhood" the man proffers. Phillips describes making "the familiar flustered attempt to answer the question. He listens, and then spoils it all. 'So my friend, you are going home to Africa. To Ghana.' *I say nothing*. No, I am not going home" (125). Neither Britain nor Africa satisfies the question of "home" for Phillips, and his geographical answer is finally represented by his wish, in death, to have his ashes "scattered in the middle of the Atlantic Ocean at a point equidistant between Britain, Africa and North America."[43] In locating himself in this in-between space, he claims that "this watery crossroads lay at the center of a place that had become my other 'home'; a place that, over the years, I have come to refer to as my Atlantic home."[44] In choosing this mid-Atlantic space as home, Phillips lands (or scatters himself) on a space marked by fluidity and movement, a space that never holds still, rejecting a genealogical or historical tracing of roots and families. And yet, this very place in the Atlantic is also the site of another watery archive, marking the millions of Africans lost in the middle passage. Both this history and the watery indeterminacy, the plurality and multiplicity of this space, appeal to Phillips.

Throughout *The Atlantic Sound*, Phillips questions an understanding of diaspora that would be based on a discourse of family. Retracing his own parents' migration as West Indian emigrants of the fifties and sixties, he recounts their dismay at discovering "that the mother country had little, if any, desire to embrace her colonial offspring" (21). Colonialism denies its own rhetoric of family when the direction of travel changes from the Caribbean to the metropole. Phillips's own generation is under no delusion that England welcomes them as children returning to a mother. But Phillips is also critical of what he sees as the falsely nostalgic rhetoric of family embodied in other diasporic "returns," and he is especially critical of the touristic commodification of this nostalgic longing. He spends several sections of *The Atlantic Sound* reporting on Panafest, a contemporary cultural festival in Ghana: "According to the publicity material, Panafest is to be a time when the diasporan family returns to Mother Africa to celebrate the arts, creativity and intellectual achievements of the Pan African world" (167). Phillips traces what he considers the falsely romantic idea(l) of an African home back to the founding of Liberia and Sierra Leone, African American political movements that he considers "clumsy experiments," where "the idealistic notion of family soon floundered against the rocks of reality" (143). Phillips casts a cold eye on those engaged in promoting a contemporary touristic reunion, arguing that "these days a great part of the responsibility for keeping the family flame burning is now being borne by those of Africa, who appear to be craving a new unity with their diasporan brothers; the same 'brothers' they helped sell into slavery" (143). Here Phillips echoes Richard Wright in his rejection of a connection to Africa based on the idea of "family"; for both men, any family relationship is made permanently impossible by the rupture of slavery. Like Wright's *Black Power*, however, Phillips's writing evokes a longing, an affective desire for what Africa may represent in terms of identity. Though he rejects the brotherhood of the Ghanaian man on the plane, Phillips sees their connections and is emotionally honest about their differences: "Like me, he is a product of British imperial adventures. Unlike me, he is an African. A Ghanaian. A whole man. A man of one place. A man who will never flinch at *the* question, 'Where are you from?' A man going home. . . . I envy his rootedness" (126). Perhaps we can say that it is Phillips's flinch that produces his envy. Though Phillips himself admits to having a "desire to actively cultivate a plural notion of home" in his mid-Atlantic placing, this desire exists in tension with his envy of what he perceives as the Ghanaian man's "wholeness" and "rootedness." Despite his embrace of a multiple and fluid identity, the flinch remains.

It seems clear that this flinch originates in the experiences of contemporary discrimination. Not only is the question of "Where are you from?" part of what makes Phillips recoil, but he also describes enduring in Leeds "a daily chorus of 'Why don't you fuck off back to where you come from?'"[45] This hostile chorus gives the "Where are you from?" question its hard edge. As we have seen in previous chapters, the languages of the state, the hate speech of "fellow" citizens, and the experiences of discrimination generate the sense of exclusion felt by black people in "white countries." These languages generate Phillips's flinch as well as his envy of the more "rooted" man.

Against the destructive "daily chorus" described above, Phillips's writing calls up other Atlantic sounds, as he listens for other choruses and harmonies in the multiple voices of the diverse literary characters he creates. As all of Phillips's writings trace the paths of these Atlantic shores and waters, he has created a literary home in diaspora. Indeed he writes, "I have chosen to create for myself an imaginary 'home' to live alongside the one that I am incapable of fully trusting. My increasingly precious, imaginary, Atlantic world."[46] Like Chester Himes, who only felt at home in his detective fiction; Michelle Cliff, who claims a Jamaican identity in her novels; Richard Wright, who uses writing to express his sense of himself as Western; or Simon Njami, who finds his landmark in the work of Chester Himes, so, too, does Caryl Phillips locate his home in the writing he produces about the diasporan world. Phillips describes the choral qualities in the voices of his characters in *Crossing the River:*

> These people were talking in harmonies I could hear. That doesn't just come from survival, but from something more than just getting to the next day. There's an underlying passion which informs the ability to survive, and it's that word that most people shy away from . . . which is a love, an affirmative quality present everywhere I looked in those children of the African diaspora, from Marvin Gaye to Jimmy Baldwin to Miles Davis.[47]

It is perhaps this reservoir of resistant love that makes the writing a more habitable space. Against the hurts of contemporary discriminations, writing enables both authors and readers to perceive a sustaining passion, to consider the ways in which survival is possible, and to imagine new futures.

Epilogue

The diaspora is a thought whose closure cannot be seen by any one individual nor imagined by any single text.

—*Kenneth Warren*

This epilogue seeks no closure; it aims to secure no singular reading of black international texts. Each text contributes its own multiple meanings to an ongoing project of diaspora literacy. Abena P. A. Busia reminds us that it is the storyteller who defines diaspora community. Through literature, she says, "We learn to translate dividing borders into a diaspora community, to transform a lack of language into diaspora literacy. Such literacy requires shared knowledge, a knowledge of histories, continuities, and discontinuities which only our storytellers in their many guises can give us."[1] Busia's words speak to the powers of literary texts to generate a sense of community, outside the "dividing borders" of national identities. James Baldwin said in 1970, "I don't believe in nations anymore. Those passports, those borders are as outworn and useless as war."[2] And yet Baldwin was the subject of great scrutiny by the U.S. government's security branches as they monitored his passport and freedom of movement.

The FBI has had a long history of surveillance of black (expatriate) writers. A file was opened on Claude McKay in 1921, on Langston Hughes in 1925, on Richard Wright in 1935, and on James Baldwin in 1960. Wright's file is 181 pages, and Baldwin's is more than 1,700 pages. In *A Question of Sedition,* Patrick Washburn writes that in September 1943 "FBI Director J. Edgar Hoover compiled a 714-page report [entitled "Survey of Racial Conditions in the United States"] which solidly linked a number of black publications and black journalists with the Communist Party."[3] Hoover's surveillance was focused on bringing sedition charges against the black press, and against black writers in general. I am particularly interested here in reading the meanings of sedition. Washburn's study shows that despite many examples of patriotism and assertions of loyalty on the part of the black press during World War II, "Such declarations of loyalty did not satisfy Hoover. The black press also was expected to give up its demands for full black rights until the end of the war."[4] Here we clearly see that black civil rights are interpreted as clashing with national (read: white) self-interest. I would argue further that Hoover interprets antiracism, and the statement of sympathy or unity with "other dark races," to be part of a cluster of attitudes that he deems "un-American ideologies," and therefore seditious.[5] U.S. national identity, as defined by Hoover, is for all intents and purposes linked to white supremacist ideology. Black political rights are equated with U.S. security threats. No wonder Himes (and so many other black writers) perceived the United States to be a place of danger for people of color, when national self-interest demanded their exclusion from the polity. The FBI's interest in and reading of black writers complicates a notion of literature as a potentially open political space.

Commenting on the global reach of U.S. surveillance, William Maxwell discusses Claude McKay's FBI file. Maxwell finds that the bureau followed McKay with a Foucauldian policing, but so, too, he argues, do pursued subjects write back. McKay's wandering is in part a direct response to the bureau's watching him, and though McKay could not return to the United States before 1935 because of the danger he felt the FBI posed, we can also see McKay as a double agent, retaining agency by being aware of how the bureau was reading him, choosing his literary forms to express resistance under the constraints of charges of sedition.[6] Maurice Wallace explains that the bureau itself deleted its own readings and policed its own interpretations: "Ironically, as Baldwin was making tracks to Europe, the bureau was making its own tracks on the pages of Baldwin's file, clearly blacking out text to cover its own traces after the 1966 Freedom of Information Act but 'marking' Baldwin just the same."[7] What of Chester Himes's FBI file? As chapter 3 showed, Himes used his detective fiction to critique U.S. racism and re-vision U.S. law enforcement practices. The FBI began watching Himes when he was a resident of the United States, with most FBI documents on Himes dating between 1944 and 1945. In Himes's file, dated 11/25/44 and characterized as an Internal Security—Sedition file, the bureau states that

> this subject first came to the attention of the Bureau as a result of a ques-
> tionable article which subject had written entitled "Negro Martyrs Are
> Needed," which appeared in the May 1944 issue of the publication "The
> Crisis." This article related to certain proposed revolutionary actions which
> subject advocated on the part of Negroes. The Criminal Division of the
> Department subsequently requested that an investigation of HIMES be
> undertaken with a view to developing data as to his general background,
> activities, inclinations, etc.[8]

This particular document follows Himes's moves to Los Angeles; his various employments in shipyards, canning companies, and so forth; his member-ships in the NAACP and the Urban League; his high-school years; and his criminal record, with many passages later blocked out. The document then quotes from several of Himes's writings, the first being a 1942 letter he wrote to the "People's World" expressing his solidarity with India's independence movement. Another article quoted in the file concerns Himes's sympathy with interned Japanese-American citizens. Later in the document the FBI writer provides synopses of a group of Himes's short stories, concluding that "all of them were found to be fiction articles and none contained any mate-rial which could be termed seditious." Later, when Himes is photographed in New York with Malcolm X in 1962, the FBI sends a letter to their legal attaché in Paris. This later file sums up the bureau's previous and current interest in Himes: "Investigation did not disclose Communist activity or affiliation on the part of Himes at that time [1944] and the Department ad-vised in 1945 no further investigation was necessary."[9] The letter also de-scribes the tracing of Himes's movement to Paris, his inclusion in a report entitled, "Possible Subversives among U.S. Personnel in France," and the fact that he and other black writers and artists were watched and even informed on by agents perhaps posing erroneously at the famous Café Tournon in 1960 and possibly other times as well. Some of the mystique surrounding the Latin Quarter and the Café Tournon as sites of the black American expatriate community are thereby dispelled by the possible presence of FBI informants and agents among its café-sipping patrons.

What are the effects of this constant watching and reading? What are the material effects of the reaches of the state on the body of the writer and the writer's work? Addison Gayle, one of Richard Wright's biographers, responds to the rumor that the CIA killed Wright by stating,

What I found [in the documents] was a pattern of harassment by agencies of the U.S. government, resembling at times, a personal vendetta more so than an intelligence-gathering investigation. I discovered that the government was guilty of producing anxiety and stressful situations, which would have produced severe hypertension in most men, let alone one so sensitive as Wright.... In retrospect, this may well have been a crime of the magnitude of assassination.[10]

More recently, James Campbell, Baldwin's biographer, has documented the global reach of the FBI's voluminous surveillance of Baldwin; he writes that Baldwin's "political engagement had been answered, in proportion, by secret and continuous surveillance, in NY, Hollywood and the American South, in Istanbul, Rome and elsewhere."[11] The covert pressures of odd phone calls and information-seeking can have the effect of silencing and limiting one's capacity to speak about U.S. racial oppression. Campbell feels that Baldwin left the United States at an important time in the civil rights movement, at the height of his own influence, due to this surveillance pressure. This policing of black literary identities is consistent with the culture of confinement represented by the high rates of incarceration in the United States. We have seen that Himes's identity as a writer was initially connected in both symbolic and material ways to his experience of imprisonment and his access to freedom. The relationship of U.S. law enforcement institutions to African American people is a dominant theme throughout his writing.

Michelle Cliff is also positioned in and by her location in North America, and she speaks of her own literary connection to the letters of George Jackson: "I thought about his prison letters as a testament to his intellectual survival, about all of us communicating from what may seem like prison."[12] Exiled Kenyan writer Micere Githae Mugo describes a community created by an even more direct conversation with prisoners during volunteer work in a maximum security prison in Ogdensburg, New York: "Free conversation with metaphorically and psychologically exiled people, even as they occupy physical space in their own home countries, definitely helps to construct a new home space for the writer in exile."[13] Mugo's and Cliff's words speak to the ways in which these communities of resistant authorship create networks and affiliations, dialogues between past prisoners and future freedoms.

The previous chapters have argued that the literary space allows for a potentially fruitful ambiguity and sometimes ambivalence that is either not possible or perhaps too painful to occupy in "real" space. The authors I have discussed in this book enact relationships to home outside the state, and often outside biological notions of "racial" identities. And yet clearly this does not mean they are utopically free of the claims made on them by the discourses of nation and race. Indeed, perhaps the only (habitable?) geo-graphical space for such freedom is the mid-Atlantic resting place that Caryl Phillips seeks in death. These texts evoke relationships to home(s) that are perhaps forever ambivalent. As Michelle Cliff states, "There is no ending to this piece of writing. . . . I and Jamaica is who I am. No matter how far I travel—how deep the ambivalence I feel about ever returning. And Jamaica is a place in which we/they/I connect and disconnect—change place."[14] Chester Himes expresses a similar ambivalence in a 1961 letter to Carl Van Vechten: "America is home; the only home I know, and I always think wist-fully it would be wonderful to go back. But I don't believe I can. . . . I do not feel despondent; up to a point I enjoy Europe but basically I am a stranger and always will be a stranger."[15] Richard Wright saw himself as an Ameri-can, with a difference that he ever sought to emphasize: "I am an American writer—but I would not be honest with you if I did not draw a hard and sharp line of distinction between the ideas I hold and the ideals (or lack of them) that prevail in my land today."[16] The black international writers I have discussed produce multiple and complex articulations of home and community. These resistant stagings of diaspora "represent an idea of action and agency more complex than either the nihilism of despair or the utopia of progress."[17] Perhaps they help lead us to the home in the heart that Richard Wright sought.

Acknowledgments

Early work on this project was supported by an American Association of University Women Dissertation Fellowship and a University of California Regents Fee Fellowship. Robert Cancel, Frances S. Foster, Rosemary George, and Winnie Woodhull were generous, critical readers of my work, as well as teachers whose example I hope I can follow. Thanks also to Ann duCille for her unfailing warmth, good humor, and professionalism. The late Sherley Anne Williams was my dissertation director; she always devoted time and care to guiding my work, and I miss her presence greatly.

I thank Michel Fabre for inviting me to attend the African Americans and Europe Conference in Paris in 1992, where I presented early versions of my work on Chester Himes and Simon Njami. Bennetta Jules-Rosette was kind enough to introduce me to Simon Njami in Paris. I would also like to thank Robert Skinner for introducing me to Lesley Himes, for sharing his knowledge about Chester Himes and about *Plan B*, and for calling my attention to Himes archival material at Xavier University Library and at the Amistad Library in New Orleans.

Later stages of this project were supported by a nonresident fellowship at the W. E. B. Du Bois Institute for Afro-American Research at Harvard University. Thanks to Henry Louis Gates Jr. for providing the opportunity and to Dorothy Aram for allowing me a leave of absence from my teaching at Emerson College during that year. Thanks to Carla Peterson for her interest in my work and her support. Shawn Smith, Marsanne Brammer, and Susan Light have always been there through thick and thin. Robin Fast and Flora Gonzalez are wonderful mentors at Emerson. Dawn Skorczewski is a true friend, great colleague, and careful reader. Ellen Goodenow is everything I could have wished for in a research assistant. Thanks to Ellen Lindstrom for her work on the index.

George Lipsitz is a model teacher, scholar, and colleague, unmatched in my mind. His intellectual rigor is an inspiration always, and his generosity and friendship have been important to every stage of my academic career. At the University of Minnesota Press I would like to thank Richard Morrison and Andrea Kleinhuber for their help throughout the publishing process.

Mike and Bev have always believed, and Lisa and Michael have made so many things possible. This book is dedicated to two who were born with this project and grew up alongside it, Lindsey and Kylie, and most of all for Tim.

Notes

Introduction

1. Both quotes are from W. E. B. Du Bois, *Dusk of Dawn: An Essay toward an Autobiography of a Race Concept*, 2.

2. Throughout the text I use the term "black" cognizant of its shortcomings as a way to describe a group of writers whose very work aims to deconstruct notions of racial categories based on false science. I will use the term borrowing Stuart Hall's definition when he says that "[t]he term black is referring to this long history of political and historical oppression; it's not referring to... genes; it's not referring to... biology" (Hall, "Race: The Floating Signifier").

3. Equiano, *The Interesting Narrative of the Life of Olaudah Equiano or Gustavus Vassa, the African*; Douglass, *Narrative of the Life of Frederick Douglass, An American Slave: Written by Himself*; Prince, *The History of Mary Prince, a West Indian Slave, Related by Herself*.

4. Griggs, *Imperium in Imperio*; Delany, *Blake; or, The Huts of America*.

5. As I was preparing this book for publication, Brent Hayes Edwards's excellent study of the international character of the Harlem Renaissance, *The Practice of Diaspora: Literature, Translation, and the Rise of Black Internationalism*, was published.

6. Brah, *Cartographies of Diaspora: Contesting Identities*, 16.

7. Busia, "Words Whispered over Voids: A Context for Black Women's Rebellious Voices in the Novel of the African Diaspora," 5.

8. Abena Busia's work on black women writers has been seminal in this field, as has the work of Gay Wilentz. Other important books analyzing the concepts of diaspora, exile, and migration using a range of texts written by black women are Davies, *Black Women, Writing and Identity: Migrations of the Subject*; and Chancy, *Searching for Safe Spaces: Afro-Caribbean Women Writers in Exile*.

9. Bhabha, *The Location of Culture*, 238. See also Fanon, *Black Skin, White Masks*.

10. Clifford, "Diasporas," 321.

11. Joan Scott's essay, "Experience," argues that experience itself cannot be seen outside of discourse or used unquestioningly as evidence. Scott explains that to understand how difference is "constituted relationally... we need to attend to the historical processes that, through discourse, position subjects and produce their experiences. It is not individuals who have experiences, but subjects who are constituted through experience. Experience in this definition then becomes not the origin of our explanation, not the authoritative (because seen or felt) evidence that grounds what is known, but rather that which we seek to explain, that about which knowledge is produced. To think about experience in this way is to historicize it as well as to historicize the identities it produces" (25–26). See also Earl Lewis's insistence that "to study African Americans requires us to historicize the processes of racial formation and identity construction. Race in turn is viewed as historically contingent and relational, with full understanding of that process dependent on our abilities to see African Americans living and working in a world of overlapping diasporas" ("To Turn as on a Pivot: Writing African Americans into a History of Overlapping Diasporas," 767).

12. Bhabha, *The Location of Culture*, 2.

13. Echeruo, "An African Diaspora: The Ontological Project," 11.

14. Denis-Constant Martin explains that "[n]arrative identity, being at the same time fictitious and real, leaves room for variations on the past—a 'plot' can always be revised—and also for initiatives in the future" ("The Choices of Identity," par. 11).

15. Hesse, "Black to the Front and Black Again: Racialization through Contested Times and Spaces," 177.

16. In *Dangerous Crossroads: Popular Music, Postmodernism, and the Poetics of Place*, George Lipsitz shows how music can teach us about "place and displacement. Laments for lost places and narratives of exile and return often inform, inspire, and incite the production of popular music" (4). Lipsitz's analysis explains how these "new discursive spaces allow for recognition of new networks and affiliations; they become crucibles for complex identities in formation that respond to the imperatives of place at the same time that they transcend them" (6). In *Scattered Belongings: Cultural Paradoxes of "Race," Nation, and Gender*, cultural anthropologist Jayne O. Ifekwunigwe studies what she calls "the everyday words of working-class and middle-class 'mixed-race' people in England." Ifekwunigwe makes these oral testimonies central to her analysis, showing how "'mixed-race' de/territorialized declarations delimit and transgress bi-racialized discourses and point the way toward a profound re-alignment of thinking about belonging" (xiii).

17. Iser, "Why Literature Matters," 18.

18. Paul Gilroy, for example, warns that "there isn't any anterior purity—there isn't any anterior, first of all, and there isn't any purity either" (quoted in Lott, "Black Cultural Politics: An Interview with Paul Gilroy," 54). Echeruo argues that even Gilroy's concept of diaspora ends up relying on "blood" in its reference to blackness ("An African Diaspora," 7). Okpewho also argues that a desire for home is betrayed throughout Gilroy's *The Black Atlantic* (introduction to *The African Diaspora*, xxii–

xxiii). I do not propose to resolve this contradiction, instead viewing these ambivalences as important sites of inquiry. The push-and-pull of a desire for home is, in fact, the very topic of this book.

19. Several critics have pointed to a similar danger in using the term "postcolonial" to refer to locations and experiences characterized by importantly diverse power dynamics. The warning here is against erasing such differences or simply subsuming them under an academically convenient rubric. Sarah Suleri writes, "The concept of the postcolonial itself is too frequently robbed of historical specificity in order to function as a preapproved allegory for any mode of discursive contestation" ("Woman Skin Deep: Feminism and the Postcolonial Condition," 758). See also McClintock, "The Angel of Progress: Pitfalls of the Term 'Post-Colonialism.'"

20. Busia, "Words Whispered over Voids," 2, 3.

21. Wilentz, "Toward a Diaspora Literature: Black Women Writers from Africa, the Caribbean, and the United States," 386. See also Wilentz, *Binding Cultures: Black Women Writers in Africa and the Diaspora*.

22. When I use the term *diaspora* (or diasporic), though I drop the qualifier *African*, I am specifically referring to African diasporic peoples and do not mean to imply a similarity with other diasporas, such as the Jewish or Greek diasporas.

23. Du Bois, *Dusk of Dawn*, 117; italics added.

24. It is important to note, however, that in 1897 in "The Conservation of Races," Du Bois had defined a race as "a vast family of human beings, *generally* of common blood and language, *always* of common history, traditions, and impulses, who are both voluntarily and involuntarily striving together for the accomplishment of certain more or less vividly conceived ideas of life" (40, italics added). For several important analyses of Du Bois's complicated and shifting arguments about race, see Appiah, "The Uncompleted Argument: Du Bois and the Illusion of Race" and Sundquist, "W. E. B. Du Bois and the Autobiography of Race." See also Posnock, *Color and Culture: Black Writers and the Making of the Modern Intellectual*; and Hall, "Race, the Floating Signifier."

25. Bammer, "Editorial," vii.

26. Ibid., viii.

27. Hesse, "Black to the Front and Black Again," 169.

28. Rosemary George's work reminds us that "[h]ome is a way of establishing difference. Homes and home-countries are exclusive" (*The Politics of Home*, 2).

29. Bammer, "Editorial," ix.

30. Ibid.

31. Tölölyan, "Rethinking *Diaspora*(s): Stateless Power in the Transnational Moment," 23.

32. See Echeruo, "An African Diaspora," for a counterargument asserting an ontological basis for diaspora identification.

33. Matsuda, "Public Response to Racist Speech: Considering the Victim's Story," 25.

34. Wright, *Black Boy (American Hunger): A Record of Childhood and Youth*, 355.

35. Collins, *Fighting Words: Black Women and the Search for Justice*, 4.

36. George, *The Politics of Home*, 5.

37. Ekeh, "Kinship and State in African-American Histories," 90.

38. Hesse, "Black to the Front and Black Again," 177.
39. Hall, "Cultural Identity and Diaspora," 234.
40. Clark, "Developing Diaspora Literacy and *Marasa* Consciousness," 53.
41. Hesse, "Black to the Front and Black Again," 179.
42. Hall, "Cultural Identity and Diaspora," 236.
43. Cliff, "Clare Savage as a Crossroads Character," 266.
44. Butler, "Sovereign Performatives in the Contemporary Scene of Utterance," 365.
45. Donald Pease describes national narratives as acting as agents of the state, constructing "imaginary relations to actual sociopolitical conditions to effect imagined communities called national peoples" ("National Identities and Postnational Narratives," 3–4). I am using Peases's term for a slightly different purpose: the community that I believe readers perceive in Himes's writing is clearly an imagined one. In addition, they are invested with a false universalism. The difference is that this *perceived* national narrative constructs a community outside the sanction of the state—even as exotically always-already marginalized outside.
46. Lorde, "Age, Race, Class, and Sex: Women Redefining Difference," 285.
47. Cliff, "An Interview with Michelle Cliff," 601, 612.
48. Njami, interview by Wendy Walters.
49. Cliff, "An Interview with Michelle Cliff," 598.
50. Ibid., 612.
51. Njami, interview by Wendy Walters.
52. Cliff, "Interview with Michelle Cliff," 615.
53. Ibid., 615, 614.
54. Wallace, "The Politics of Location: Cinema/Theory/Literature/Ethnicity/Sexuality/Me," 50, 52.
55. Two other early Afro-British writers are Ukasaw Gronniosaw and Ignatius Sancho. For excerpts of their work, see Phillips, *Extravagant Strangers: A Literature of Belonging*, 1–8.
56. Bhabha, *Location of Culture*, 241–42.
57. Clark, "Developing Diaspora Literacy and *Marasa* Consciousness," 42.
58. Sommer, "Resisting the Heat: Menchu, Morrison, and Incompetent Readers," 411.
59. Ibid., 421.
60. I am using the word *coalition* in the way described by Bernice Johnson Reagon in her influential essay, "Coalition Politics: Turning the Century," when she reminds us that a coalition is not an exclusionary home with a nipple and a bottle for comfort (359).

1. "On the Clifflike Margins of Many Cultures"

1. Wright, "Black Boy in France," 32.
2. Ibid. In Wright's autobiography he recounts reading Mencken in a segregated southern library: "Yes, this man was fighting, fighting with words. He was using words as a weapon, using them as one would use a club. Could words be weapons? Well,

yes, for here they were. Then, maybe, perhaps, I could use them as a weapon?" (*Black Boy (American Hunger): A Record of Childhood and Youth*, 293).

3. The restored text of Wright's complete autobiography was published as *Black Boy (American Hunger): A Record of Childhood and Youth* in 1993, as noted above.

4. Nina Kressner Cobb's article, "Richard Wright and the Third World," is one of the few critical works that places these texts in dialogue. She briefly discusses *White Man, Listen!* in relation to Wright's later works *Black Power, Pagan Spain*, and *The Color Curtain*.

5. Cobb, "Richard Wright in the Third World," 239n18.

6. Wright, *White Man, Listen!* 79.

7. Ibid., 81.

8. Ibid., 83.

9. Ibid., 81, 87.

10. Ibid., 99.

11. Alexander, "'Can You Be BLACK and Look at This?': Reading the Rodney King Video(s)," 78.

12. Harris, *Exorcising Blackness: Historical and Literary Lynching and Burning Rituals*, 95.

13. Wright, "I am an American, but."

14. Harris, *Exorcising Blackness*, 70.

15. Ibid., 70.

16. Paul Gilroy's chapter, "'Without the Consolation of Tears': Richard Wright, France, and the Ambivalence of Community," from *The Black Atlantic*, presents important readings of Wright's later works. Gilroy argues for examining Wright's "route from the particular to the general, from America to Europe and Africa" in order "to get us out of a position where we have to choose between the unsatisfactory alternatives of Eurocentrism and black nationalism" (186). I am arguing that Wright's work creates a space between racial essentialism and national identity that can be called *diaspora*.

17. Harris, *Exorcising Blackness*, 185.

18. Wright, "Blueprint for Negro Writing," 48.

19. Harris, *Exorcising Blackness*, 101.

20. Ibid., 103–4.

21. Wright, "Blueprint for Negro Writing," 48.

22. Wright, *Black Power: A Record of Reactions in a Land of Pathos*, 5–6.

23. Ibid., xxxvi.

24. Throughout *Black Power*, Wright uses terms like "the African," though indeed his travel was largely confined to the Gold Coast region. His broad continental generalizations are just one reason that many readers find this text problematic.

25. Scholars have shown that Wright's title references Nkrumah's political rise to power over British colonialists, not the phrase used in the United States in the 1960s, which was not a part of the U.S. civil rights vocabulary in 1953. Other titles he considered were "Richard Wright in Africa," "The White Man's Grave," "Stranger in Africa," "A Journey in a Land of Pathos," "What Is Africa to Me?" "This Heritage," "Black Brothers," "Dark Heritage," "Africa Turns Black," "Ancestral Land,"

and "Ancestral Home." See Fabre, *The Unfinished Quest of Richard Wright*, 401, 404. These titles indicate his back-and-forth shifts regarding questions of diasporic connection and/or distance.

26. Wright, *Black Power*, 6. Subsequent references to *Black Power* will be cited in the text.

27. Appiah, "Long Way from Home," 188, 190.

28. See Hughes, *The Big Sea*; Golden, *Migrations of the Heart: An Autobiography*; and Harris, *Native Stranger: A Black American's Journey into the Heart of Africa*, among others.

29. For critical work exploring the connections between traveling subjects, tourism, and colonialism, see George, *The Politics of Home: Postcolonial Relocations and Twentieth-Century Fiction*; Kaplan, *Questions of Travel: Postmodern Discourses of Displacement*; and Pratt, *Imperial Eyes: Travel Writing and Transculturation*. Pratt's final chapter also contains a short section on *Black Power*, though she and I read Wright's touristic position in Africa differently; see *Imperial Eyes*, 221–24.

30. As two examples of Wright's lack of identification with black women's suffering, recall his treatment of Bessie in *Native Son* or his tales in *Black Boy (American Hunger)* of exploiting poor women in Chicago when he worked as an insurance salesman.

31. Drake, "Diaspora Studies and Pan-Africanism," 460.

32. Singh, introduction to *Black Power*, xxvi. For further details about Wright's participation both in the Bandung conference and the Paris Conference of Negro African Writers, see James Campbell's chapter, "Black on Black," from his *Exiled in Paris: Richard Wright, James Baldwin, Samuel Beckett, and Others on the Left Bank*.

33. See, for example, Lipsitz, *The Possessive Investment in Whiteness: How White People Profit from Identity Politics*; Hill, *Whiteness: A Critical Reader*; and Bay, *The White Image in the Black Mind: African-American Ideas about White People, 1830–1925*.

34. Wright's work here can be linked to the work of Frantz Fanon, specifically Fanon's *Peau Noire, Masques Blancs*, which was published in Paris in 1952 (later translated as *Black Skin, White Masks*). In the fourth chapter, "The So-Called Dependency Complex of Colonized Peoples," Fanon presents a similar analysis of the colonizer's initiation of racialized subjectivity when he explains that "[t]he arrival of the white man in Madagascar shattered not only its horizons but its psychological mechanisms. As everyone has pointed out, alterity for the black man is not the black but the white man" (97). As we have seen in Wright's Ghana travels, however, there are clearly moments when alterity for Wright is the black African. This is his complicated positioning between the colonizer and the African, which will become clearer when we consider the type of Western diasporic identity that Wright articulates. See Gilroy, *Black Atlantic*, 245n65, for a reference to correspondence between Wright and Fanon.

35. Though examples are too numerous to mention, the following critical volumes provide further information: Ashcroft, Griffiths, and Tiffin, *The Empire Writes Back: Theory and Practice in Post-Colonial Literatures*; Williams and Chrisman, *Colonial Discourse and Postcolonial Theory: A Reader*; and Bhabha, *The Location of Culture*.

36. Segments of this debate are excerpted and reprinted in Chinua Achebe "The African Writer and the English Language," and Ngũgĩ wa Thiong'o, "The Language of African Literature," in Williams and Chrisman, *Colonial Discourse and Post-Colonial Theory*.

37. The phrase "English is a foreign anguish" comes from Marlene Nourbese Philip's poem, "Discourse on the Logic of Language," in her *She Tries Her Tongue, Her Silence Softly Breaks*, 55–59.

38. For more information on this shadowing, see Campbell, "Black on Black."

39. For more on FBI and CIA interest in the writings of Baldwin and McKay, see Wallace, "'I'm Not Entirely What I Look Like': Richard Wright, James Baldwin, and the Hegemony of Vision; Or, Jimmy's FBEye Blues"; and Maxwell, "F.B. Eyes: The Bureau of Investigation Reads Claude McKay."

40. Wright, quoted in Fabre, *Unfinished Quest*, 407.

41. Wright, "The Position of the Negro Artist and Intellectual in American Society."

42. Unpublished interview, Richard Wright Papers, Box 3 Folder 32, Yale Collection of American Literature, Beinecke Rare Book and Manuscript Library.

2. The Postcolonial as Post-Enlightenment

1. In her article, "Race, Privilege, and the Politics of Re(Writing) History: An Analysis of the Novels of Michelle Cliff," Belinda Edmondson explains that in the Jamaican context, both the protagonist of *Abeng* and the author might be considered "Jamaica white." She says, "Though from all evidence Cliff regards herself as black or mixed, in Jamaica she is considered, socially and economically speaking, 'white'" (191n7).

2. Chambers, *Migrancy, Culture, Identity*, 24.

3. Gilroy, *The Black Atlantic: Modernity and Double Consciousness*, 31.

4. Owens, "The Discourse of Others: Feminists and Postmodernism," 58.

5. Cliff, *Abeng*; subsequent references will be cited parenthetically in the text.

6. Lionnet, *Autobiographical Voices: Race, Gender, Self-Portraiture*, 18.

7. Smith and Watson, *De/Colonizing the Subject: The Politics of Gender in Women's Autobiography*, xxi.

8. Hall, "Old and New Identities, Old and New Ethnicities," 49.

9. Kaplan, "Resisting Autobiography: Out-Law Genres and Transnational Feminist Subjects," 130. Lorde, *Zami*.

10. Harpham, "So...What *Is* Enlightenment? An Inquisition into Modernity," 537.

11. Gilroy, *Black Atlantic*, 55.

12. Chow, *Writing Diaspora: Tactics of Intervention in Contemporary Cultural Studies*, 60, 34, 52.

13. Haraway, "Situated Knowledges: The Science Question in Feminism and the Privilege of Partial Perspective," 586.

14. Lionnet, "Of Mangoes and Maroons: Language, History, and the Multi-Cultural Subject of Michelle Cliff's *Abeng*," 339.

15. hooks, "Marginality as a Site of Resistance," 342.

16. Mercer, "Diaspora Culture and the Dialogic Imagination: The Aesthetics of Black Independent Film in Britain," 55.

17. Johnson, "A-beng: (Re)Calling the Body In(To) Question," 121.

18. For a thorough discussion of resistance and popular cultures in Jamaica, see Cooper, *Noises in the Blood: Orality, Gender, and the "Vulgar" Body of Jamaican Popular Culture*.

19. Mair, "Recollections of a Journey into a Rebel Past," 59.

20. Mercer, "Diaspora Culture," 59; and Clark, "Developing Diaspora Literacy and *Marasa* Consciousness," 43, 45.

21. Hall, "Old and New Identities," 58.

22. Chambers, *Migrancy*, 38.

23. Glissant, *Caribbean Discourse: Selected Essays*, 26, 245.

24. This denial of representation, a specific resistance to totalizing as well as to objectifying, characterizes the work of Antiguan writer Jamaica Kincaid. Her two novels, *Annie John* and *Lucy*, for example, exist in dynamic tension with her trenchant critique, *A Small Place*. The latter work completely undercuts any kind of nostalgic or fetishistic representation of the Caribbean as an Edenic site.

25. Cliff, "An Interview with Michelle Cliff," 604.

26. Cliff acknowledges Zora Neale Hurston's work as a source for *Abeng*, and the description of this funeral is very similar to a funeral description in chapter 4 of *Tell My Horse: Voodoo and Life in Haiti and Jamaica*: "Plaintive tunes, mournful songs are sung now. A new and most doleful arrangement of 'Lead Kindly Light' fairly drips tears" (50).

27. Elsewhere I develop a discussion of the dynamic uses of the Legend of the Flying Africans in novels by Paule Marshall and Toni Morrison. See Walters, "'One of Dese Mornings, Bright and Fair, / Take My Wings and Cleave De Air': The Legend of the Flying Africans and Diasporic Consciousness."

28. Hayden White, quoted in Owens, "The Discourse of Others," 66.

29. For a historical overview of the racist components of Enlightenment thought, see Emmanuel Eze's excellent collection, *Race and the Enlightenment: A Reader*.

30. Owens, "The Discourse of Others," 66.

31. Chambers, *Migrancy, Culture, Identity*, 41.

32. Jamaica Kincaid, quoted in Cudjoe, "Jamaica Kincaid and the Modernist Project: An Interview," 226–31.

33. Grewal, "Autobiographic Subjects and Diasporic Locations: *Meatless Days* and *Borderlands*," 234.

34. Spivak, "Who Claims Alterity?" 282.

35. Glissant, *Caribbean Discourse*, 105–6, 154.

36. For a development of this argument with respect to Cliff's second novel, *No Telephone to Heaven*, see Walters, "Michelle Cliff's *No Telephone to Heaven*: Diasporic Displacement and the Feminization of the Landscape."

37. Cliff, "Caliban's Daughter: The Tempest and the Teapot," 40.

38. Owens, "The Discourse of Others," 80.

39. Gilroy, *Black Atlantic*, 99.

40. Robinson, "It Takes One to Know One: Passing and Communities of Common Interest," 721.

41. Lyotard, *The Postmodern Condition: A Report on Knowledge*, 81–82.

42. Alexander, "'Can You Be BLACK and Look at This?': Reading the Rodney King Video(s)," 94.

43. Spillers, "Mama's Baby, Papa's Maybe: An American Grammar Book," 67.

44. Elizabeth Alexander's "'Can You Be BLACK and Look at This?': Reading the Rodney King Video(s)" discusses the work of visual artist Pat Ward Williams in depth. Williams's 1987 work, *Accused/Blowtorch/Padlock*, depicts images of a torture/lynching as printed in *Life* magazine. Around the images Williams writes out her own anguished questions about the identity of the photographer, the act of looking, and the subjectivity of the viewer: "WHO took this picture?... How can this photograph exist?... Can you be BLACK and look at this?"

45. Haraway, "Situated Knowledges: The Science Question in Feminism and the Privilege of Partial Perspective," 585.

46. Lionnet, "Inscriptions of Exile: The Body's Knowledge and the Myth of Authenticity," 34.

47. Wynter, "Sambos and Minstrels," 152.

48. de Lauretis, "Eccentric Subjects: Feminist Theory and Historical Consciousness," 145.

49. Both *Abeng* and *No Telephone to Heaven* concern the life of Clare Savage. *No Telephone* follows Clare as she migrates from Jamaica to the United States to Britain, and finally back to the island. Cliff's third novel, *Free Enterprise*, marks a departure, as it does not concern Clare but instead focuses on a more U.S.-based history of diaspora and the life of African American Mary Ellen Pleasant.

50. Hodge, "Challenges of the Struggle for Sovereignty: Changing the World Versus Writing Stories," 206.

3. Harlem on My Mind

1. Muller, *Chester Himes*, 15. *For Love of Imabelle* was published in the United States by Fawcett in 1957, then again by Avon in 1965 with the title *A Rage in Harlem*, and in France in 1958 as *La Reine des Pommes*. Himes's win represented the first time the prize had been awarded to a non-French author.

2. Himes, *My Life of Absurdity: The Later Years*, 150.

3. Himes quoted in Williams, "Chester Himes—My Man Himes," 315.

4. Himes, *My Life of Absurdity*, 110.

5. Himes, quoted in Fabre, *From Harlem to Paris: Black American Writers in France, 1840–1980*, 215. Perhaps it is ironic that Himes saw Wright as the single famous black American writer when he sailed for Paris—ironic since at that time Wright himself was in Paris (having moved there in 1947) and indeed Wright became the first contact for Himes when he docked. Wright met Himes's train in Paris and Himes brought to his friend "good bond paper... as well as complimentary copies from Harper's of Wright's new novel, *The Outsider*" (Margolies and Fabre, *The Several Lives of Chester Himes*, 77).

6. Margolies and Fabre, *The Several Lives of Chester Himes*, 36.

7. Both H. Bruce Franklin and Edward Margolies discuss Himes's prison experiences as influential on his detective story writing. See Franklin, *Prison Literature in America: The Victim as Criminal and Artist*, 223–24; and Margolies, *Which Way Did He Go? The Private Eye in Dashiell Hammett, Raymond Chandler, Chester Himes, and Ross Macdonald*, 59.

8. Quoted in Sallis, *Chester Himes: A Life*, 110. The publishing history of Himes's prison novel sheds much light on his reasons for resenting the U.S. publishing industry. The original manuscript was titled *Yesterday Will Make You Cry*, and was cut so severely that *Cast the First Stone* barely resembles it. *Yesterday Will Make You Cry* was only published in its originally intended form in 1998, with an introduction by Melvin Van Peebles explaining some of the changes. See Sallis, chapter 10, for more on the differences between the two books.

9. Malcolm X, *Malcolm X Speaks: Selected Speeches and Statements*, 8.

10. Johnson, "American Prisons and the African-American Experience: A History of Social Control and Racial Oppression," 6.

11. Ibid., 6.

12. Quoted in Kelley, "But a Local Phase of a World Problem: Black History's Global Vision, 1883–1950," 54.

13. Robert Johnson's analysis of U.S. prisons and racial oppression reminds us that the main residence on slave plantations was also called the "Big House," and he adds that the walled maximum security prisons of the northern United States "could be thought of as walled ghettos, not unlike urban ghettos, which were the source of so many of their inmates. . . . Big House prisons originally were modeled on factories and their inmates were thought of as 'slaves of the state' well into the twentieth century" ("American Prisons and the African-American Experience: A History of Social Control and Racial Oppression," 28).

14. Himes, quoted in Williams, "Chester Himes—My Man Himes," 329.

15. John Roberts expresses the need for an analysis of African American folk heroes "as symbols of black cultural identity." He explains that "African American folk heroic creation is a normative cultural activity linked to black culture-building in America" (*From Trickster to Badman: The Black Folk Hero in Slavery and Freedom*, 2, 4). This is the sense in which I use the term "folk heroic creation."

16. Himes, "Negro Martyrs Are Needed," 174.

17. Roberts, *From Trickster to Badman*, 197.

18. I present a fuller discussion of the folk basis of neighborhood residents' strategies of self-defense and a more complete analysis of Coffin Ed and Grave Digger as linked to folk heroic precursors in "Limited Options: Strategic Maneuverings in Himes's Harlem."

19. Johnson, "American Prisons and the African-American Experience," 6.

20. I am grateful to the late Sherley Anne Williams for reminding me of Toomer's poem.

21. Farah Jasmine Griffin reads Toomer's poem in similar terms: "The song of the slaves exists side by side with the terror inflicted upon them. The slaves are dark purple plums. One plum is plucked by the poet to become a seed nourished in

him and eventually a poem of the race" ("*Who Set You Flowin'?*" *The African-American Migration Narrative*, 148).

22. David Margolick says that "the song's popularity extended to Europe, where Holiday... performed it several times during a 1954 tour" (*Strange Fruit: The Biography of a Song*, 96). See also Farah Jasmine Griffin's discussion of Holiday's European experiences in *If You Can't Be Free, Be a Mystery* (97–115).

23. Angela Davis asserts that "Strange Fruit" "put the elements of protest and resistance back at the center of contemporary black musical culture" (quoted in Margolick, *Strange Fruit*, 7).

24. René Micha, "Les Paroissiens de Chester Himes," 1520. The original reads: "C'est la vision même qui nous transporte:... qui offre une beauté comique. Ut pictura poesis.... Nous poussons une porte: sur les murs blanchis à la chaux des graffiti forment une longue fresque, toujours la même: des organes génitaux démésures sur des corps minuscules, tel un verger de fruits estranges" (my translation).

25. For a discussion of this type of fetishism, see Julien and Mercer, "Introduction: De Margin and De Centre." The phrase "eroticised othering" is theirs.

26. Malcolm X noted in 1964, "Harlem is a police state; the police in Harlem, their presence is like occupation forces, like an occupying army. They're not in Harlem to protect us; they're not in Harlem to look out for our welfare; they're in Harlem to protect the interests of the businessmen who don't even live there" (*Malcolm X Speaks: Selected Speeches and Statements*, 66).

27. Cawelti, "The Study of Literary Formulas," 142.

28. Roberts, *From Trickster to Badman*, 50.

29. Ibid., 53.

30. Quoted in Fabre, "Écrire: une tentative pour révéler l'absurdité de la vie," 20. The original publication reads: "Cerceuil et Fossoyeur seraient des traîtres a leur race s'ils étaient les personnages réalistes. Ce qui n'est pas le cas: ils représentent le type de policier qui devrait exister, celui qui vit dans la communauté, la connait bien et fait respecter la loi de façon humaine. Je crois en eux. Je les ai créés: deux personnages qui seraient les ennemis des Noirs dans la réalité, mais que j'ai voulu sympathique" (my translation). Himes did not speak French; Michel Fabre translated his responses for publication in *Le Monde*.

31. "Absurd" was one of Himes's favorite words to describe the politics of race in America. The second volume of his autobiography is entitled *My Life of Absurdity* and it begins with a paragraph that states, "If one lives in a country where racism is held valid and practiced in all ways of life, eventually, no matter whether one is a racist or a victim, one comes to feel the absurdity of life" (1).

32. Hogue, "Sixties' Social Movements, the Literary Establishment, and the Production of the Afro-American Text," 50.

33. Himes, "Now Is the Time! Here Is the Place!" 273.

34. Lipsitz, *The Possessive Investment in Whiteness: How White People Profit from Identity Politics*, 5. Lipsitz's excellent book provides a comprehensive examination of the tragic consequences that the possessive investment in whiteness has had and continues to have for the possibilities of democratic freedom in America. Lipsitz provides an important analysis of housing laws and loan policies that have made the

concept of being at home in America and owning a home in America impossible for so many people of color.

35. Williams, "Chester Himes—My Man Himes," 346.

36. Lee, "Hurts, Absurdities and Violence: The Contrary Dimensions of Chester Himes," 103.

37. Himes, "Negro Martyrs Are Needed," 174.

38. Fabre, "Écrire," 21. The original reads: "Il y a plusieurs années, de nombreuses émeutes ont éclaté en Amérique, suivies d'émeutes spontanées apres l'assassinat de Martin Luther King et de batailles entre les Pantheres noires et la police. J'ai pensé que toute cette violence inorganisée que les Noirs déchainent en Amérique n'était rien d'autre que des coups de feu tirés a l'aveuglette, et j'ai intitulé mon roman Blind Man with a Pistol. Tel était mon commentaire sur l'inefficacité de ce type de violence" (my translation).

39. Williams, "Chester Himes—My Man Himes," 311.

40. Fabre, "Écrire," 21.

41. Himes, "Prediction," in Black on Black, 281.

42. Williams, "Chester Himes—My Man Himes," 312. Plan B in fact remained unpublished in the United States until 1993, when a resurgence in Himes scholarship led Michel Fabre and Robert Skinner to publish Himes's somewhat incomplete manuscript.

43. Himes, "Negro Martyrs Are Needed," 159. It is important to note that in 1944, when Himes was still living in the United States, his revolutionary proclamations are spoken in terms that include him: he uses the pronoun "us" instead of "them," seeing himself as a part of the revolutionary movement that he seems to stand outside of in his later pronouncements.

44. Johnson, "American Prisons," 8. Johnson cites the following statistics, supported by multiple studies: "By 1970, African-Americans comprised 40.7 percent of the state prison population and a mere 12 percent of the general population.... This means that in 1970, blacks were more than three times more likely to go to prison than one would expect, given their prevalence in the general population.... By 1996, African-Americans were overrepresented in state prisons at a rate of more than four times their prevalence in the general population, accounting for more than 50 percent of the state prison population (and just less than 50 percent of the state and federal systems combined), but only 12 percent of the general population" (8).

45. Himes's literary expression of black revolutionary ideologies should be seen within a tradition; his voice obviously is not the first, nor does it stand alone. In an interview in Black World, Hoyt Fuller calls Himes's attention to his literary company in Sam Greenlee's The Spook Who Sat by the Door and another novel whose author is unnamed, Black Commandoes (Fuller, "Chester Himes: Traveler on the Long, Rough, Lonely Old Road"). I would also add Sutton Griggs's Imperium in Imperio to this discussion of revolutionary discourse. Griggs's novel exists as an interesting precursor for Plan B since it, too, involves two heroes who disagree over particular revolutionary ideologies, with death as the result.

46. Himes, My Life, 360.

47. Darryl Dickson-Carr's African American Satire: The Sacredly Profane Novel

analyzes the history of African American satire writing. *Plan B* should certainly be read within this tradition.

4. "A Landmark in a Foreign Land"

1. Simon Njami, in personal communication with the author, April 21, 1993.

2. I refer throughout this essay to Marlene Raderman's translation of Njami's novel, entitled *Coffin & Co.* The French edition, which I also use for comparison, is *Cerceuil & Cie.*

3. Jules-Rosette, *Black Paris: The African Writers' Landscape,* 148.

4. Quoted in ibid.,162.

5. Ibid., 152.

6. Ibid., 157.

7. Simon Njami, in personal communication with the author, April 21, 1993.

8. One of the effects of Himes's statement, and its reverberations in other aspects of postcolonial writing, is that French itself as a category must be expanded in response to this pressure placed on any (false) claims to exclusivity. Cameroonian writer Calixthe Beyala explains that she and other Parisianism writers "are an incontestable element in defense of the French language. This is not the French of Baudelaire, but a reconfigured language that will enrich French culture, language, and values, as in the case of any métissage. Because of this, African literature is the literature of tomorrow that will give life to French culture and make the [French] language more dynamic" (quoted in Jules-Rosette, *Black Paris,* 205).

9. Himes, "Harlem ou le cancer d'Amérique," (my translation). The original French reads: "Vous pouvez manger comme un Américain, vous habiller comme un Américain, parler comme un Américain, perser [sic, penser?] comme un Américain. Mais si vous êtes Noir, vous êtes moins Américain que ne l'est un étranger" (63).

10. Henderson, "In Another Country: Afro-American Expatriate Novelists in France, 1945–1974."

11. Muller, *Chester Himes,* 37–38.

12. The name of the paper speaks to the cultural location in which Njami defines himself. He has described himself as a "citizen of the world," and I think it is interesting that his protagonist "writes for the *World.*" This is a cultural location very different from that described by Richard Wright when he speaks of "the Westernized and tragic elite of Asia, Africa, and the West Indies—the lonely outsiders who exist on the clifflike margins of many cultures" (*White Man, Listen!* dedication page). Nearly thirty-five years after Wright, Njami's diasporic intellectual works and exists in a hub, not on a margin. Njami's quote comes from an unpublished interview with the author, 1993. See also Wright, *White Man, Listen! Lectures in Europe, 1950–1956.*

13. Jules-Rosette, *Black Paris,* 149.

14. The original French for this passage also uses the words "slave" and "family" to describe the demands made by the "community" on the expatriate subject: "La 'communauté,' cette grande famille hypothétique et abstraite de laquelle on voulait le rendre esclave" (Njami, *Cerceuil & Cie,* 67).

15. Himes, *My Life of Absurdity: The Later Years,* 381.

16. Her name is also a pun, since fay or o'fay is slang for white folks, pig-latin for "foe."

17. Henderson, "In Another Country," 189.

18. Himes, *A Case of Rape*, 85.

19. Ibid.

20. Henderson, "In Another Country," 213.

21. Ibid., 216.

22. In the original French, this passage does not contain such explicit play on the "literary" and "fictional" nature of Dubois's and Smith's alter egos, but Raderman's translation is consistent with the overall spirit of the text. The French reads: "Plus jamais ils ne porteraient les défroques de Cercueil et de Fossoyeur. Chester Himes s'en retournerait dans son trou de dépit. A eux deux, en terre étrangere et sans appui logistique, sans l'aide narquoise des hommes du capitaine Brice, sans le fichier de la Criminelle, sans même la couverture du lieutenant Anderson, ils feraient passer le goût du sang à ces assassins de Negres qui fricotaient avec les gangsters de la honte et les racistes pilleurs de chambres d'hôtel" (Njami, *Cerceuil & Cie*, 240).

23. Brah, *Cartographies of Diaspora: Contesting Identities*, 196.

24. John Dalberg-Acton, quoted in Anderson, "Exodus," 315.

25. Keith and Pile, introduction to *Place and the Politics of Identity*, 18.

26. Himes, *My Life*, 40.

27. In his work on Mexican migration and social space, Roger Rouse addresses the limits of the term *community* in its implication of "a single and internally consistent set of rules, values, or beliefs." See Rouse, "Mexican Migration and the Social Space of Postmodernism," 10.

28. Simon Njami, quoted in Jules-Rosette, *Black Paris*, 198.

29. In his autobiography, Himes explains the genesis of *Cotton Comes to Harlem*, which he had originally titled *Back to Africa*: "I thought the Back to Africa program in the U.S. was one of the most absurd things the black people of America had ever supported. How were the black Americans going back to Africa? Who was to take them? Who was to support them? Protect them? Feed them? It was an opium pipe smoker's dream. But it was perfect for a con. And that was my story" (Himes, *My Life*, 258).

30. Quoted in Williams, "Chester Himes—My Man Himes," 306.

31. Jules-Rosette, *Black Paris*, 9.

32. Chatterjee, "The Nationalist Resolution of the Women's Question," 234.

33. Calixthe Beyala is an important female Cameroonian author, also a writer influenced by Parisianism. Beyala's seventh novel, *Les Honneurs Perdus* (1996), received the literary Grand Prix from the Académie Française in 1996. Providing feminist analyses of expatriate black women's experience, Beyala's novels also depict "the alienation, isolation, and entrapment of African women, both in African cities and Paris." See Jules-Rosette, *Black Paris*, 170.

34. The French reads, "Ne t'avise pas d'avancer, petit connard" (Njami, *Cerceuil & Cie*, 193).

35. In Himes's *A Case of Rape*, the white woman, Elizabeth Hancock, is shown not to have been on an island in her white identity either. Himes's novel shows the social space of whiteness to be falsely safe, since it is actually Elizabeth's white husband who rapes her repeatedly before she meets her former lover, African American Scott Hamilton, and his other black male friends. The court only sees the stereotype

of a black male rapist and cannot see the cruelty of Elizabeth's white husband, veiled by the mask of marriage and the mask of whiteness.

36. Himes, *My Life*, 126, original italics.

37. Martin and Mohanty, "Feminist Politics: What's Home Got to Do with It?" 196.

38. Carole Boyce Davies and Anne Adams Graves's *Ngambika: Studies of Women in African Literature* is a collection of essays addressing the ways that the specific histories of African women are represented in literature. *Women in Africa and the Diaspora*, by Rosalyn Terborg-Penn, Sharon Harley, and Andrea Benton Rushing, is concerned more with history and economics than literary representations.

39. Brah, *Cartographies of Diaspora*, 184.

40. Safran, "Diasporas in Modern Societies: Myths of Homeland and Return," 94.

41. Gilroy, *"There Ain't No Black in the Union Jack": The Cultural Politics of "Race" and Nation*, 158.

42. Ibid.

43. Margolies and Fabre relate a famous incident at the Café Tournon in Paris when Baldwin and Wright got into an argument over Baldwin's critique of Wright: "Baldwin ... responded [to Wright's taking him to task] that 'the sons had to kill the fathers'" (*The Several Lives of Chester Himes*, 79). Wright's papers at Yale also describe this scene, saying that Himes, who had come to the café with Wright, got up and walked around the block, wanting no part of the confrontation between Wright and Baldwin (Richard Wright Papers, Yale Collection of American Literature, Beinecke Rare Book and Manuscript Library).

44. In the original French, this passage again places the postcolonial female in an exploited position, specifying, "Les voisins de la résidence ministérielle étaient rares, et sans doute plus occupés a déguster leur potage en détaillant les appas de la soubrette expatriée qu'à scruter les trottoirs" (Njami, *Cerceuil & Cie*, 254).

45. I discuss this feminist rewriting of nostalgia further in Walters, "Michelle Cliff's *No Telephone to Heaven*: Diasporic Displacement and the Feminization of the Landscape."

46. Lipsitz, *Dangerous Crossroads: Popular Music, Postmodernism and the Poetics of Place*, 123.

47. Lahens, "Exile: Between Writing and Place," 745.

48. The fact that Himes's detective novels first appeared in French generated the interest of Cameroonian scholar Ambroise Kom, whose writing about Himes draws entirely different connections between Harlem and Africa than we have seen in the work of Njami. See Kom, "Chester Himes et Sembene Ousmane: un même message aux Peuples Noirs," and *Le Harlem de Chester Himes*.

49. Bhabha, *The Location of Culture*, 6 (original italics).

5. History's Dispersals

1. Brah, *Cartographies of Diaspora: Contesting Identities*, 16.

2. Phillips, "Crossing the River: Interview with Caryl Phillips," 29. Phillips here refers to his parents as part of the Windrush generation, those who came to England and in some ways prospered, and to himself as one who was raised in Leeds and educated at Oxford. Perhaps he also refers to himself as a descendant of a slave who was able to survive the middle passage.

3. The prevalence of a tourist industry around the coastal slave forts depends on this emotional connection to the site of the first rupture of African identity. Phillips writes critically about this touristic practice in *The Atlantic Sound*.

4. Phillips describes his reading of *Native Son* this way: "If I had to point to any one moment that seemed crucial in my desire to be a writer, it was then, as the Pacific surf began to wash up around the deck chair" (*The European Tribe*, 7). He reiterates Wright's "profound, seminal" effect on him again in *A New World Order: Essays* (18).

5. *The European Tribe*, 28.

6. See Phillips's chapter "Dinner at Jimmy's" in *The European Tribe*, 39–44.

7. This strategy is similar to the work that Toni Morrison performs in *Beloved*. She moves from the shocked horror of a newspaper clipping about infanticide to the fleshed-out story of a mother's love. Phillips's narrator, however, remains somewhat distant and unlikable, and we do not identify nearly so much with him as we do with Morrison's Sethe.

8. For more on the life and letters of Philip Quaque, see Priestley, "Philip Quaque of Cape Coast."

9. Phillips, "Crossing the River: Interview with Caryl Phillips," 26.

10. Ibid.

11. Robert Reid-Pharr describes a willful forgetting as a form of agency that enables African Americans to live with American history. He qualifies this description, adding, "You're not going to forget it; but rather to *behave as if* you've forgotten it. And if this weren't the case, it would be a *very* bloody country" ("Nobody's Fault But Mine: James Baldwin and the Promise of American Alienation").

12. See Gilroy, *The Black Atlantic: Modernity and Double Consciousness*, and Lipsitz, *Dangerous Crossroads: Popular Music, Postmodernism and the Poetics of Place*, for excellent discussions of the creative potential for resistance articulated in the diasporic circulation of popular music.

13. Phillips, "Crossing the River," 28.

14. Hall, "Cultural Identity and Diaspora," 236.

15. I borrow the section's subtitle from the recent prison writings of Mumia Abu-Jamal; see his *Live from Death Row*.

16. Studies of U.S. incarceration rates and the racialization of the prison population have shown that in the year 2001, the United States "managed to replicate—at least on a statistical level—the shame of chattel slavery in this country: The number of black men in prison (792,000) has already equaled the number of men enslaved in 1820. With the current momentum of the drug war fueling an ever expanding prison-industrial complex, if current trends continue, only 15 years remain before the United States incarcerates as many African-American men as were forced into chattel bondage at slavery's peak in 1860" (Boyd, "The Drug War Is the New Jim Crow," 1).

17. "By 2000, non-whites were 66 percent of the prison population while accounting for 30 percent of the American population, according to federal officials" (Roach, "From the Classroom to the Courtroom: Scholars Assess Race and Class in the American Criminal Justice System," 1).

18. Phillips, "Worlds Within: An Interview with Caryl Phillips," 602.

19. Dent and Davis, "Conversations: Prison as a Border: A Conversation on Gender, Globalization and Punishment," 1236–37.

20. "With 5 percent of the world's population, the United States now holds 25 percent of the world's prisoners, winning it the dubious title of the world's leading jailer. The rate at which we lock up our citizens now surpasses every other country that has ever kept such statistics" (Boyd, "The Drug War Is the New Jim Crow"), 1.

21. Malcolm X, *Malcolm X Speaks: Selected Speeches and Statements*, 63.

22. Sarvan and Marhama, "The Fictional Works of Caryl Phillips: An Introduction," 39.

23. Jackson, *Soledad Brother: The Prison Letters of George Jackson*, 62.

24. Malcolm X, *The Autobiography of Malcolm X*, 179.

25. Ibid., 174; Jackson, *Soledad Brother*, 115.

26. Jonathan Jackson Jr., foreword to Jackson, *Soledad Brother*, xiv.

27. Ibid., 190.

28. Jonathan Jackson Jr., foreword to Jackson, *Soledad Brother*, xix. In his study of prison literature in the United States, H. Bruce Franklin concurs that Jackson's murder at San Quentin, ten months after the publication of *Soledad Brother*, was linked to his developing internationalist vision and critique of American politics. See Franklin, *Prison Literature in America: The Victim as Criminal and Artist*, 241.

29. See chapter 1, n. 58.

30. George Jackson comments on the educational level of prison guards and police: "United States prisons are the last refuge of the brainless.... The cop, as I've stated before, is a guy who can do no other type of work, who can feed himself only by feeding upon this garbage dump" (*Soledad Brother*, 220–21).

31. See Kojève, *Introduction to the Reading of Hegel: Lectures on the Phenomenology of the Spirit*, 9, 17–21, for a discussion of recognition in Hegel's concept of the master-slave relationship.

32. Jackson, *Soledad Brother*, 19.

33. Ibid., 56.

34. Malcolm X, *Malcolm X Speaks: Selected Speeches and Statements*, 40.

35. Jackson, *Soledad Brother*, 106.

36. Ibid., 168.

37. Ibid., 223.

38. Ibid., 309–10.

39. The previously cited Critical Resistance work continues this international analysis of prisons, as well as its own prison abolition strategies. Davis explains that an international perspective is mandatory in "reconceptualizing the relationship between the prison industrial complex and globalization—from a discussion of how the prison is affected by the globalization of the economy (where the prison fits into globalization) to using the prison as a contingent historical institution that not only prefigures globalization but allows us to think today about the intersections of punishment, gender, and race, within and beyond the borders of the United States" (Dent and Davis, "Conversations," 1236).

40. See Jackson, *Soledad Brother*, 26, 115, 140, 313.

41. *The European Tribe* is Phillips's 1987 travel narrative about Europe, a chapter of which is devoted to "Anne Frank's Amsterdam." In this chapter, Phillips recalls a

television program he watched when he was fifteen: "I watched the library footage of the camps and realized both the enormity of the crime that was being perpetrated, and the precariousness of my own position in Europe. The many adolescent thoughts that worried my head can be reduced to one line: 'If white people could do that to white people, then what the hell would they do to me?'" (67).

42. W. E. B. Du Bois, *Dusk of Dawn: An Essay Toward an Autobiography of a Race Concept,* 117.

43. Phillips, *A New World Order,* 304.

44. Ibid.

45. Ibid., 309.

46. Ibid., 308.

47. Phillips, "Crossing the River: Interview with Caryl Phillips," 28.

Epilogue

1. Busia, preface to *"Testimonies of Exile:* On Territories, Tied Tongues, and Translations," 195.

2. Baldwin, "Why I Left America: Conversation: Ida Lewis and James Baldwin," 414.

3. Washburn, *A Question of Sedition: The Federal Government's Investigation of the Black Press during World War Two,* 167.

4. Ibid., 174.

5. Natalie Robins explains that "[t]o the FBI...the embryonic civil rights movement was simply a communist plot; the Bureau remained blind to the causes and widespread nature of blacks' discontent. Consequently, it sought to pin a Red label on anyone who demanded equal rights for blacks, and all politically active blacks were considered security threats" (*Alien Ink: The FBI's War on Freedom of Expression,* 282).

6. Maxwell, "F.B. Eyes: The Bureau of Investigation Reads Claude McKay."

7. Wallace, "'I'm Not Entirely What I Look Like': Richard Wright, James Baldwin and the Hegemony of Vision; or, Jimmy's FBEye Blues," 302.

8. Federal Bureau of Investigation, File No. 100–22661, p. 2. Chester Himes archives, Amistad Research Center, Tulane University, New Orleans, La.

9. Ibid. Letter, dated August 8, 1962.

10. Quoted in Robins, *Alien Ink: The FBI's War on Freedom of Expression,* 286.

11. Campbell, "I Heard It Through the Grapevine," 157.

12. Cliff, "History as Fiction, Fiction as History," 197.

13. Mugo, "Exile and Creativity: A Prolonged Writer's Block," 98.

14. Cliff, "If I Could Write This in Fire I Would Write This in Fire," 30.

15. Chester Himes, quoted in Margolies and Fabre, *The Several Lives of Chester Himes,* 119.

16. Richard Wright Papers, Yale Collection of American Literature, Beinecke Rare Book and Manuscript Library. Indeed, in 1897 Du Bois had asked, "Am I an American or am I a Negro? Can I be both?" (Du Bois, "The Conservation of Races," 43).

17. Bhabha, "Freedom's Basis in the Indeterminate," 57.

Works Cited

Abu-Jamal, Mumia. *Live from Death Row*. New York: Avon Books, 1995.

Achebe, Chinua. "The African Writer and the English Language." In Williams and Chrisman, *Colonial Discourse and Post-Colonial Theory*, 428–34.

Alexander, Elizabeth. "'Can You Be BLACK and Look at This?' Reading the Rodney King Video(s)." *Public Culture* 7, no. 1 (Fall 1994): 77–94.

Anderson, Benedict. "Exodus." *Critical Inquiry* 20, no. 2 (Winter 1994): 314–27.

Appadurai, Arjun. *Modernity at Large: Cultural Dimensions of Globalization*. Minneapolis: University of Minnesota Press, 1996.

Appiah, Anthony. "A Long Way from Home: Wright in the Gold Coast." In *Richard Wright*, edited by Harold Bloom, 173–90. New York: Chelsea House, 1987.

———. "The Uncompleted Argument: Du Bois and the Illusion of Race." In *"Race," Writing, and Difference*, edited by Henry Louis Gates Jr., 21–37. Chicago: University of Chicago Press, 1985.

Ashcroft, Bill, Gareth Griffiths, and Helen Tiffin. *The Empire Writes Back: Theory and Practice in Post-Colonial Literatures*. London: Routledge, 1989.

Baker, Houston A. *Turning South Again: Re-Thinking Modernism/Re-Reading Booker T.* Durham, N.C.: Duke University Press, 2001.

Baldwin, James. *Notes of a Native Son*. Boston: Beacon Press, 1955.

———. "Why I Left America: Conversation: Ida Lewis and James Baldwin." In *New Black Voices: An Anthology of Contemporary Afro-American Literature*, edited by Abraham Chapman, 409–19. New York: New American Library, 1972. First published in *Essence*, October 1970.

Bammer, Angelika. "Editorial," in *The Question of "Home,"* special issue of *New Formations* 17 (Summer 1992): vii–xi.

Bay, Mia. *The White Image in the Black Mind: African-American Ideas about White People, 1830–1925*. New York: Oxford University Press, 2000.

Berry, Jay R. "Chester Himes and the Hard-Boiled Tradition." *The Armchair Detective* 15, no. 1 (1982): 38–43.

Bhabha, Homi K. "Freedom's Basis in the Indeterminate." *October* 61 (Summer 1992): 46–57.

———. "Frontlines/Borderposts." In *Displacements: Cultural Identities in Question*, edited by Angelika Bammer, 269–72. Bloomington, Ind.: Indiana University Press, 1994.

———. *The Location of Culture*. London: Routledge, 1994.

———. "The World and the Home." *Social Text* 31/32 (10), nos. 2 and 3 (1992): 141–53.

Boyd, Graham. "The Drug War Is the New Jim Crow." *NACLA Report on the Americas* 35, no. 1 (July/August 2001). http://archive.aclu.org/issues/drugpolicy/NACLA_Article.html

Brah, Avtar. *Cartographies of Diaspora: Contesting Identities*. London: Routledge, 1996.

Busia, Abena P. A. "Preface to *Testimonies of Exile*: 'On Territories, Tied Tongues, and Translations.'" In *The Word behind Bars and the Paradox of Exile*, edited by Kofi Anyidoho with a foreword by Jane I. Guyer, 188–200. Evanston, Ill.: Northwestern University Press, 1997.

———. "Words Whispered over Voids: A Context for Black Women's Rebellious Voices in the Novel of the African Diaspora." In *Black Feminist Criticism and Critical Theory*, vol. 2 of *Studies in Black American Literature*, edited by Joe Weixlmann and Houston A. Baker Jr., 1–41. Greenwood, Fla.: Penkevill Publishing Co., 1988.

Butler, Judith. *Gender Trouble: Feminism and the Subversion of Identity*. New York: Routledge, 1990.

———. "Sovereign Performatives in the Contemporary Scene of Utterance." *Critical Inquiry* 23 (Winter 1997): 350–77.

Campbell, James. "Black on Black." In Campbell, *Exiled in Paris: Richard Wright, James Baldwin, Samuel Beckett, and Others on the Left Bank*.

———. *Exiled in Paris: Richard Wright, James Baldwin, Samuel Beckett, and Others on the Left Bank*. New York: Scribner, 1995.

———. "I Heard It through the Grapevine." *Granta* (March 2001): 157.

Cawelti, John. "The Study of Literary Formulas." In *Detective Fiction: A Collection of Critical Essays*, edited by Robin Winks, 121–43. Englewood Cliffs, N.J.: Prentice-Hall, 1980.

Chambers, Iain. *Migrancy, Culture, Identity*. London: Routledge, 1994.

Chancy, Myriam J. A. *Searching for Safe Spaces: Afro-Caribbean Women Writers in Exile*. Philadelphia: Temple University Press, 1997.

Chatterjee, Partha. "The Nationalist Resolution of the Women's Question." In *Recasting Women: Essays in Indian Colonial History*, edited by Kumkum Sangari and Sudesh Vaid, 233–53. New Brunswick, N.J.: Rutgers University Press, 1990.

Chester Himes Papers. Amistad Research Center, Tulane University, New Orleans, La.

Chow, Rey. *Writing Diaspora: Tactics of Intervention in Contemporary Cultural Studies*. Bloomington: Indiana University Press, 1993.

Clark, Vè Vè A. "Developing Diaspora Literacy and Marasa Consciousness." In *Comparative American Identities: Race, Sex, and Nationality in the Modern Text*, edited by Hortense J. Spillers, 40–61. New York: Routledge, 1991.

Cliff, Michelle. *Abeng*. New York: Dutton, 1984.

———. "Caliban's Daughter: The Tempest and the Teapot." *Frontiers* 12, no. 2 (1991): 36–51.

———. *Claiming an Identity They Taught Me to Despise*. Watertown, Mass.: Persephone Press, 1980.

———. "Clare Savage as a Crossroads Character." In Cudjoe, *Caribbean Women Writers*, 263–68.

———. *Free Enterprise*. New York: Dutton, 1993.

———. "History as Fiction, Fiction as History." *Ploughshares* 20, nos. 2–3 (Fall 1994): 196–202.

———. "If I Could Write This in Fire I Would Write This in Fire." In *Home Girls: A Black Feminist Anthology*, edited by Barbara Smith, 15–30. New York: Kitchen Table: Women of Color Press, 1983.

———. "An Interview with Michelle Cliff." By Meryl Schwartz. *Contemporary Literature* 34, no. 4 (Winter 1993): 595–619.

———. *No Telephone to Heaven*. New York: Vintage, 1987.

Clifford, James. "Diasporas." *Cultural Anthropology* 9, no. 3 (1994): 302–38.

———. "Traveling Cultures." In *Cultural Studies*, edited by Lawrence Grossberg, Cary Nelson, and Paula Treichler, 96–116. New York: Routledge, 1992.

Cobb, Nina Kressner. "Richard Wright in the Third World." In *Critical Essays on Richard Wright*, edited by Yoshinobu Hakutani, 228–39. Boston: Hall, 1982.

Collins, Patricia Hill. *Fighting Words: Black Women and the Search for Justice*. Minneapolis: University of Minnesota Press, 1998.

Cooper, Carolyn. *Noises in the Blood: Orality, Gender, and the "Vulgar" Body of Jamaican Popular Culture*. Durham, N.C.: Duke University Press, 1995.

Cudjoe, Selwyn R., ed. *Caribbean Women Writers: Essays from the First International Conference*. Wellesley, Mass.: Calaloux Press, 1990.

———. "Jamaica Kincaid and the Modernist Project: An Interview." In Cudjoe, *Caribbean Women Writers: Essays from the First International Conference*, 215–32.

Davies, Carole Boyce. *Black Women, Writing and Identity: Migrations of the Subject*. London: Routledge, 1994.

Davies, Carole Boyce, and Anne Adams Graves, eds. *Ngambika: Studies of Women in African Literature*. Trenton, N.J.: Africa World Press, 1986.

Delany, Martin R. *Blake; or, The Huts of America*. Edited by Floyd J. Miller. Boston: Beacon Press, 1970. First published as a serialized novel in 1861–62.

de Lauretis, Teresa. "Eccentric Subjects: Feminist Theory and Historical Consciousness." *Feminist Studies* 16, no. 1 (Spring 1990): 115–50.

Dent, Gina, and Angela Davis. "Conversations: Prison as a Border: A Conversation on Gender, Globalization, and Punishment." *Signs: A Journal of Women in Culture and Society* 26, no. 4 (Summer 2001): 1235–41.

Dickson-Carr, Darryl. *African American Satire: The Sacredly Profane Novel.* Columbia: University of Missouri Press, 2001.

Douglass, Frederick. *Narrative of the Life of Frederick Douglass, An American Slave: Written by Himself.* 1845. Reprint, edited by Houston A. Baker Jr., New York: Viking Penguin, 1982.

Drake, St. Clair. "Diaspora Studies and Pan-Africanism." In *Global Dimensions of the African Diaspora,* edited by Joseph E. Harris, 451–514. Washington, D.C.: Howard University Press, 1993.

Du Bois, W. E. B. "The Conservation of Races." In *The Oxford W. E. B. Du Bois Reader,* edited by Eric J. Sundquist, 38–47. New York: Oxford University Press, 1996.

———. *Dusk of Dawn: An Essay toward an Autobiography of a Race Concept.* 1940. Reprint, New York: Schocken Books, 1968.

———. *The Souls of Black Folk.* 1903. Reprint, New York: Penguin, 1989.

Echeruo, Michael J. C. "An African Diaspora: The Ontological Project." In Okpewho, Davies, and Mazrui, *The African Diaspora: African Origins and New World Identities,* 3–18.

Edmondson, Belinda. "Race, Privilege, and the Politics of (Re)Writing History: An Analysis of the Novels of Michelle Cliff." *Callaloo* 16, no. 1 (1993): 180–91.

Edwards, Brent Hayes. *The Practice of Diaspora: Literature, Translation, and the Practice of Black Nationalism.* Cambridge, Mass.: Harvard University Press, 2003.

Ekeh, Peter P. "Kinship and State in African-American Histories." In Okpewho, Davies, and Mazrui, *The African Diaspora: African Origins and New World Identities,* 89–155.

Equiano, Olaudah. *The Interesting Narrative of the Life of Olaudah Equiano or Gustavus Vassa, the African.* In *The Classic Slave Narratives,* edited by Henry Louis Gates Jr. New York: NAL/ Penguin, 1987.

Eze, Emmanuel Chukwudi. *Race and the Enlightenment: A Reader.* Cambridge, Mass.: Blackwell, 1997.

Fabre, Michel. "Écrire: une tentative pour révéler l'absurdité de la vie." *Le Monde,* 13 November 1970, 20.

———. *From Harlem to Paris: Black American Writers in France, 1840–1980.* Urbana: University of Illinois Press, 1991.

———. *La Rive Noire: De Harlem a la Seine.* Paris: Lieu Commun, 1985.

———. *The Unfinished Quest of Richard Wright.* Translated by Isabel Barzun. 2d ed. Urbana: University of Illinois Press, 1993.

Fanon, Frantz. *Black Skin, White Masks.* 1952. Translated by Charles Lam Markmann. New York: Grove, 1967.

Federal Bureau of Investigation. File No. 100–22661. Chester Himes archives. Amistad Research Center, Tulane University, New Orleans, La.

Ferguson, Russell, Martha Gever, Trinh T. Minh-ha, and Cornel West, eds. *Out There: Marginalization and Contemporary Cultures.* New York: New Museum of Contemporary Art, 1990.

Franklin, H. Bruce. *Prison Literature in America: The Victim as Criminal and Artist.* Westport, Conn.: Lawrence Hill, 1978.

Fuller, Hoyt. "Chester Himes: Traveler on the Long, Rough, Lonely Old Road." *Black World* 21 (March 1972): 4–22, 87–98.

George, Rosemary Marangoly. *The Politics of Home: Postcolonial Relocations and Twentieth-Century Fiction*. Cambridge: Cambridge University Press, 1996.

Gikandi, Simon. *Writing in Limbo: Modernism and Caribbean Literature*. Ithaca, N.Y.: Cornell University Press, 1992.

Gilroy, Paul. *The Black Atlantic: Modernity and Double Consciousness*. Cambridge, Mass.: Harvard University Press, 1993.

———. *"There Ain't No Black in the Union Jack": The Cultural Politics of "Race" and Nation*. London: Hutchinson, 1987.

———. "'Without the Consolation of Tears': Richard Wright, France, and the Ambivalence of Community." In Gilroy, *The Black Atlantic: Modernity and Double Consciousness*, 146–86.

Glissant, Edouard. *Caribbean Discourse: Selected Essays*. Translated by J. Michael Dash. Charlottesville: University Press of Virginia, 1989.

Golden, Marita. *Migrations of the Heart: An Autobiography*. New York: Ballantine Books, 1983.

Greenlee, Sam. *The Spook Who Sat by the Door*. 1969. Reprint, Detroit: Wayne State University Press, 1990.

Grewal, Inderpal. "Autobiographic Subjects and Diasporic Locations: *Meatless Days* and *Borderlands*." In *Scattered Hegemonies: Postmodernity and Transnational Feminist Practices*, edited by Inderpal Grewal and Caren Kaplan, 231–54. Minneapolis: University of Minnesota Press, 1994.

Griffin, Farah Jasmine. *"Who Set You Flowin'?" The African-American Migration Narrative*. New York: Oxford University Press, 1995.

———. *If You Can't Be Free, Be a Mystery: In Search of Billie Holiday*. New York: Free Press, 2001.

Griggs, Sutton. *Imperium in Imperio*. 1899. Reprint, New York: Arno, 1969.

Hall, Stuart. "Cultural Identity and Diaspora." In *Identity: Community, Culture, Difference*, edited by Jonathan Rutherford, 222–37. London: Lawrence and Wishart, 1990.

———. "The Formation of a Diasporic Intellectual II." In *Hurricane Hits England: An Anthology of Writing about Black Britain*, edited by Onyekachi Wambu, 86–90. New York: Continuum, 2000.

———. "The Local and the Global: Globalization and Ethnicity." In *Culture, Globalization, and the World-System: Contemporary Conditions for the Representation of Identity*, edited by Anthony D. King, 19–39. Binghamton: Department of Art and Art History, SUNY, 1991.

———. "Old and New Identities, Old and New Ethnicities." In *Culture, Globalization, and the World-System: Contemporary Conditions for the Representation of Identity*, edited by Anthony D. King, 41–68. Binghamton: Department of Art and Art History, SUNY, 1991.

———. "Race, the Floating Signifier." Undated video. Media Education Foundation.

———. "What Is This 'Black' in Black Popular Culture?" In *Black Popular Culture: A Project by Michele Wallace*, edited by Gina Dent, 21–33. 1983. Reprint, New York: New Press, 1998.

Haraway, Donna. "Situated Knowledges: The Science Question in Feminism and the Privilege of Partial Perspective." *Feminist Studies* 14, no. 3 (Fall 1988): 575–99.

Harpham, Geoffrey Galt. "So . . . What *Is* Enlightenment? An Inquisition into Modernity." *Critical Inquiry* 20, no. 3 (Spring 1994): 524–56.

Harris, Eddy L. *Native Stranger: A Black American's Journey into the Heart of Africa*.
New York: Vintage Books, 1992.

Harris, Trudier. *Exorcising Blackness: Historical and Literary Lynching and Burning Rituals*. Bloomington: Indiana University Press, 1984.

Henderson, Mae. *In Another Country: Afro-American Expatriate Novelists in France,
1945–1974*. PhD diss., Yale University, 1983.

Hesse, Barnor. "Black to the Front and Black Again: Racialization through Contested
Times and Spaces." In Keith and Pile, *Place and the Politics of Identity*, 162–82.

Hill, Mike, ed. *Whiteness: A Critical Reader*. New York: New York University Press,
1997.

Himes, Chester. *Blind Man with a Pistol*. 1969. Reprint, New York: Vintage, 1989.

———. *A Case of Rape*. Washington, D.C.: Howard University Press, 1984.

———. *Cast the First Stone*. New York: Signet, 1952.

———. *Cotton Comes to Harlem*. 1965. Reprint, New York: Vintage, 1988.

———. "Dilemma of the Negro Novelist in the U.S." In *Beyond the Angry Black*,
edited by John A. Williams, 51–58. New York: Cooper Square Publishers, 1966.

———. "Harlem ou le cancer d'Amérique." *Présence Africaine* 45 (Spring 1963):
46–81.

———. *If He Hollers Let Him Go*. 1945. Reprint, New York: Thunder's Mouth
Press, 1986.

———. *Lonely Crusade*. 1947. Reprint, New York: Thunder's Mouth Press, 1986.

———. *My Life of Absurdity: The Later Years*. 1976. Reprint, New York: Paragon,
1990.

———. "Negro Martyrs Are Needed." *The Crisis* 51 (May 1944): 159, 174.

———. "Now Is the Time! Here Is the Place!" *Opportunity* 20 (September 1942):
271–73, 284.

———. *Plan B*. Paris: Lieu Commun, 1983.

———. *Plan B*. Edited by Michel Fabre and Robert E. Skinner. Jackson: University
of Mississippi Press, 1993.

———. "Prediction." In *Black on Black: Baby Sister and Selected Writings*. Garden
City, N.Y.: Doubleday, 1973.

———. *A Rage in Harlem*. New York: Vintage, 1991. Originally published in 1957
as *For Love of Imabelle* (Greenwich, Conn.: Fawcett World Library).

———. *The Real Cool Killers*. 1959. Reprint, New York: Vintage, 1988.

———. *Yesterday Will Make You Cry*. New York: W. W. Norton, 1998.

Hodge, Merle. "Challenges of the Struggle for Sovereignty: Changing the World
Versus Writing Stories." In Cudjoe, *Caribbean Women Writers: Essays from the
First International Conference*, 202–8.

Hogue, W. Lawrence. *Discourse and the Other: The Production of the Afro-American
Text*. Durham, N.C.: Duke University Press, 1986.

———. "Sixties' Social Movements, the Literary Establishment, and the Production of the Afro-American Text." In *Discourse and the Other: The Production of
the Afro-American Text*. Durham, N.C.: Duke University Press, 1986.

Holiday, Billie. *Lady Sings the Blues*. With William Duffy. New York: Avon, 1956.

————. "Strange Fruit." April 20, 1939. *Billie Holiday: Strange Fruit.* Atlantic Records, SD 1614.

hooks, bell. "Marginality as a Site of Resistance." In Ferguson, Gever, Minh-ha, and West, *Out There: Marginalization and Contemporary Cultures,* 341–43.

————. "Postmodern Blackness." In *Yearning: Race, Gender, and Cultural Politics,* 23–31. Boston: South End, 1990.

Hughes, Langston. *The Big Sea.* 1940. Reprint, New York: Thunder's Mouth Press, 1986.

Hurston, Zora Neale. *Tell My Horse: Voodoo and Life in Haiti and Jamaica.* 1938. Reprint, New York: Harper Perennial, 1990.

————. *Their Eyes Were Watching God.* 1937. Reprint, Urbana: University of Illinois Press, 1978.

Ifekwunigwe, Jayne O. *Scattered Belongings: Cultural Paradoxes of "Race," Nation, and Gender.* London: Routledge, 1999.

Iser, Wolfgang. "Why Literature Matters." In *Why Literature Matters: Theories and Functions of Literature,* edited by Rudiger Ahrens and Laurenz Volkmann, 13–22. Heidelberg: Universitatsverlag C. Winter, 1996.

Jackson, George. *Soledad Brother: The Prison Letters of George Jackson.* 1970. Reprint, Chicago: Lawrence Hill Books, 1994.

Jameson, Fredric. "Postmodernism, or The Cultural Logic of Late Capitalism." *New Left Review* 146 (1984): 53–92.

Johnson, Lemuel A. "A-beng: (Re)Calling the Body In(To) Question." In *Out of the Kumbla: Caribbean Women and Literature,* edited by Carole Boyce Davies and Elaine Savory Fido, 111–42. Trenton, N.J.: Africa World Press, 1990.

Johnson, Robert. "American Prisons and the African-American Experience: A History of Social Control and Racial Oppression." *Corrections Compendium* 25, no. 9 (September 2000): 6–10, 28–30.

Jules-Rosette, Bennetta. *Black Paris: The African Writers' Landscape.* Urbana: University of Illinois Press, 1998.

Julien, Isaac, and Kobena Mercer. "Introduction: De Margin and De Centre." *Screen* 29, no. 4 (Autumn 1988): 2–10.

Kaplan, Amy, and Donald Pease, eds. *Cultures of United States Imperialism.* Durham, N.C.: Duke University Press, 1993.

Kaplan, Caren. "Deterritorializations: The Rewriting of Home and Exile in Western Feminist Discourse." *Cultural Critique* 6 (Spring 1987): 187–98.

————. *Questions of Travel: Postmodern Discourses of Displacement.* Durham, N.C.: Duke University Press, 1996.

————. "Resisting Autobiography: Out-Law Genres and Transnational Feminist Subjects." In Smith and Watson, *De/Colonizing the Subject: The Politics of Gender in Women's Autobiography,* 115–38.

Kelley, Robin D. G. "But a Local Phase of a World Problem: Black History's Global Vision, 1883–1950." *Journal of American History* 86, no. 3 (1999): 1045–77.

Keith, Michael, and Steve Pile, eds. *Place and the Politics of Identity.* London: Routledge, 1993.

Kincaid, Jamaica. *Annie John.* New York: Farrar, Straus, and Giroux, 1985.

————. *Lucy.* New York: Farrar, Straus, and Giroux, 1990.

———. *A Small Place*. New York: Farrar, Straus, and Giroux, 1988.

King, Russell, John Connell, and Paul White, eds. *Writing across Worlds: Literature and Migration*. London: Routledge, 1995.

Kojève, Alexandre. *Introduction to the Reading of Hegel: Lectures on the Phenomenology of the Spirit*. Edited by Allan Bloom and translated by James H. Nichols Jr. New York: Basic Books, 1969.

Kom, Ambroise. "Chester Himes et Sembene Ousmane: un même message aux Peuples Noirs." *L'Afrique littéraire et artistique* 42 (1976): 20–30.

———. *Le Harlem de Chester Himes*. Quebec, Canada: Editions Naaman, 1978.

Lahens, Yanick. "Exile: Between Writing and Place." Translated by Cheryl Thomas and Paulette Richards. *Calalloo* 15, no. 3 (1992): 735–46.

Lee, A. Robert. "Hurts, Absurdities, and Violence: The Contrary Dimensions of Chester Himes." *Journal of American Studies* 12, no. 1 (April 1978): 99–114.

Levine, Lawrence. *Black Culture and Black Consciousness: Afro-American Folk Thought from Slavery to Freedom*. Oxford: Oxford University Press, 1977.

Lewis, Earl. "To Turn as on a Pivot: Writing African Americans into a History of Overlapping Diasporas." *American Historical Review* 100 (June 1995): 765–87.

Lionnet, Françoise. *Autobiographical Voices: Race, Gender, Self-Portraiture*. Ithaca, N.Y.: Cornell University Press, 1989.

———. "Inscriptions of Exile: The Body's Knowledge and the Myth of Authenticity." Translated by Joseph Heath. *Callaloo* 15, no. 1 (1992): 30–40.

———. "Of Mangoes and Maroons: Language, History, and the Multi-Cultural Subject of Michelle Cliff's *Abeng*." In Smith and Watson, *De/Colonizing the Subject: The Politics of Gender in Women's Autobiography*, 321–45.

Lipsitz, George. *Dangerous Crossroads: Popular Music, Postmodernism, and the Poetics of Place*. London: Verso, 1994.

———. *The Possessive Investment in Whiteness: How White People Profit from Identity Politics*. Philadelphia: Temple University Press, 1998.

Locke, Alain, ed. *The New Negro*. 1925. Reprint, New York: Atheneum, 1992.

Lorde, Audre. "Age, Race, Class, and Sex: Women Redefining Difference." In Ferguson, Gever, Minh-ha, and West, *Out There: Marginalization and Contemporary Cultures*, 281–87.

———. *Zami: A New Spelling of My Name*. Freedom, Calif.: Crossing Press, 1982.

Lott, Tommy. "Black Cultural Politics: An Interview with Paul Gilroy." *Found Object* 4 (Fall 1994): 46–81.

Lowe, Lisa, and David Lloyd. Introduction to *The Politics of Culture in the Shadow of Capital*, 1–32. Durham, N.C.: Duke University Press, 1997.

Lyotard, Jean-François. *The Postmodern Condition: A Report on Knowledge*. Translated by Geoff Bennington and Brian Massumi. Minneapolis: University of Minnesota Press, 1984.

Mair, Lucille Mathurin. "Recollections of a Journey into a Rebel Past." In Cudjoe, *Caribbean Women Writers: Essays from the First International Conference*, 51–59.

Malcolm X. *The Autobiography of Malcolm X*. 1964. With Alex Haley. Reprint, New York: Ballantine Books, 1965.

———. *Malcolm X Speaks: Selected Speeches and Statements*. Edited by George Breitman. New York: Grove Press, 1965.

Margolick, David. *Strange Fruit: The Biography of a Song*. New York: Ecco Press, 2001.

Margolies, Edward. "Experiences of the Black Expatriate Writer: Chester Himes." *CLA Journal* 15, no. 4 (June 1972): 421–27.

———. *Which Way Did He Go? The Private Eye in Dashiell Hammett, Raymond Chandler, Chester Himes, and Ross Macdonald*. New York: Holmes and Meier, 1982.

Margolies, Edward, and Michel Fabre. *The Several Lives of Chester Himes*. Jackson: University Press of Mississippi, 1997.

Marshall, Paule. *The Chosen Place, The Timeless People*. 1969. Reprint, New York: Vintage Books, 1984.

———. *Praisesong for the Widow*. New York: Dutton, 1983.

Martin, Biddy, and Chandra Talpade Mohanty. "Feminist Politics: What's Home Got to Do with It?" In *Feminist Studies/Critical Studies*, edited by Teresa de Lauretis, 191–212. Bloomington: Indiana University Press, 1986.

Martin, Denis-Constant. "The Choices of Identity." *Social Identities* 1, no. 1 (1995).

Matsuda, Mari J. "Public Response to Racist Speech: Considering the Victim's Story." In *Words That Wound: Critical Race Theory, Assaultive Speech, and the First Amendment*, edited by Mari J. Matsuda, Charles R. Lawrence III, Richard Delgado, and Kimberlè Williams Crenshaw, 17–51. Boulder, Colo.: Westview Press, 1993.

Maxwell, William J. "F.B. Eyes: The Bureau of Investigation Reads Claude McKay." Paper delivered at African American Literature and Culture Society Meeting, Salt Lake City, Utah, 27 October 2000.

McClintock, Anne. "The Angel of Progress: Pitfalls of the Term 'Post-Colonialism.'" *Social Text* 10, nos. 2 and 3 (1992): 84–98.

Mercer, Kobena. "Diaspora Culture and the Dialogic Imagination: The Aesthetics of Black Independent Film in Britain." In *Critical Perspectives on Black Independent Cinema*, edited by Mbye B. Cham and Claire Andrade-Watkins, 50–61. Cambridge, Mass.: MIT Press, 1988.

Micha, René. "Les Paroissiens de Chester Himes." *Les Temps Modernes* 20 (February 1965): 1507–23.

Morrison, Toni. *Beloved*. New York: Plume, 1987.

———. *Jazz*. New York: Alfred A. Knopf, 1992.

Mugo, Micere Githae. "Exile and Creativity: A Prolonged Writer's Block." In *The Word behind Bars and the Paradox of Exile*, edited by Kofi Anyidoho, 80–99. Evanston, Ill.: Northwestern University Press, 1997.

Muller, Gilbert H. *Chester Himes*. Boston: Twayne, 1989.

Njami, Simon. *Cercueil & Cie*. Paris: Lieu Commun, 1985.

———. *Coffin & Co*. Translated by Marlene Raderman. Berkeley: Black Lizard, 1987.

———. Interview by Wendy Walters. La Jolla, April 21, 1993, unpublished.

Nora, Pierre. "Between Memory and History: *Les Lieux de Mémoire*." *Representations* 26 (Spring 1989): 7–25.

Okpewho, Isadore, Carol Boyce Davies, and Ali Mazrui, eds. *The African Diaspora: African Origins and New World Identities*. Bloomington: Indiana University Press, 1999.

Owens, Craig. "The Discourse of Others: Feminists and Postmodernism." In *The Anti-Aesthetic: Essays on Postmodern Culture*, edited by Hal Foster, 57–82. Port Townsend, Wash.: Bay Press, 1983.

Pease, Donald. "National Identities and Postnational Narratives." *boundary 2* 19, no. 1 (Spring 1992): 1–13.

Pierpont, Claudia Roth. Book review of *Cambridge*. *The New Yorker* (10 August 1992): 76–79.

Philip, Marlene Nourbese. *She Tries Her Tongue, Her Silence Softly Breaks*. Charlottetown, Prince Edward Island: Ragweed Press, 1989.

Phillips, Caryl. *The Atlantic Sound*. New York: Vintage, 2000.

———. *Cambridge*. 1991. Reprint, New York: Vintage International, 1993.

———. "Crisscrossing the River: An Interview with Caryl Phillips." By Carol Margaret Davison. *ARIEL: A Review of International English Literature* 25, no. 4 (October 1994): 91–99.

———. *Crossing the River*. 1993. Reprint, New York: Vintage, 1995.

———. "Crossing the River: Interview with Caryl Phillips." By Maya Jaggi. *Wasafiri* 20 (1994): 25–30.

———. *The European Tribe*. Boston: Faber and Faber, 1987.

———, ed. *Extravagant Strangers: A Literature of Belonging*. New York: Vintage International, 1997.

———. *Higher Ground: A Novel in Three Parts*. 1989. Reprint, New York: Vintage, 1995.

———. *A New World Order: Essays*. New York: Vintage International, 2002.

———. "Worlds Within: An Interview with Caryl Phillips." By C. Rosalind Bell. *Callaloo* 14, no. 3 (1991): 578–606.

Posnock, Ross. *Color and Culture: Black Writers and the Making of the Modern Intellectual*. Cambridge, Mass.: Harvard University Press, 1998.

Pratt, Mary Louise. *Imperial Eyes: Travel Writing and Transculturation*. London: Routledge, 1992.

Priestley, Margaret. "Philip Quaque of Cape Coast." In *Africa Remembered: Narratives by West Africans from the Era of the Slave Trade*, edited by Philip D. Curtin, 99–139. Madison: University of Wisconsin Press, 1968.

Prince, Mary. *The History of Mary Prince, a West Indian Slave, Related by Herself*. Edited by Moira Ferguson. Rev. ed. Ann Arbor: University of Michigan Press, 1997.

Reagon, Bernice Johnson. "Coalition Politics: Turning the Century." In *Home Girls: A Black Feminist Anthology*, edited by Barbara Smith, 356–68. New York: Kitchen Table: Women of Color Press, 1983.

Reid-Pharr, Robert. "Nobody's Fault But Mine: James Baldwin and the Promise of American Alienation." Lecture presented at Harvard University, December 10, 2001.

Richard Wright Papers. Yale Collection of American Literature, Beinecke Rare Book and Manuscript Library.

Roach, Ronald. "From the Classroom to the Courtroom: Scholars Assess Race and Class in the American Criminal Justice System." In *Black Issues in Higher Edu-*

cation, http://www.findarticles.com/cf_dls/mODXK/24_18/82770920/print.jhtml. (accessed January 17, 2002).

Roberts, John W. *From Trickster to Badman: The Black Folk Hero in Slavery and Freedom*. Philadelphia: University of Pennsylvania Press, 1989.

Robins, Natalie. *Alien Ink: The FBI's War on Freedom of Expression*. New York: William Morrow and Co., 1992.

Robinson, Amy. "It Takes One to Know One: Passing and Communities of Common Interest." *Critical Inquiry* 20, no. 4 (Summer 1994): 715–36.

Rouse, Roger. "Mexican Migration and the Social Space of Postmodernism." *Diaspora* 1, no. 1 (Spring 1991): 8–23.

Safran, William. "Diasporas in Modern Societies: Myths of Homeland and Return." *Diaspora* 1, no. 1 (Spring 1991): 83–99.

Sallis, James. *Chester Himes: A Life*. New York: Walker and Company, 2000.

Sarvan, Charles P., and Hasan Marhama. "The Fictional Works of Caryl Phillips: An Introduction." *World Literature Today* 65, no. 1 (Winter 1991): 35–40.

Scott, Joan. "Experience." In *Feminists Theorize the Political*, edited by Judith Butler and Joan Scott, 22–40. New York: Routledge, 1992.

Smith, Sidonie, and Julia Watson, eds. *De/Colonizing the Subject: The Politics of Gender in Women's Autobiography*. Minneapolis: University of Minnesota Press, 1992.

Sommer, Doris. "Resisting the Heat: Menchú, Morrison, and Incompetent Readers." In Kaplan and Pease, *Cultures of United States Imperialism*, 407–32.

Spillers, Hortense J. "Mama's Baby, Papa's Maybe: An American Grammar Book." *Diacritics* 17, no. 2 (Summer 1987): 65–81.

Spivak, Gayatri. "Who Claims Alterity?" In *Remaking History*, edited by Barbara Kruger and Phil Mariani. Seattle: Bay Press, 1989.

Suleri, Sarah. "Woman Skin Deep: Feminism and the Postcolonial Condition." *Critical Inquiry* 18 (Summer 1992): 756–69.

Sundquist, Eric. "W. E. B. Du Bois and the Autobiography of Race." In *The Oxford W. E. B. Du Bois Reader*, 3–36. New York: Oxford University Press, 1996.

Terborg-Penn, Rosalyn, Sharon Harley, and Andrea Benton Rushing, eds. *Women in Africa and the Diaspora*. Washington, D.C.: Howard University Press, 1989.

Tölölyan, Khachig. "Rethinking *Diaspora*(s): Stateless Power in the Transnational Moment." *Diaspora* 5, no. 1 (1996): 3–36.

Toomer, Jean. *Cane*. 1923. Reprint, New York: Harper and Row, 1969.

Thiong'o, Ngũgĩ wa. "The Language of African Literature." In Williams and Chrisman, *Colonial Discourse and Postcolonial Theory*, 435–55.

Walker, Margaret. *Richard Wright: Daemonic Genius*. New York: Amistad, 1988.

Wallace, Maurice. "'I'm Not Entirely What I Look Like': Richard Wright, James Baldwin, and the Hegemony of Vision; Or, Jimmy's FBEye Blues." In *James Baldwin Now*, edited by Dwight A. McBride, 289–306. New York: New York University Press, 1999.

Wallace, Michele. "The Politics of Location: Cinema/Theory/Literature/Ethnicity/ Sexuality/ Me." *Framework* 36 (1989): 42–55.

Walters, Wendy W. "Limited Options: Strategic Maneuverings in Himes's Harlem." *African American Review* 28, no. 4 (Winter 1994): 615–31.

————. "Michelle Cliff's *No Telephone to Heaven:* Diasporic Displacement and the Feminization of the Landscape." In *Borders, Exiles, Diasporas,* edited by Elazar Barkan and Marie-Denise Shelton, 217–33. Stanford, Calif.: Stanford University Press, 1998.

————. "'One of Dese Mornings, Bright and Fair,/Take My Wings and Cleave De Air': The Legend of the Flying Africans and Diasporic Consciousness." *MELUS* 22, no. 3 (Fall 1997): 3–29.

Warren, Kenneth W. "Appeals for (Mis)recognition: Theorizing the Diaspora." In Kaplan and Pease, *Cultures of United States Imperialism,* 392–406.

Washburn, Patrick S. *A Question of Sedition: The Federal Government's Investigation of the Black Press during World War Two.* New York: Oxford University Press, 1986.

Washington, Booker T. *The Story of the Negro: The Rise of the Race from Slavery.* Vol. 1. New York: Negro Universities Press, 1909.

Wideman, John Edgar. "Doing Time, Marking Race." *The Nation* 261, no. 14, October 30, 1995.

Wilentz, Gay. *Binding Cultures: Black Women Writers in Africa and the Diaspora.* Bloomington: Indiana University Press, 1992.

————. "Toward a Diaspora Literature: Black Women Writers from Africa, the Caribbean, and the United States." *College English* 54, no. 4 (April 1992): 385–419.

Williams, Eric. *Capitalism and Slavery.* 1944. Reprint, New York: Russell and Russell, 1961.

Williams, John A. "Chester Himes—My Man Himes." In *Flashbacks: A Twenty-Year Diary of Article Writing,* 292–352. Garden City, N.Y.: Anchor/Doubleday, 1973.

Williams, Patrick, and Laura Chrisman, eds. *Colonial Discourse and Post-Colonial Theory: A Reader.* New York: Columbia University Press, 1994.

Williams, Raymond. *Keywords: A Vocabulary of Culture and Society.* New York: Oxford University Press, 1976.

Woodson, Carter G. "Fifty Years of Negro Citizenship as Qualified by the United States Supreme Court." *Journal of Negro History* 6 (January 1921).

Wright, Richard. *Black Boy (American Hunger): A Record of Childhood and Youth.* 1944. Reprint, New York: Harper Perennial Restored Edition, 1993.

————. "Black Boy in France," an interview with Richard Wright. By William Gardner Smith. *Ebony* 8, no. 9 (July 1953): 32–42.

————. *Black Power: A Record of Reactions in a Land of Pathos.* 1954. Reprint, New York: Harper Perennial, 1995.

————. "Blueprint for Negro Writing." 1937. Reprinted in *African American Literary Theory: A Reader,* edited by Winston Napier, 53–65. New York: New York University Press, 2000.

————. *The Color Curtain: A Report on the Bandung Conference.* 1956. Reprint, Jackson: University of Mississippi Press, 1995.

————. "I am an American, but." Richard Wright Papers, Box 5 Folder 107, Yale Collection of American Literature, Beinecke Rare Book and Manuscript Library.

————. "The Literature of the Negro in the U.S." In Wright, *White Man, Listen! Lectures in Europe, 1950–1956,* 71–109.

————. *Native Son.* 1940. Reprint, New York: Harper Perennial, 1993.

———. *Pagan Spain*. 1956. Reprint, New York: Harper Perennial, 1995.

———. "The Position of the Negro Artist and Intellectual in American Society." Richard Wright Papers, Box 3 Folder 41, Yale Collection of American Literature, Beinecke Rare Book and Manuscript Library.

———. *White Man, Listen! Lectures in Europe, 1950–1956*. 1957. Reprint, New York: Harper Perennial, 1995.

Wynter, Sylvia. "Sambos and Minstrels." *Social Text* 1, no. 1 (1979): 149–56.

Index

Wendy W. Walters is assistant professor in the Writing, Literature, and Publishing Department at Emerson College in Boston.